The Grand Tour of Kerry

The Grand Tour of Kerry

Compiled by

PENELOPE DURELL
&
CORNELIUS KELLY

CAILLEACH BOOKS

Published by
CAILLEACH BOOKS
Allihies, Beara, County Cork

ISBN 0-9537823-1-X

Cover design by Anissa Fox
Cover illustration: Mucross Friary by Gabriel Beranger (front) and Lakes of Killarney by Dennis Sullivan (back).
Typesetting by Carrigboy Typesetting Services, Durrus, County Cork
Printed by ColourBooks Ltd., Baldoyle, Dublin

Contents

Introduction			vii
Giraldus Cambrensis	Welsh bishop	*c.*1186	1
Thomas Stafford	Elizabethan soldier	1601	2
Dionisio Massari	Vatican emissary	1645	5
William Petty	Political economist	1685	9
Samuel Molyneux	Astronomer	1709	10
Charles Smith	County historian	1756	12
Richard Pococke	Bishop of Ossory	1758	16
Richard Twiss	Traveller and writer	1775	21
Arthur Young	Agriculturalist	1776	23
Daniel Beaufort	Cartographer	1778	27
Jacques Louis de Bougrenet	French Royalist	1797	29
George Holmes	Landscape artist	1797	38
Isaac Weld	Topographer	1800	42
John Carr	Traveller & writer	1805	45
Edward Dubois	Satirist	1807	49
James Bell	Methodist preacher	*c.*1807	52
Lewis Dillwyn	Naturalist	1809	54
Thomas Moore	Poet	1823	57
Alexander Nimmo	Pioneering engineer	1824	59
Walter Scott	Novelist	1825	60
John Lockhart	Biographer	1825	61
H. von Pückler-Muskau	German prince	1828	63
William Wordsworth	Poet	1829	67
Jonathan Binns	Agriculturalist	1835	68
Georgiana Chatterton	Writer	1838	70
Michael Condon	Catholic priest	1839	75
W. M. Thackeray	Author of *Vanity Fair*	1842	77
Johann G. Kohl	German geographer	1842	83
Asenath Nicholson	American missionary	1845	89
William Bennett	Famine aid worker	1847	95
Thomas Carlyle	Man of letters	1849	97
Thomas B. Macaulay	Historian	1849	103
John Windele	Antiquarian	1851	104
Harriet Martineau	Social philosopher	1852	106
Isabella Beeton	Cookery writer	1860	110

Daniel Gooch	Engineer & inventor	1865	111
William W. Barry	Barrister	1865	113
Bernard H. Becker	Journalist	1880	116
E. de Mandat-Grancey	French baron	1887	119
Marie-Anne de Bovet	French novelist	1889	121
Bertha Beatty	Kerry-born author	*c.*1890	124
John M. Synge	Playwright	1903	126
Michael M. Shoemaker	American writer	1908	135
George Bernard Shaw	Dramatist	1910	138
Robin Flower	Celtic scholar	1910	141
Stephen Gwynn	Author	1912	144
Harold Speakman	American travel writer	1924	147
John J. Welsh	American traveller	1928	151
H. V. Morton	Travel writer	1930	153
Signe Toksvig	Danish writer	1932	158
Virginia Woolf	Bloomsbury novelist	1934	159
Padraic Colum	Poet & playwright	1937	161
Robert Lloyd Praeger	Botanist	1937	163
Sean O'Faolain	Author	1939	169
Richard Hayward	Ballad singer & writer	1944	172
J. P. Donleavy	Author of *The Ginger Man*	*c.*1947	180
Olivia Manning	Novelist	1950	183
Frank O'Connor	Short story writer	1950	192
Honor Tracy	Novelist	*c.*1950	193
Oriana Atkinson	American author	1955	201
Kate O'Brien	Novelist	1958	204
Brendan Behan	Author of *Borstal Boy*	1962	207
Robert Mitchum	American actor	1969	211
Rebecca West	Feminist writer	1971	211
Philip Ward	Author & publisher	1972	213
Peter Somerville-Large	Writer & traveller	1980	216
Edna O'Brien	Novelist	1986	218
Niall Williams & Christine Breen	Writing team	1990	221

Sources & Text Credits 223

Picture Credits 226

Acknowledgements 227

Index 228

Introduction

According to legend, the Milesians, one of the first groups to arrive in Ireland, sailed up the Kenmare River and made landfall in what is now County Kerry. They discovered a land of rugged beauty with widespread woodlands where oak, hazel, rowan, holly and birch flourished. Travelling inland they found a district of lakes set among encircling hills. Farther north still the beginning of the broad Central Plain awaited them.

Many millennia after the legendary arrival of the Milesians, the area still bears abundant traces of people who either visited or settled in Kerry before written records were kept. The most ancient copper mines in northwest Europe are to be found near Killarney, and traders and fishermen have been visiting its coasts since prehistoric times. However it was not until the late 12th century that Welsh bishop Giraldus Cambrensis penned the earliest description extant of County Kerry. Since then eight centuries of travellers have recorded their experiences in the area and their impressions of the striking landscape.

These visitors were drawn to Kerry for a variety of reasons. At around the time Cambrensis was writing his *Topographia Hiberniae*, the O'Sullivans migrated to the Iveragh Peninsula, squeezed out of their ancestral lands in Tipperary by the incoming Normans. Later the Normans also moved westward, and families such as the Walshes and Fitzmaurices settled in the rich lands around Tralee. The Spanish came to fish in the sheltered bays and to trade in towns like Dingle, which county historian Charles Smith described in 1756: 'Several of the houses were built in the Spanish fashion, with ranges of stone balcony windows.' In 1588, when four vessels of the Spanish Armada went aground off the Kerry coast, the shipwrecked sailors found refuge ashore. The 16th and 17th centuries brought visitors on military and diplomatic missions. Thomas Stafford, a soldier who served with the military commander George Carew during the Elizabethan wars, wrote a dramatic account of a siege in North Kerry. Italian Dionisio Massari left us a vivid description of his experiences after he landed in Kenmare in 1645 on a mission with Cardinal Rinuccini to safeguard Catholicism in Ireland.

In 1652 the surrender of Ross Castle to the Parliamentary forces symbolised the end of an era for the aristocratic Gaelic families of Kerry. They were either in exile, subsumed into Norman or English families or reduced to poverty. Nevertheless, in the remote valleys and hills, the old Gaelic peasant way of life survived, and in time those with an interest in the ancient culture came to learn Irish and to research folktales. Folklorist

The road from Bantry to Killarney, completed in 1839 under the supervision of Scottish engineer Alexander Nimmo, included several tunnels through Esk Mountain.

Thomas Crofton Croker, who was to provide much of the material that Thomas Moore turned into poetry, visited in 1825 – perhaps encouraged by Moore, who on visiting Killarney two years earlier, had remarked: 'the softness, the luxuriance, the variety of colouring, the little gardens that every small rock inhabits . . . is unequalled anywhere else.' It was to West Kerry that John Millington Synge went to study the rhythms of language that were to mark his plays. Robin Flower, the Keeper of Manuscripts at the British Museum, travelled to the Blasket Islands and was to devote the rest of his life to translating the rich literature he found there.

Beginning in the 18th century, the cult of the picturesque started to draw tourists to Kerry. Killarney, with its beautiful lakes, dramatic ravines, mysterious woodlands and romantic legends, was the principal destination for most. Originally a plantation town with 40 houses, it started to expand in the 1750s when Lord Kenmare took steps to provide accommodations in the town and boats for hire on the lakes. The town was soon bustling with tourists, being rowed out on the lakes or taking the excursion to the Gap of Dunloe. Soon there were so many printed descriptions of the area that Richard Twiss, when preparing for his 1775 visit read all the following accounts: '. . . Charles Smith's *History of Kerry*, of which twenty-five pages describe the lake, and are illustrated by a print. . . . Thirty pages in Bush's *Hibernia Curiosa*, thirty more in Derrick's *Letters*, and three letters written by the late Mr. Ockenden, which are added to those of Derrick.'

But, although Killarney was the jewel in the Kerry crown, other places in the county also attracted visitors – the home of Daniel O'Connell near Caherdaniel, for example. In the 19th century many travellers went there hoping to meet the Liberator. In 1828 German prince Hermann von Pückler-Muskau sent advance word and received an invitation. American missionary Asenath Nicholson was less fortunate in 1845 – she arrived unannounced during O'Connell's absence and was turned away in a storm.

In the 19th century, travel and tourism entered a new phase with greatly improved communications. In 1833 Charles Bianconi started his coach service to Kerry and by 1836 the service extended as far west as Caherciveen. A road connecting Bantry with Kenmare and Killarney was built in 1839 under the supervision of Scottish engineer Alexander Nimmo. To carry it across the Roughty River at Kenmare, architect Sir Samuel Brown designed the first public suspension bridge in Ireland. The railway line to Killarney opened in 1853, and 40 years later Valentia was the most westerly railhead in Europe. In the mid 1860s the Transatlantic Telegraph Cable was laid at Valentia, connecting Europe with North America. When Queen Victoria visited Kerry in August 1861, with Prince Albert and four of their children, including the future Edward VII Killarney became a fashionable tourist destination.

The visual attractions of County Kerry have ensured that there were many famous authors among the visitors. This collection is enriched by the words of such writers as Walter Scott, who visited in 1825 with Maria Edgeworth; William Wordsworth, who at nearly 60, rode from Kenmare to Bantry Bay and back in one day; George Bernard Shaw, who spent many summer holidays at Parknasilla; Brendan Behan, who worked on the restoration of Daniel O'Connell's birthplace; and Rebecca West, who visited the homes and burial places of her ancestors. Other writers too,

though less known, have also contributed greatly to the large body of writing about Kerry. In their responses to what they saw, they reveal much about their own characters and about the attitudes and prejudices of the day. But whether they came to study the old culture, to write books or reports, to help relieve famine, to draw or paint, to find antiquities, to visit friends or find ancestral roots, to search for plants or rocks, or to make a film, they have all been moved by the singular beauty of County Kerry.

Penelope Durell & Cornelius Kelly

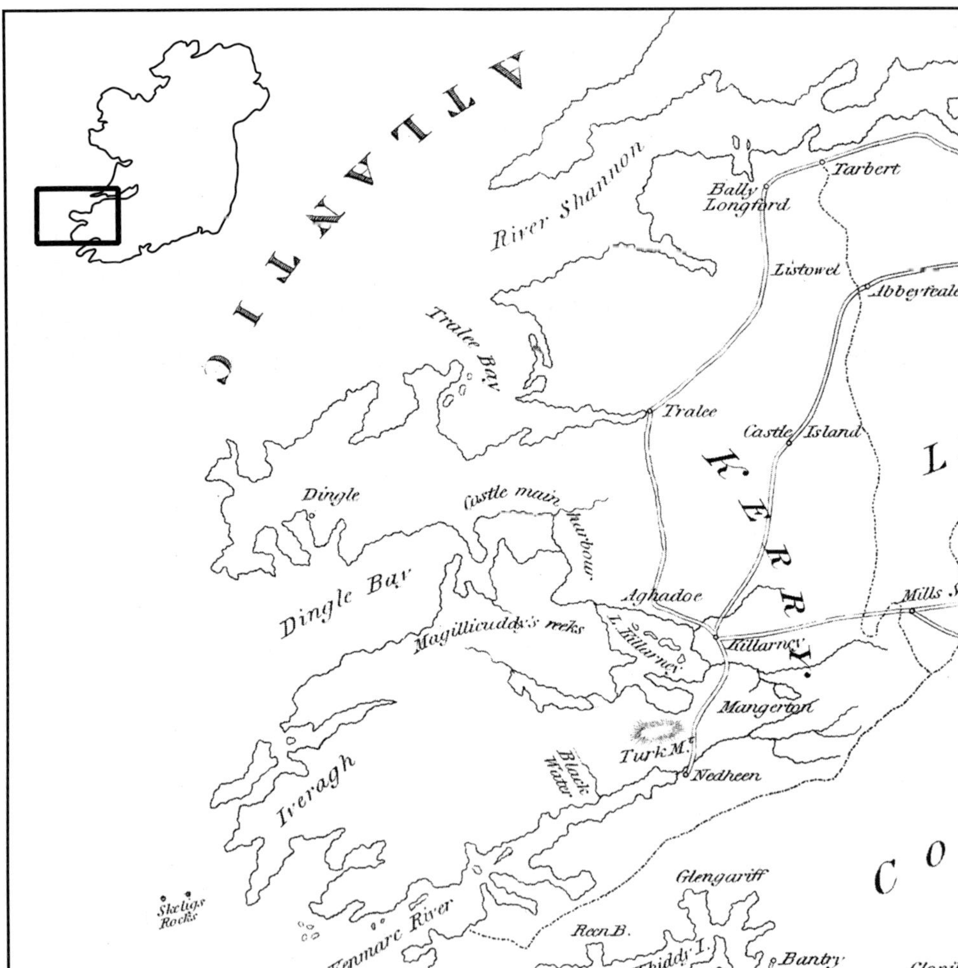

County Kerry from an 1800 map by Isaac Weld.

According to tradition, St. Finan founded the monastery on Skellig Michael in the 6th century.

Giraldus Cambrensis

*c.*1186

BETTER KNOWN AS Giraldus Cambrensis, Gerald de Barri was born in Pembrokeshire, Wales around 1146. He made several journeys to France, studying and lecturing. He was ordained shortly after his return to England, and in 1184 he became one of Henry II's chaplains. The king sent him to Ireland in 1185 to accompany his son Prince John. Cambrensis stayed in Ireland for two years and, on his return, he read his work *Topographia Hiberniae* publicly at Oxford over three successive days. It is one of the earliest travel descriptions of Ireland – often painting a fantastic picture of the country.

In the southern part of Munster, in the neighbourhood of Cork, there is an island with a church dedicated to St Michael, famed for its orthodox sanctity from very ancient times. There is a stone outside the porch of this church, on the right hand and partly fixed in the wall, with a hollow in its surface, which every morning, through the merits of the saint to whom the church is dedicated, is filled with as much wine as will conveniently suffice for the service of the masses on the day ensuing, according to the number of priests there who have to celebrate them.

From *Topographia Hiberniae*

Thomas Stafford

1601

THOMAS STAFFORD, WHO was almost certainly the natural son of Sir George Carew, president of Munster, served under Carew during Queen Elizabeth's war in Ireland. He accompanied Carew to England, and lived with him in the capacity of secretary. When Carew died in 1629 he bequeathed to Stafford his large collection of manuscripts relating to Ireland – including the original of *Pacata Hibernia*, a day-by-day account of the military campaign. When published a few years later, the book was under Carew's authorship, although it seems to have been the work of Stafford.

Sir Charles Wilmot, knowing that FitzMaurice the Lord of Lixnaw had only one castle, called Listoell, wherein to shelter himself, finding no other means to compass the same, determined to besiege it, and intimated so much to the President by his letters, requesting his advice and allowance therein, who returned answer, that he desired nothing more than to have that castle got for the Queen, and, for the manner, left the managing thereof wholly to his discretion. He settled before it upon the fifth of November, attempting to get it by a mine; in which, after he had wrought five or six days, and brought it underneath the castle wall, being ready to make a bed for the placing of the powder, suddenly the spring broke forth in such abundance that work became fruitless; thereupon new ground was sought, which proved good; the foundation of the castle was undermined as far as the middle of the cellar, which the ward perceiving, made humble suit to be permitted to depart with their lives, which Sir Charles absolutely refused; but if they would simply surrender themselves, the castle, and all things in it, to his discretion, he would then stay further proceeding in his work, otherwise they might look within very few hours to be blown up. The ward, which were eighteen in number, came forth, and upon their knees submitted themselves unto him, whom he caused to be apprehended. The women and small children he suffered to depart; of the weaponed men he hanged nine, so many of ours being lost at the siege, which continued more than three weeks; the residue he detained, until he had acquainted the President with all these accidents, who gave present order for the execution of the rest; for they had been all of them formerly protected, except one Sir Dermond MacBrodie, a priest, whose life was saved upon this occasion. It chanced that within this castle, at the rendering thereof, there was, unknown to Sir Charles, the Lord of Lixnaw's eldest son, a child of five years of age. The warders, upon their coming forth, disarrayed this child of all his clothes, and, having besmeared his face with dust and dirt, committed him to an old woman, who, bringing the infant naked and disfigured at her back, conveyed him away without suspicion. Sir Charles, receiving advertisment of this escape, sent out some soldiers and some provincials, whom he most trusted, for the recovery of him, but in vain; they all returned with lost labour. At last he bethought himself that peradventure some of the prisoners could direct him in the pursuit, and, questioning the priest concerning the child, he answered that he could best resolve him, for that himself had given directions to the woman where she should bestow the child till she might deliver him to his father. 'Why, then,' said Sir Charles, 'will you not conduct me to him? Know you not that it is in my power to hang you or to save you? Yes, and I assure you, if you will not guide me to the place where he lies hidden, I will cause you to be instantly hanged.' The priest answered that it was all one to him, whether he died this day or tomorrow; but yet if he might have his word, for the sparing of his own life and the child's, he would reveal his knowledge; otherwise the Governor might do his pleasure. Sir Charles, though very unwilling to grant the priest's life, yet the earnest desire he had to get the child into his hands caused him to agree thereto. The priest, being put into a handlock, is sent with a captain and a good guard of soldiers about this business, who guided them to a wood, six miles from the castle, by reason of thick briars and thorns almost impassable, in the midst whereof there is a hollow cave within the ground, not much unlike, by description, Cacus's den, or the mouth of Avernus, in which desolate place they found that old woman and this young child, whom they brought to the governor, and the priest and child were shortly after sent to the President. In this castle were got all the Lord of Lixnaw's goods, besides store of provisions for the war, who were plentifully provided for six months with such kind of victual as the country yields; and it was said that the Baron himself would have set up his rest in the castle, which he held impregnable against any force, the cannon excepted, but it would seem his heart failed him no less than his expectations. While these things were in doing, Sir Richard Percy drew

The castle at Castlemaine, or Castle Magne, was built on a rock in the river Maine in 1215 by brothers John and Maurice FitzGerald.

his company forth from Kinsale into Kinalmekagh, and there took a prey of two hundred cows, and got the killing of some rebels.

In the beginning of this month William FitzGerald, the Knight of Kerry, came to the President with a letter in his favour from Sir Charles Wilmot, dated the thirtieth of October, wherein he witnessed for him that ever since he was received under protection he had demeaned himself not only like a good subject, in doing no harm, but that he had endeavoured to his uttermost to annoy the enemy, and had lately in token of his obedience delivered unto Sir Charles his castle at the Dingle. The testimony wrought so much with the President that he used him very kindly, and returned him home with great contentment.

From *Pacata Hibernia*

Dionisio Massari

1645

In October 1645 Monsignor Dionisio Massari (born 1597), dean of Fermo in Italy, sailed to Ireland from France with Papal Nuncio Giovanni Battista Rinuccini. En route their ship evaded capture by English and Dutch vessels, and they landed safely near Kenmare. Rinuccini was on a mission from Rome to aid the Confederate Catholics and to safeguard the public exercise of the Catholic religion. In his contemporary correspondence Massari provides a vivid account of their journey. He returned to Italy in November 1646 and was later appointed secretary of Propaganda to the Vatican.

The place in which we now found ourselves was so full of reefs and shoals that our captain would not venture near land at that late hour, and so we had to remain on sea all night. The next day, however, the 22nd, feast of the martyr St. Philip, Bishop of Fermo, we touched land near the mouth of the river Maire, not far from Kenmare, towards the west of the kingdom but in the province of Munster. As the frigate was unable to make very close to shore because of a strong land wind blowing in our teeth, we had the Nuncio conveyed ashore in the ship's boat. His Excellency was immediately conducted to a shepherd's hut in the neighbourhood, while I with some of the servants and a few soldiers remained on board to take care of the frigate, and look after our money and baggage, the others going on shore to attend the Nuncio.

Next morning, leaving the frigate well guarded, I also went on shore to rejoin my chief and congratulate him on his safe arrival in the land of his nunciature after the many trials and adventures of the journey. An immense crowd of people had gathered around him from the neighbouring districts, and I was enabled to form some idea of the size of the population, though to judge from the wild and mountainous appearance of the region one would be inclined at first sight to imagine that there could be comparatively few inhabitants in the locality. His Excellency celebrated Mass in the hut which had sheltered him during the night. He received many presents from the people of the neighbourhood, such as beer, bread, cheese, butter and the like, and being anxious to have me taste of the produce of the country, he made me remain for dinner. After dinner he directed me to return to the frigate, intimating at the same time that he would soon let me have his further orders and instructions. Of course I promptly obeyed.

Next day his Excellency set out by road for Ardtully, while I proceeded by sea in the same direction, but hugging the shore pretty close, as the wind was still unfavourable. The Nuncio was attended by two companies of soldiers, one of infantry and the other mounted and well armed, as also by the chief of Ardtully who with some relatives and friends had come to meet him.

I sailed on as long as there was water enough, and when the tongue of the sea became too narrow I had the anchor cast. In the meantime the Nuncio safely reached his destination at Ardtully.

I am unable to convey an adequate idea of the beauty and wonderful variety of those spots lying amidst the stern mountains of Munster. I particularly enjoyed the sight of several rivulets, one of which sprung out from the summit of a high hill and, falling down a ravine into a deep abyss, at once became a large torrent. I noticed woods, springs, beauty spots, and the finest and safest harbours I have ever seen in all my travels. Happening to go ashore one day to enjoy the charm of a valley lying between two noble mountains I chanced upon a harbour so capacious and secure as to be able to afford shelter and protection to a large fleet against the most violent hurricane.

As I stood lost in admiration of the marvellous beauty that nature had wrought in this place, I suddenly found myself surrounded by more than four hundred persons, and imagining they were heretics I thought for a moment I was a lost man; but I soon found they were all fine Catholics, men, women, and children, who had gathered in from the surrounding districts. They formed a circle round me, and detained me till each one had kissed the crucifix I wore on my breast. They showed me many signs of kindness and affection, lifting up their arms to heaven in token of welcome and of thanksgiving to God for our safe arrival. They then led me with gentle violence to a cabin situated in the depths of a wood where

I was welcomed by a matron of grave and noble appearance and of most courteous bearing. I was at once put to sit on two feather pillows and I may confess that as I sat down I thought for a moment the ground had given way beneath me. I was then handed a generous noggin of fresh milk, and whether it was owing to the thirst or to the excellency of the beverage I took a second drink of it with infinite relish.

County Kerry, from Thomas Stafford's 1633 book, Pacata Hibernia, the military report of the Elizabethan Munster War.

All present knew how to make the sign of the cross, and there was not a child of even the tenderest years but could recite in Latin the Our Father, the Hail Mary and the Creed, while to my astonishment many could repeat the Ten Commandments.

Fortunately there was one among them who knew Spanish, and he not only interpreted what they were saying in the Irish tongue, but also conveyed my answers to them to their evident satisfaction.

Even after many hours I had great difficulty in tearing myself away from them, and then all insisted on accompanying me to the waterside. On the way they let me see that they regarded it as a privilege to attend me, give me a hand over difficult places, or even touch the hem of my garments. Some would not part with me till they had waded some distance into the water, while there were others who in a small boat of their own came with me as far as the frigate and having asked to see the room which the Nuncio had occupied, they set to kiss it all over in token of their great devotion and reverence for the Holy Apostolic See.

Next day I received orders from his Excellency to land part of the arms and bring them to Ardtully, whither I also was to proceed, sending on the frigate to Limerick with the rest of our retinue and the baggage, all of which was duly seen to.

Ardtully is a small but strong castle standing in the midst of some 200 cabins, inhabited by such large families that it was a marvel to see so many people in so small a place. Its chief (McFineen) is the owner of an iron mine in the vicinity and has built two excellent mills or factories there, one near the pit and the other a short distance away for the work of smelting and finishing the product, out of which he is said to make a handsome profit.

Leaving Ardtully we set out for the Viscount Muskerry's castle at Macroom, strong in situation and of almost impregnable construction. We were unable, however, to reach Macroom that day and had to rest the night in a shepherd's hut within a wood. We lay any way at all on straw scattered over the floor, a roaring fire protecting us from the great cold of the mountains. The Nuncio, however, was more fortunate in having with him his own bed which had been brought in two serviceable cases all the way from Rome. As far as was in their power the humble peasants of the place displayed wonderful courtesy, and treated his Excellency to cheese, butter, and exquisite milk in great plenty, which in that wild region reminded one of manna.

After Mass next morning in a rural church called St. Gobinet's not far away, we set out for Macroom. As the wear and tear of the long journey had led to a troublesome skin affection on his Excellency he was unable to travel on horseback and had to be carried that day and the next on a rude litter of wood and oziers by twelve men turn about, until a proper Sedan chair could be provided. He was attended all the time by two squads of cavalry and a company of foot soldiers, as well as by those who looked after the baggage, consisting of some twenty-two trunks and boxes.

From *My Irish Campaign*

William Petty

1685

POLITICAL ECONOMIST William Petty (1623–1687) was born at Romsey in Hampshire and went to sea at an early age. After studying in France and Holland, he matriculated as a student of medicine at Leyden. He returned to England and gained a reputation with the invention of a manifold letterwriter. In 1652 Petty came to Ireland as Physician-General of the army and reformed its medical services. His next task was the creation of the first scientific map of Ireland. Known as the Down Survey because it was measured down on maps, its purpose was to facilitate the confiscation and regrant of Irish properties. Petty himself received lands in South Kerry and founded the town of Kenmare.

I say that the more Pilchards (I meant at Killmare) were taken, the better price they yield; And I say again 'tis true. For when they bee few, merchants will not come to fetch them; and when we have not enough of them to load a ship, nor other goods to make up a freight, our Pilchards are undervalued. But quitting the Instance of Pilchards, I say that in Holland and Zeeland (the thickest peopled Countrys I know), the worth of men and of their days labour is greater than in Kerry and Connaught, and there also are fewer beggars.

From a letter to Robert Southwell

William Petty

Samuel Molyneux

1709

ASTRONOMER SAMUEL MOLYNEUX (1689–1728) was the only son of William Molyneux, the founder of the Dublin Philosophical Society and a friend of William Petty. Born at Chester, Samuel entered Trinity College in 1705 and while there received private tuition from George Berkeley. He undertook to finish a project of his father's, the writing of a description of Ireland for an atlas. With this goal he set off for Kerry in July 1709, with Petty's son, Baron Shelburne. Near Ballyheigue they went searching for the semi-precious stones that had been recently discovered there. In 1712 Molyneux went to London and became private secretary to the future King George II.

I went to Mr Crosbys of Baliheigh, about 6 mile from Lixnaw, to see the rock where the blew-Kerry stones are found. It is about 3 or 4 mile west of Ballyheigh, situated on the west point of Kerry head or Teduff mountains (which mountains bound on the south the mouth of River Shannon and on the north the bay of Brandon), calld Carcarbery you descend by the scragginess of the rock some 20 or 30 f: down a very dreadfull praecipice before you come to the first considerable vein of Chrystall. From the top of the rock to the sea there are five or six different veins, all at near aequall distances about some 2 or 3 inches perpendicular thickness each and running so farr horisontally into the rock that they are not yet exhausted where they have come at them. Over every vein and below runs a layr of a red earth of about 5 or 6 inches thickness which lys between it and the rock and accompanys it every where. The rock is a black colourd stone, as commonly. This is what you observe on yr right hand as you climb down the praecipice, where you have a fair prospect of the whole N. W. surface of that part of the rock. I climbed to the 2 or 3rd vein and there gatherd some large pieces of the vein, which is all solid and pretty plain at top and bottom, the chrystalls shooting in towards the center, where they meet and intermicx. What I gatherd here and in all the veins I saw in the surface of the rock to the right hand were perfectly clear, transparent, colourless Hexagonall chrystalls, but I am told that on the left hand descending further they meet, as they describe it, in the same reddish kind clay with the purple stones or Amethysts and that they find these to be water petryfyd or incrustated with this colourd stone, being all easily broken between ones fingers and water coming out from within, so that in severall clusters of em as big as ones hand (more or less) you shall not it may be have a solid stone of the bigness of ones little finger end. They find also, I hear, of these stones in this place of a yellow colour like the Orientall Amethyst. This I have only by Hearsay, for the descent was all ready so dangerous and frightfull to me that I did not venture any lower without the usuall help of a rope and basket and so lost the sight of the blue or lower quarry, as they call it. I was scarce climb'd up to the top again, when we saw arising here from the sea a very thick vapour or fog which rise to the top of the mountains and blew along em with the wind, so thick you could scarce see yr hand. This has often catchd people below picking Chrystalls and constraind em to wait severall hours for a return, but it was my good fortune to escape. There is another place also, some 2 mile from this, up the Shannon, where these stones are also pickd from the rocks, but this I had not time to visit. They shewd also here a place where in a rank western storm a ship was left by the waves whole on land, some 30 or 40 f. high from high water mark. Here it lay in so good condition and so long that all the people but the master, who was sick, came out safe on dry land, when a second as violent wave came and carryd back the ship and dashd it on the rocks below into a 1,000 pieces. We passd in going to Ballyheigh near Ardfert, where is an old round tower or steeple belonging to the church but very low one, oft mistaken by sea men for a like one which stands in Scatery Island at the bottom of the Shannon Mouth bay as this does at the bottom of Brandon bay, which, and indeed the whole sea hereabouts, is so very high and tempestuous, tho the most calm day it could be, that lying on the beak you might feel the earth tremble under you and by the noise one would think all the cannons in Europe could not aequall it; yet I am told the rowling of this sea is nothing comparable to that off Brandon head, which they here say is worse than the bay of Biscay; they are both so tempestuous, no boat ever passes here at all. Another of these round steeples also stands at Ratou near Lixnaw, near an old church, its door raisd high from the ground. We passed also by a place they call Magheryes or the 3 stones, from 3 very large tall stones, a large one in the middle and 2 smaller ones at each side, on the top of a hill which overlooks a vast country, probably a Danish remain. At Killahen also on this road stands another remain of antiquity, a very large ancient cross, but without any figure carv'd on't or any inscription. Captn Fitsmorris gave me at Balliheigh some fullers clay which He gathers at his house at Banno in that neighbourhood and tells t'is found in all qualitys to aequall the English but that t'is more gritty and not so tough as theirs. From hence we returnd the same way to Lixnaw. Ld Kerry gave me 2 samples of different coall which he has found on his land, in the mountains at a place calld Bololina. The vein is considerably thick and worth diggin, but that it dipps, but he hopes he shall find it run levell in another. With 2 mile down hill of land carriage he can bring it to his river here, the Breuke, and laden it into boats of 30 Tun to which this river is navigable to this height. He shewd me also some excellent slate, which he has from a slate quarry at Broadford in C. Clare, also severall chymney pieces of a very pretty colourd red and white marble, which he had from Killarny. The grain is not very fine and the stone looks as if it would splinter, but these faults, I believe, might be helpd by using more skillfull raisers, polishers and other artists. If so 'twill be little inferior to Italian. He has also a black sort of marble at Lixnaw, of which all the walls of his house are built, but this will not take with his workman any kind of polish.

From a manuscript at Trinity College, Dublin

Charles Smith

1756

A NATIVE OF WATERFORD, Charles Smith (*c.*1715–1762) worked for many years as an apothecary in Dungarvan. His first book, *The Antient and Present State of the County of Down*, was published in 1744. The first county history on such a large scale, it established Smith's reputation. He then embarked on a series of county histories and set up the Dublin Physico-Historical Society to facilitate publication. Histories of Cork and Waterford followed. Although the Society disbanded, Smith wrote another county history, *The Antient and Present State of the County of Kerry*, from which this account is taken.

Corckaguiny is generally subdivided into 2 parts or half baronies; they give that name to the southern and western part of this peninsula; and the northern side which is very coarse and mountainous is called Litteragh.

In the southern division, are also large tracts of mountain, which have been formerly cultivated up to the top. Several of them, which are but poor barren rocks, have great numbers of inclosures and marks of culture on their sides, which are now neglected; and this is a further circumstance that tends to prove that it hath been better peopled formerly than at present.

The country people are prepossessed with an opinion, that most of the old fences in these wild mountains, were the work of the antient Danes, and that they made a kind of beer of the heath which grows there; but

The main street in Dingle, photographed by Robert French a century and a half after Charles Smith's visit. (Lawrence Collection R10460)

these inclosures are more modern than the time when that Northern nation inhabited Ireland. Many of them were made to secure cattle from wolves, which animals were not entirely extirpated, until about the year 1710; as I find by presentments for raising money for destroying them in some old grand jury books: and the more antient inclosures were made about corn fields, which were more numerous before the importation of potatoes, into Ireland, than at present.

The feet of these mountains have several small brooks flowing from them, into both bays, near which, the industrious inhabitants have cultivated several large tracts of ground, that produce good crops of barley, oats, and wheat. They are encouraged to pursue agriculture because of the convenience of sea sand, which is an excellent manure; and this barony is thereby esteemed, the granary of the whole county.

To the other new roads already mentioned, that lately made from Castlemain to Dingle ought to be added; the greater part being quite new, and laid out in as direct a line as could possibly be drawn between the two places. The former road besides it's having been uneven, rocky, and rugged for carriages, went in so winding a course that the distance by the chain was 31 Irish measured miles, estimated only at 20; but the new way is but 22 Irish miles; by which travellers have not only an excellent road between the places, but also 9 miles less to travel.

To the S. of this road is Inch-Island, as it is called, although properly an isthmus. It lies on the N. side of the entrance of Castlemain harbour, and consists of one continued range of sand-hills, some of which are 30, or 40 feet high. They are covered with a long kind of sedgy grass that renders them compact, and binds the sand together. When the country people cut and carry away this sedge, as they frequently do for thatch, and other purposes, the sea and wind make great irruptions into the sand-banks. Between these hills the ground is quite covered with Yellow Ladies Bed-Straw, a plant called in England, Cheese Rennet; Gerard, who was a Cheshire man, says, that in his country, especially about Nantwich, they use it instead of rennet, esteeming that the best cheese was made from it. . . . The cattle fed on this island being mostly kine, thrive exceedingly well upon this plant. Towards the southern point of the island, considerable quantities of white peas grow spontaneously, the seed of which was probably scattered here by some ship-wreck. There are also great quantities of Eryngo or Sea-Holly, Colt's foot, Star of the Earth; and other sea-plants on this peninsula, but very little grass. The sand here is very white, hard, and of a fine grain; the air when I was on this isthmus was very hot and parching, occasioned by the reflection of the solar beams from the sand-banks: and it was with some labour that I measured a base line, in order to adjust the distances and bearings of the points and head-lands of the adjoining bay, which hath been for many years infamous for ship-wrecks; and never laid down with the least degree of truth, in any former sea-chart or map.

A few winters ago there happened a great storm in this place, whereby the sand was blown about so furiously, that a large herd of cows were driven off the peninsula, the poor animals chusing rather to betake themselves to the inraged ocean, where many of them were drowned, than to be overwhelmed on shore. Some of them swam across the bay, near two miles, through the highest waves imaginable, and saved their lives.

The castle of Minard, which stands on the sea-coast, midway between this isthmus and Dingle, was built by the knights of Kerry. There is a good quarry of brown free-stone, at no great distance from it, of which the coin-stones of several of the old buildings in this county are composed.

Dingle is the only town in this barony. Q. Elizabeth incorporated it, in 1586; and granted to it the same privileges which the town of Drogheda enjoyed, with a superiority over the harbours of Ventry, and Smerewick; and she gave the inhabitants 300 *l.* to wall the place. K. James I renewed its privileges; and granted it a charter bearing date March 2d. in the 4th. year of his reign, at Westminster. The Irish formerly called it Daingean ni Cushy, i.e. the fastness or castle of Hussey, an old English family, to whom one of the Fitz-Geralds, earls of Desmond, had formerly granted a considerable tract of land in these parts: viz, from Castle-Drum to Dingle; and, others say, he gave him as much as he could walk over in his jack-boots in one day. Hussey built a castle here, which is said to have been the first that was erected in this place, the vaults of which are now used as the town gaol. It was forfeited by the earl of Desmond, or at least by one of his followers, on his rebellion; and was granted to the earl of Ormond, with divers other lands contiguous to it; from whom, Fitz-Gerald, knt. of Kerry bought it, who also had a large old castle in this town. Several of the houses were built in the Spanish fashion, with ranges of stone balcony windows, this place being formerly much frequented by ships of that nation, who traded with the inhabitants, and came to fish on this coast; most of them are of stone, with marble door, and window frames: on one is an inscription signifying that the house was built by one RICE, *anno* 1563; and on a stone beneath two roses are carved these words, AT THE ROSE IS THE BEST WINE. Many of them have dates on them as old as Q. Elizabeth's time, and some earlier; but the best modern edifice in this town belongs to the knight of Kerry, at the back of which are large gardens, regularly disposed and kept in good order. Lime being scarce here, the town walls were built of clay mortar, and are gone much to decay. The town stands at the bottom of a small, but safe harbour, at the mouth of which large vessels may ride secure: the channel lies on the west side, and ships of an hundred tuns may come up to the town. The entrance of the harbour was formerly defended by a small fort or block-house, which has been many years demolished. Here is a barrack for a company of foot, and a tolerable good Saturday market. There was formerly an antient monastery in this town, which was a cell of the abbey of Killagh, near Castlemain.

From *The Antient and Present State of the County of Kerry*

Richard Pococke

1758

Born at Southampton in 1704, Richard Pococke followed the family tradition and became a clergyman. His real love though was travelling and he made tours in Britain, mainland Europe, Egypt, and the Middle East. He first visited Kerry in 1749, and again in 1758, while Bishop of Ossory, he undertook another tour of the southwest. His observations of his journey, recorded in letters to his sister Elizabeth, lay forgotten for two centuries in the Bodleian Library until discovered by Cork County Librarian Pádraig Ó Maidín.

Dingle, Aug. 14th 1758. Dear Madam, We set out on the 5th & in two miles came to Dunkeron castle, a quarter of a mile from the river are foundations of a wall in the wood, which they say is circular enclosing two acres. It seems some notes on Wallis's Geography mention Dunkeron, as the Ierne of Ptolemy call'd by him the Capital, I think of Munster: We went on & I took a view of Temple no Church, which is not very old. We came to the Blackwater, where the fall appead [sic] better than before, & we went down it to a rock near which we saw them fish for Salmon & take 32 at one draft in a Sein net. We had two of them roasted & din'd on the rock, in this Romantic place, in the middle of fine wood & rock. We came on to Dr Blands house at Sneim harbor, & saw the great waterfall but little better than before.

We perform'd the Divine office on the 6th & crossed the river Sneim & over two mountains to that part of Kilcrohan parish call'd Poolansbay. On the top of the first mountain, I observ'd a circular fort with a stone wall round it; & the second to have been another on the rampart about 3 yards from it. It was about 40 feet in Diameter; as I conjecture, as well as another I saw in the valley to the right at the foot of the second hill; here the wall was entire & there is a set in about six feet from the ground, this part might have a flat covering on it, but what is singular, the wall is about 8 feet higher, & round within are eight figures of steps to the top of the wall in this manner as to go up to annoy the enemy, & by 'em to be supplied with Stones it may be or other materials for that purpose. We came on near to St Crohans Cave over us towards the top of the hill, & turning to the South, we pass'd by another round fort entirely ruin'd, & at the Castle of Bonaneer came to the east side of Poleen ragh bay, this castle was made with a set out on every side, so as to receive the gabel end of a roof. We came to Mr Orpins little cabin; a most beautiful situation, in view of the little Islands in the bay, with hills rocks also cover'd with

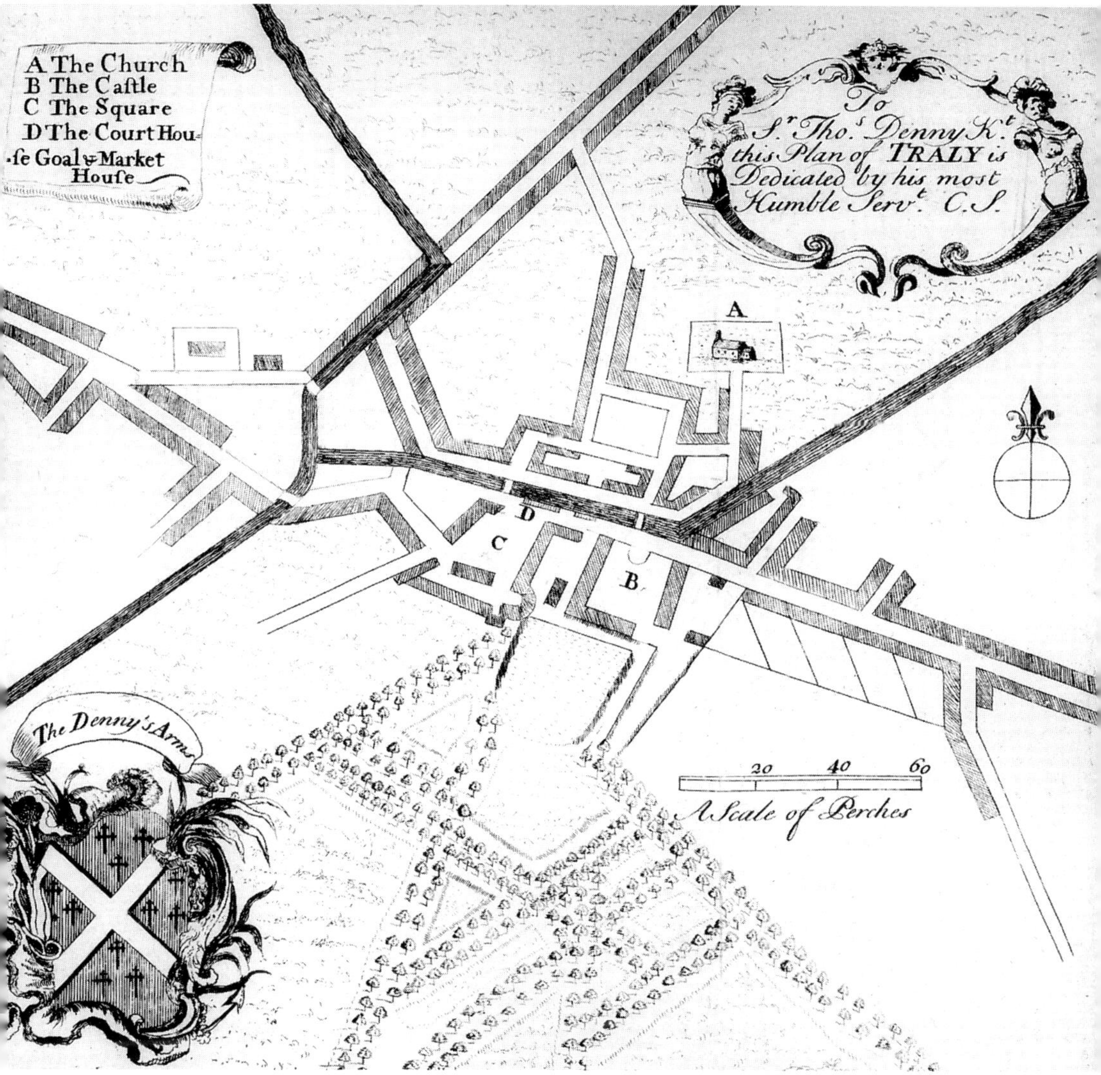

This plan of Tralee appeared in Charles Smith's 1756 book, The Antient and Present State of the County of Kerry.

such Shrubs, & wood as one would plant on them in a garden. A little beyond is an eminence with a circle of Stones & to the South a pretty Strand of white Sand, very rich in broken Shells; here we saw many of the little yellow periwinkles; nothing can be imagin'd more Romantic then this situation having the sea to the South & rocky mountains every other way at about five miles distance; & one beautiful hill near like a Pyramid.

On the 7th we cross'd to the same Castle & ascended up the hill to the North & coming to a Stream, we ascended near to the top of the mountain to St Crohan's Cave, which is about ten feet long & six broad & five high;

it is in a Vein of red, brown & green Stone, with a great mixture of Sparr, & the people by their devotions have worn it so smooth as to give it a polish. They hold a pattern here on the 1st of August St Crohans day. They say St Keran founded the see of Ossory liv'd for some time in this Cave; & some say that he composed his rules here, for the monastick life. Near this I was shown a Wolf trap fill'd up; it was a round hole about six feet diameter, & on this they put a hurdle, with a Swivel in the middle & a bait on it, laying a little fern on, the wolf coming to the bait the hurdle turn'd & let him down. They say a Fox pursued a Sheep into this hole & fell in it & got out, being not so deep as formerly, that an Eagle descended to the Sheep & was caught not being able to get on the wing. We had a fine view from the mountain & saw the Dursey Island in its whole length & very plainly Baley dungan bay no secure harbor to the west of Colagh bay where we embark'd after we left Beer haven. We saw what we took to be a small circle of Stones lower down & came to the foot of the hill to Kilcrohan church, a very old good building, near which is his well & an ash tree, which they say is always green, concerning wch I doubt. The Church has the narrow window with the true arch & that to the east is divided by two, by a Stone across the middle of it. We came on & cross'd over a hill, to Baley Carney Castle, & soon came to a white Strand over which we cross'd half a mile to Mr Connels house so well shelter'd by the hills & sand tho' very near the bay, that trees grow well about it, & especially orchards. We walk'd along the Strand to the Peninsula call'd Abbey Island, where there is an ancient church a sort of Hall & Dormitory & two other buildings adjoyning to it: they say this land was given to two Monks of the Abbey of [ ] on a vow. It is a charming spot of ground producing fine herbage & Elecampane. On the green sod near the strand, I saw a plant very common in Hamps. with stalks of yellow flowers on it in clusters, the flowers not so big as a pin's head, they call it Dah divell (sand bank dye) the root of it dying a fine red & is used by the common people for dying stockins &c: on this herbage are most beautiful streak'd snails. Juniper also crawls on the ground & so it does in Hog Island. I here also saw the Cornish Daw, which they likewise have at Beerhaven. This Strand is call'd Aghamore (the great Eddy). In these parts they manure for potatoes with dry fern. I was inform'd that at Argroure bay & at Cloheen, they have a coral sand of a brownish colour, & a gentlemen assur'd me he had seen it grow to a shell about two inches long & of a reddish colour. The Kites here are white & their wings tip't with black. They have the large Eagle in great plenty, & the rock Eagle which are smaller. The Sea Pye is a beautiful bird the head & wings black the belly & neck white, & the back grey, the long bill & legs red, about as big as a Pheasant. They have

The bridge on the Blackwater, drawn by Isaac Weld during his 1800 tour of Kerry.

another extraordinary sea Bird the Ganett as large as a Goose, it is grey the first year, the wings all black the next year, & afterwards the tip of the wings only black, they have a brown bill something like that of a gull, like them they fly over the skulls of fish & dart down with such force into the water, as to throw up a spout about six feet high; if the prey is near the surface they do not go with such force, when they rise they shake their wings to dry 'em & then soon in again, to take another; 'tis said, sometimes when they are gorg'd they cant rise, & may be easily knock'd down with an oar: They also put a prey on a board on the end of a boat, a little under water on which they come with such force as to kill themselves: they brood on the little Skelig, & 'tis sd are so bold, as like geese to come & fly at the oars & bite 'em, as people land. They take the young ones & sell 'em dear for their fat, which the people use to make rush lights. On Puffin Island they take Puffins when young & sell 'em dear salted, & they are allow'd to be eat in Lent as fish, as all other sorts of birds are that live altogether on fish. The Great Hog Island which we saw belongs to Lord Orrery, & there is a vein of Ore in it, Lead & Copper as I was inform'd; & they find large pieces & lumps of Chrystal in that Vein.

I must give you some Idea of a Milesian feast & manner of living. We had a dram offer'd before dinner, & had at the upper end Bacon & fowls & cabbage, at the lower a large roasted Turkey, on one side a leg & Loyn of mutton boyl'd & cabbage, on the other a boyl'd Cod, pease on one side, Lobsters on the other & 2 dishes of Potatoes on each side below, & a large dish of Stew'd apples in the middle, all succeeded by a large bowl of punch & wines. The Breakfast the remnants of the day before, Cold Turkey, chickens minc'd Turkey, a dish of fryed Mutton & of Boyl'd Salmon, a large wooden bowl of potatoes at a side table, covered with a cloth to keep 'em warm, boy'd eggs at the tea table, & a dram before they sat down, I am &c.

From *Richard Pococke's Irish Tours*

For centuries pilgrims and visitors to Skellig Michael have endured a steep climb up the ancient stone stairs to the monastery.

Richard Twiss

1775

RICHARD TWISS (1747–1821) was born in Rotterdam, the son of an English merchant. Having an adequate fortune, he devoted himself to travel, spending several years on journeys throughout the continent. His book on his travels in Spain and Portugal was published to great acclaim. He next turned his attentions to Ireland, but his *A Tour in Ireland in 1775* was very unpopular for its unflattering portrait of the country. The Irish had their revenge by manufacturing a chamber pot called the Twiss – the bottom a portrait of Twiss and the words 'Let everyone ——, on lying Dick Twiss.'

I had previously provided myself with every account which had been published relative to the celebrated lake, on the edge of which this town is built, which accounts I perused attentively, in order to be enabled to form distinct ideas of what I was to see. These were Smith's *History of Kerry*, of which twenty-five pages describe the lake, and are illustrated by a print. Thirty pages in Bush's *Hibernia Curiosa*, thirty more in Derrick's *Letters*, and three Letters written by the late Mr. Ockenden, which are added to those of Derrick. After these I read a poem, entitled *Killarney*, of fifty pages in quarto, written by Mr. John Leslie, and inspected six very fine prints of the lake, engraven from drawings of Jonathan Fisher, and published in London in 1770. Thus prepared I applied to lord Kenmare for leave to make use of one of his boats, and his lordship very politely ordered me to be accommodated with a six-oared barge.

It may not be improper to remark here, that it is customary to employ two days in seeing the lake, (or rather the two lakes, as they are divided into upper and lower) though a single day might prove sufficient, were it possible to prevail on the watermen to work; but as they are as obstinate here as they are everywhere else, travellers must comply. Sails are never used, as the sudden gusts of wind, which frequently issue from the mountains, would overset the boats.

These men are each paid eighteen pence, and at least five shillings to the boatswain, per day, besides which two brace of French horns reside in Killarney, one of which must be taken into the boat: the *corni primi* must be paid a guinea per day, the *corni secondi* are at half price.

All these people must likewise be maintained with provisions, and liquors of every kind; and they are always voracious and insatiable. Eight or ten pounds of gunpowder must be purchased, which are afterwards discharged from a small cannon by the boat-men, this causing the *strepitoso* of the

Ross Castle, the last castle in Munster to hold out against the Parliamentary Army, surrendered to Edmund Ludlow's forces in 1652.

explosion to succeed to the *amoroso* of the horns; so that altogether the two days which I spent on the lake cost me about eight guineas.

The first fair weather-day after my arrival in Killarney, I walked four miles to the foot of the mountain of Mangerton, after which I had two miles to climb to the summit; it is supposed to be one of the highest mountains in Ireland, as by the experiment of the barometer (Mr. Smith says) it is found to be 1020 yards perpendicular above the lake; but I was assured that it is not more than 800 yards, and that the mountain of Knock-mele-down, between Kilworth and Clonmell, is a hundred yards higher; however, all these dwindle into hills, upon comparison with the Pike of Teneriffe, which is 5132 yards, or almost three English miles in height.

The summit of Mangerton is chiefly a bog or swamp, composed of red moss and water, but tolerably firm. From the side of the mountain, about half way up, I viewed the lower lake, with its islands, as distinctly as in a map, and from the top beheld the ocean, the mouth of the river Kenmare, and the Skelig Isles; that which is called the Great Skelig stands about ten miles from the shore.

From *A Tour in Ireland*

Arthur Young

1776

ALTHOUGH BORN IN WHITEHALL, London, Arthur Young (1741–1820) was to achieve fame as an agriculturalist. A precocious child, he started a history of England while still at school and went on to write pamphlets, travel books and four novels. When in his early twenties Young found himself in possession of a small farm, he took up farming. In spite of some early successes, this venture eventually failed. In 1776 he went to Ireland to research a book on conditions there. Unfortunately, on his journey back to England, his servant stole his trunk along with all the notes of his trip. Young had to rely on memory to write his book but, from the following excerpt, it seems that the Kerry landscape had made a lasting impression.

September 26th, left Nedeen, and rising the mountainous region, towards Killarney, came to a tract of mountain-bog, one of the most improveable I have any where seen. It hangs to the south, and might be drained with the utmost ease. It yields a coarse grass, and has nothing in it to stop a plough. Lord Shelburne's agent, Mr. Wray, told me, that there are vast tracts of such in the barony of Iveragh. There is common gravel on the spot, and limestone in plenty, within half a mile of Nedeen.

Soon entered the wildest and most romantic country I had any where seen; a region of steep rocks and mountains, which continued for nine or ten miles, till I came in view of Mucross. There is something magnificently wild in this stupendous scenery, formed to impress the mind with a certain species of terror. All this tract has a rude and savage air, but parts of it are strikingly interesting; the mountains are bare and rocky, and of a great magnitude; the vales are rocky glens, where a mountain-stream tumbles along the roughest bed imaginable, and receives many torrents, pouring from clefts, half overhung with shrubby wood; some of these streams are seen, and the roar of others heard, but hid by vast masses of rock. Immense fragments, torn from the precipices by storms and torrents, are tumbled about in the wildest confusion, and seem to hang rather than rest upon projecting precipices. Upon some of these fragments of rock, perfectly detached from the soil, except by the side on which they lie, are beds of black turf, with luxuriant crops of heath, &c., which appeared very curious to me, having no where seen the like; and I observed very high in the mountains, much higher than any cultivation is at present, on the right hand, flat and cleared spaces of good grass among the ridges of rock, which had probably been cultivated, and proved that these mountains were not incapable from climate of being applied to useful purposes.

From one of these heights, I looked forward to the lake of Killarney at a considerable distance, and backward to the river Kenmare; came in view of a small part of the upper lake, spotted with several islands, and surrounded by the most tremendous mountains that can be imagined, of an aspect savage and dreadful. From this scene of wild magnificence, I broke at once upon all the glories of Killarney; from an elevated point of view I looked down on a considerable part of the lake, which gave me a specimen of what I might expect. The water you command (which, however, is only a part of the lake) appears a bason of two or three miles round; to the left it is inclosed by the mountains you have passed, particularly by the Turk, whose outline is uncommonly noble, and joins a range of others, that form the most magnificent shore in the world: on the other side is a rising scenery of cultivated hills, and Lord Kenmare's park and woods; the end of the lake at your feet is formed by the root of Mangerton, on whose side the road leads. From thence I looked down on a pretty range of inclosures on the lake, and the woods and lawns of Mucross, forming a large promontory of thick wood, shooting far into the lake. The most active fancy can sketch nothing in addition. Islands of wood beyond seem to join it, and reaches of the lake, breaking partly between, give the most lively intermixture of water: six or seven isles and islets form an accompanyment, some are rocky, but with a slight vegetation, others contain groups of trees, and the whole thrown into forms, which would furnish new ideas to a painter. Farther is a chain of wooded islands, which also appear to join the main land, with an offspring of lesser ones scattered around.

Arrived at Mr. Herbert's at Mucross, to whose friendly attention I owed my succeeding pleasure. There have been so many descriptions of Killarney written by gentlemen who have resided some time there, and seen it at every season, that for a passing traveller to attempt the like, would be in vain; for this reason I shall give the mere journal of the remarks I made on the spot, in the order I viewed the lake.

September 27th, walked into Mr. Herbert's beautiful grounds, to Oroch's hill, in the lawn that he has cleared from that profusion of stones which lie under the wall; the scene which this point commands is truly delicious; the house is on the edge of the lawn, by a wood which covers the whole peninsula, fringes the slope at your feet, and forms a beautiful shore to the lake. Tomis and Glená are vast mountainous masses of incredible magnificence, the outline soft and easy in its swells, whereas those above the Eagle's Nest are of so broken and abrupt an outline, that nothing can be imagined more savage, an aspect horrid and sublime, that gives all the impressions to be wished to astonish, rather than please the mind. The Turk exhibits noble features and Mangerton's huge body rises above the whole. The cultivated tracts towards Killarney, form a shore in contrast to the terrific scenes I have just mentioned; the distant boundary of the lake, a vast ridge of distant blue mountains towards Dingle. From hence entered the garden, and viewed Mucross abbey, one of the most interesting scenes I ever saw; it is the ruin of a considerable abbey, built in Henry VIth's time, and so entire, that if it were more so, tho' the *building* would be more perfect, the *ruin* would be less pleasing; it is half obscured in the shade of some venerable ash trees; ivy has given the picturesque circumstance, which that plant alone can confer, while the broken walls and ruined turrets throw over it

The last mournful forces of decay,

heaps of sculls and bones scattered about, with nettles, briars and weeds sprouting in tufts from the loose stones, all unite to raise those melancholy impressions, which are the merit of such scenes, and which can scarcely any where be felt more completely. The cloisters form a dismal area, in the centre of which grows the most prodigious yew tree I ever beheld, in one great stem, two feet diameter, and fourteen feet high, from whence a vast head of branches spreads on every side, so as to form a perfect canopy to the whole space; I look for its fit inhabitant – it is a spot where

The moping owl doth to the moon complain.

This ruin is in the true stile in which all such buildings should appear; there is not an intruding circumstance – the hand of dress has not touched it – melancholy is the impression which such scenes should kindle, and it is here raised most powerfully.

From the abbey we passed to the terrass, a natural one of grass, on the very shore of the lake; it is irregular and winding; a wall of rocks broken into fantastic forms by the waves: on the other side, a wood, consisting of all sorts of plants, which the climate can protect, and through which a variety of walks are traced. The view from this terrass consists of many parts of various characters, but in their different stiles complete; the lake opens a spreading sheet of water, spotted by rocks and islands, all but one or two wooded, the outlines of them are sharp and distinct; nothing can be more smiling than this scene, soft and mild, a perfect contrast of beauty to the sublimity of the mountains which form the shore: these rise in an outline, so varied, and at the same time so magnificent, that nothing greater can be imagined . . . .

The Eagle's Nest, on the wooded crags above the Long Range strait connecting the Lakes of Killarney.

Returned to breakfast, and pursued Mr. Herbert's new road, which he has traced through the peninsula to Dynis island, three miles in length; and it is carried in so judicious a manner through a great variety of ground, rocky woods, lawns, &c, that nothing can be more pleasing; it passes through a remarkable scene of rocks, which are covered with woods; from thence to the marble quarry, which Mr. Herbert is working; and where he gains variety of marbles, green, red, white, and brown, prettily veined; the quarry is a shore of rocks, which surround a bay of the lake, and forms a scene, consisting of but few parts, but those strongly marked: the rocks are bold, and broken into slight caverns; they are fringed with scattered trees, and from many parts of them wood shoots in that romantic manner, so common at Killarney. Full in front Turk mountain rises with the proudest outline, in that abrupt magnificence which fills up the whole space before one, and closes the scene.

From *A Tour in Ireland in 1775*

Daniel Beaufort

1788

GEOGRAPHER DANIEL BEAUFORT (1739–1821) was born in England, the son of a refugee Huguenot minister. He came to Ireland at eight when his father accompanied the viceroy, Lord Harrington. Educated at Trinity College, he took holy orders and succeeded his father as rector of Navan. Beaufort played a major role in the foundation of the Royal Irish Academy, but he is better remembered as a geographer for his *Memoir of a Map in Ireland*, published in 1792. He married Mary Waller of County Meath and their son, hydrographer Francis, originated the Beaufort Scale.

August 18th. This morning we assembled at 7 1/2 for our grand boating party but the day being extremely wet we sat down to Vingt un after breakfast. At Eleven it began to clear up, the boatman urged us to go, & we all drove down to Ross Castle. We were all very conveniently in the Barge of 8 Oars with a part of the band which Col. Jacques of the 51 lent us, & in another boat were our Servants & provisions. We reached the Eagle's nest, & were put on shore opposite to it, while our band went into a recess behind it. We heard their musick reverberated from the rock & quite softened, but loud enough & very true. From the rock above our heads some small cannon were fired, precisely opposite the Eagle's nest which repeated the report enlarging it to that of a rowling peal of Thunder. Poor Mrs. Pennyfeather was obliged to stop her ears so afraid she is of a Gun. A very heavy shower assailed us, & determined us to return to Dinas. On our way we saw a pair of Eagles soaring above us & at the Eagle's nest the royal bird itself upon it which our repeated shouts put to flight. It was half after Six when we arrived at Dinas. We dined heartily & merrily on our cold repast & when the musick,

Daniel Beaufort

the boatmen & servants were all replete set off for Ross Castle, by the brightest Moonlight. The water was smooth, the night calm & our passage delightfully harmonious in every sense. William in landing his aunt out of the boat fell on his head in the water. Our boatmen plied their oars so lustily that we reached shore by 9 & got drest quick & went to the Assembly which was much larger than the last. Mrs. Pennyfeather being extremely well dressed made an elegant appearance and we afterwards supped together. Did not get to bed till two.

19th. Showery again this morning yet we got to breakfast by 9 & at ten set off for Ross Castle, embarked again in two boats & proceeded to the foot of Glena near Dinas, where a large company was assembled in boats to see a Staghunt, with which O'Donoghue complimented Mrs. Pennyfeather. As soon as we arrived a gun was fired & the hounds laid on. We soon heard their tongue, & by the course of the sound in the wood, and that of the men who were placed to man the Mountain, we were guided on Westward, and the whole fleet of fifteen sail was in motion. In about an hour we perceived the stag come down from the wood, refresh himself in

The Lakes of Killarney

the lake, and then run along the shore for a mile, when he turned again into the wood. Our Boatmen anxious to catch him if he should take Sail rowed with such spirit as to pass all the rest. But they also passed the stag, for he had doubled, & tho we made haste back we were only in time to see him once more take sail, when he was soon taken up by Mr. Galway's boat, & tied there. The whole party attended him from hence to Stag Island near which he was untied & thrown into the lake, from which he swam to the shore of that Island, & lay down.

The boats dispersed now different ways – we to Innisfallen, where we had a cold dinner prepared, & fared sumptuously after walking round that Beautiful Island & observing the noble trees that adorn it, particularly a vast *holly* and a great *Yew*, the former large & lofty as an Oak & measuring 10 feet in circumference. While we were here Mr. Mahony brought over the hunted stag to this Isle in his boat to secure him from the Mountaineers who would have slain him for his hide. He had been hunted once before, the tip of one ear being cut off – & now the tip of each is gone. We passed our time here agreably till near 9 when we returned as before. When we landed at Innisfallen a crowd of apple women & nutsellers etc. were assembled there before us, just as if it were a fair, or rather like the savages coming down to barter with our ships in distant Islands.

From a manuscript at Trinity College, Dublin

Jacques Louis de Bougrenet

1797

A BRETON ROYALIST, Jacques Louis de Bougrenet, Chevalier de la Tocnaye, fled to England to escape the French Revolution. Although he spoke no English on arrival, he nevertheless managed to persuade several wealthy patrons to buy subscriptions to a book he planned to write – about a walk around Great Britain. With this successfully accomplished, de Bougrenet was persuaded by a wealthy Irishman, Burton Conyngham, to undertake the same venture in Ireland. Armed with letters of introduction, he spent nine months on his tour, and always managed to find himself a comfortable bed for the night.

I presented myself at the house of Lord Kenmare and passed there eight most agreeable days, during which I enjoyed several excursions on the lake. The soul most indifferent to beauty cannot but be charmed by this delightful spot.

Generally the visitor is taken about two miles from Killarney to the island of Ross, which is the largest island of the lake, and is only separated from the shore by a narrow stream crossed by a bridge. On this island is the castle of Prince O'Donoghue, to whom this country belonged in old times, and the inhabitants believe that they can still see him, on horseback, crossing the water on a certain day of the year. Following the coast to the east, the peninsula of Muckross is reached, and here is one of the most beautiful places I have ever seen in its singular *mélange* of wood and plain.

The venerable ruins of the Abbey inspire a sentiment of religious melancholy which is almost agreeable. The yew which is planted in the middle of a cloister covers it entirely with its branches and allows only a few rays of light to fall on the tombs at its feet. The natives here are persuaded that the mortal who would have the temerity to cut its branches, or even to pierce it, would inevitably perish during the year. They have a most extreme feeling of devotion to the saint of the place, and they make long pilgrimages to this spot, and perform here penitences which, as elsewhere in Ireland, consist in making the tour of the buildings a certain number of times while reciting prayers. They bury their dead here also, bringing them often from great distances. Interments are only made on the southern and eastern sides of the church. The north is commonly reputed to be the devil's side, and the west is reserved for children dying without baptism, and for soldiers and strangers. They look upon it as scandalous impiety to carry away any remains of coffins. In the Abbey are two large vaults entirely filled with them, while they allow bones to be scattered here and there where the spade of the gravedigger has placed them; but nothing in the world would induce them to touch one of these. In a corner outside the church they appear in a hideous pile. Although, at the time of the Reformation, the rich divided the Abbey spoils, they have never attempted to displace the burying-place. It is always round the ruins of an old church that the peasants wish to be buried, and nothing can be done to make them accept any other situation. Here attempts have been made often to find another burying-place, but such attempts have never succeeded. Nevertheless, it is a very necessary thing, for, beside the fact that over the rock there is hardly earth enough to cover the dead, the cemetery is so full that it should be closed, at any rate for some time. This crowding does not trouble the peasantry; they are content that the dead of a year or two should give place to those of to-day, and I have seen in this horrible vault more that one skull still covered with hair.

A few years ago a man of rather good appearance made his home in one of the ruined chambers of this Abbey. He made his bed out of boards which had formed part of coffins, and placed them in the embrasure of the window, which was the only covered part of the chamber. Soon he acquired a reputation for singular holiness, and the peasants carried food to him, while the rich invited him sometimes to their table, where he comported himself with the manner of a man accustomed to the best society. When he was asked for a reason for his penitence, he replied that he could never do enough to expiate his crimes. He was a fine-looking man, and it is reported that when a lady regarded him with some attention he said, 'Take care of those eyes, they have done a great deal of harm.' He lived about two years in this melancholy solitude, and then disappeared. Many conjectures have been formed as to who this singular personage could be, and many stories have been made to account for his conduct during his stay at Muckross, but they were only stories and doubtless with little foundation.

The peninsula of Muckross divides the lake of Killarney into two parts. The smaller one is very beautiful in its disposition and diversity. There is a spot on the mountain called the Eagle's Nest, where in reality eagles are to be found, and where the curious are amused by the extraordinary repercussion of an echo which does not repeat itself as others, but pauses for some time, and afterwards repeats the sound of a cannon shot like a roll of thunder. The banks of the little river which is followed for four or five miles on the way to the larger lake are very interesting, and this lake contrasts, by the wild and savage mountains which surround it, with the smaller lake, of which the banks are well cultivated.

The visitor is carried down the river to the lower lake, and brought to the O'Sullivan waterfall in the middle of the wood, afterwards being taken to Innisfallen, a charming island, on which at one time was an abbey. This island belongs to Lord Kenmare; and when one is fortunate enough to be numbered in the parties which he and My Lady arrange for visitors, after having admired the beauties of nature, homage should be rendered here to the hosts' politeness and their friendly hospitality.

There are some deer in the woods, and sometimes one of them is hunted in the mountains, and after many winds and turns, finishes by jumping into the lake, where the boats and dogs follow it and force it to land on one of the islands.

Numerous companies of people come here from all parts of Ireland, drawn by the beauty of the spot, but they only stay as long as is necessary to see this beauty. An effort ought to be made to keep them in the country by arranging some amusements, or finding mineral waters; these last established would greatly increase the wealth of the country, and I do not know of any place more agreeable and more fit for re-establishing broken health. There is a fountain of excellent mineral water in Lord

Kenmare's park. Unfortunately, it has not yet attracted the fancy or attention of the disciples of Hippocrates, but that will come with time. The town is agreeable enough – it seems to be new, and is built nearly in the formation of the letter T.

Walking early one morning I heard dreadful cries, the sound coming from a house. Led by natural instinct and by curiosity I entered, and found myself immediately in a room among a crowd of fifty or more women, who cried and wept over an uncovered bier, on which lay the pale figure of an old man, dead two days earlier. Four of these women, in particular, cried louder than others, tearing their hair and often embracing the corpse. I remarked that at the end of a quarter of an hour, as they became fatigued, they passed into a neighbouring chamber, and were replaced by four others, who immediately commenced to cry and weep in desperate fashion, and this they continued until the first four, restored by a good glass of whisky, were able to return and take up their wailing.

This sort of an assembly is called 'a wake,' and every peasant who dies is sure of having it every night up to the moment of his interment – all his friends and his acquaintances round him, crying, weeping, singing his praises in impromptu Irish verse, and drinking to his health. It is a rather costly custom, but the poor do not feel that they can, with decency, dispense with it. It was different formerly, for, according to the ancient Brehon laws, the quantity of drink and meat consumed were regulated according to the rank of the dead person, in order to prevent families from ruining themselves in trying to surpass the doings of others. This explains perfectly the answer of a good woman who had just lost her husband, and who was reproached with having allowed him to die without sending for the doctor. 'Oh,' said she, 'I thought 'twas plenty for a poor woman like me to pay the cost of the burying.'

I think, perhaps, the poor woman was right. The doctor is for the rich, a sort of moralist who urges his patient to moderate his pangs, and repair by attention to diet the effects of his excess; but for the poor peasant who has never in his life done anything to excess, and whose best remedy would be, perhaps, nourishing food, of what use could the doctor's advice be to him? If he cure him of his malady, he would kill him with hunger through the charges he would make for his services. His wife would then have double expense.

I was witness here, a few days after, of a somewhat strange scene. Hearing the funeral bell, I went out to observe the procedure. It was the funeral of a poor woman who was being carried to her last resting-place, the coffin surrounded by a prodigious number of females who wept and chanted their 'hu lu lu' in chorus, the men looking on rather indifferently.

A favourite view of many artists was the southwest facade of Muckcross Abbey. Isaac Weld drew it in 1800.

When the funeral arrived at the head of the 'T,' that is at the end of the principal street of the town, a singular dispute occurred between the husband and the brother of the deceased. One of the parting ways led to the Abbey of Muckross, where it was the custom for the family of the husband to bury their dead; the other led to Aghadoe, where were buried the family of the brother. The latter assumed the right to direct the funeral towards Aghadoe, while the husband wished to go in the other direction to Muckross. The friends of the two parties took hold in turn of the remains of the poor woman, each wishing them to be carried to the side they favoured; but each finding themselves unable to succeed, by common accord they deposited the bier on the street and commenced a vigorous fight to determine by blows of sticks to which side the remains should be carried. I was at the time with the minister of the parish, Mr. Herbert, who was also a Justice of the Peace. With great courage he threw himself into the middle of the fight, seized the collars of the two principal combatants, and, after some explanation, he decided that the husband had the right to decide where his wife should be buried. He allowed the husband then to go without letting go hold of the brother-in-law, and the funeral moved in the direction of Muckross. I remarked that neither fight nor controversy which followed arrested the cries of the wailing women, who continued to beat their breasts, tear their hair, and cry 'hu lu lu' as if neither fight nor controversy proceeded. When I saw the Justice of the Peace throw himself into the middle of the crowd, I must say I imagined that the combatants would unite to tear him to pieces, as a stranger meddling with things which did not belong to him. I mounted on a little wall more conveniently to see the punishment, but I was soon disabused; the peasants showed the greatest respect to the magistrate, and submitted promptly to his decision. This was no doubt the best thing that could happen, and the magistrate did his duty, but it was so amusing to me to find the people fighting over a dead woman, that I rather regretted that the business was so soon terminated.

I went one day to the summit of Mangerton, from which there is a view over a great extent of country, although that is far from being a sight of all the kingdoms of the earth. The eye wanders over arid mountains and parts of little lakes. That of Killarney appeared beautiful, with the serpentine peninsula of Muckross cutting it in two. Nearly at the summit of the mountain was a little round pool called 'The Devil's Punch-Bowl,' where I drank to the health of the patron, and to the health of his children; that is to say the bulk of humanity, pretty girls particularly.

As this town is much frequented in summer, beggars come from all parts. They build miserable huts along the road and importune the passers-by. I have often thought that this annoyance could easily be abolished by the establishment of a small House of Industry, in which the beggars should be forced to work.

It would not be very difficult to join the lake with the sea by a canal which could be brought to the Bay of Kenmare, or by taking the bed of the river to that of Dingle. If it were taken to Kenmare this would be better, as the bay is much safer and deeper than that of Dingle, which is sandy. To one or other there would be not more than seven or eight miles of cutting to do, and the connection would add much to the importance of the town and neighbouring country by encouraging commerce.

On the road to Tralee I was accosted by a man who pointed out to me three old castles which had belonged to three brothers who were the masters of this country, and had been chased from it by the English. I asked why they had been chased, and his answer was 'It was because they were not the stronger.' This is what may be called the argument *ad hominem*.

Tralee is rather a nice place, and is not wanting in trade. These coasts, as far as Limerick, were formerly the principal residence of the Danes, who seemed to have scattered, nearly at every step, their round forts, which the inhabitants call by the name of *rath* or *lis*. There are four of them, not more than two hundred feet from each other, near the mouth of the river in the Bay of Tralee. This town is well frequented by bathers, and the people who come to drink the mineral waters found a mile or two away.

I came to Ardfert, where I presented myself to the Dean, Mr. Grave, and was received as usual with that charming hospitality which always makes me forget, immediately, the fatigues of the road. Ardfert was formerly a bishopric; at present it is united to that of Limerick. In old times there were here many ecclesiastical establishments; the ruins of the old cathedral are the most remarkable remains, although nothing very great. The air of the place is said to be extraordinarily healthy. This has induced a celebrated surgeon to choose it for his place of burying; his tomb is constructed, and his epitaph engraved on it while he is still alive.

In ancient times there stood, in the cemetery of this cathedral, a high round tower with not more than the ordinary appearance of wear. It crushed itself, if the expression may be used, some twelve or fifteen years ago. I say 'crushed' because one would expect that such a building would naturally fall to one side or the other, but in this case the stones appear to tumble straight down, forming a large mass on the spot where the tower had stood. I went a little distance to see the venerable ruins of a Franciscan abbey, and, passing through the scattered debris of remains, I found myself in the presence of the two most beautiful and amiable ladies of Ireland, Lady Glandore and Mrs. Woodcock, who had resolved to be cruel enough to society to absent themselves from it for more that a year. I do not know whether it was their good example which affected me so much at the moment. Certain it is that never in my life did I feel such a desire to become a hermit.

At a little distance there is to be found one of those holy wells round which the inhabitants perform their devotions. This well is very famous, and the people come from afar. They pretend or assert that it can cure all evils, and the devotion consists in going round the well, bare-footed, seven times while reciting prayers, kneeling for a moment at each turn before a black stone, which seems to have been a tombstone, and, while kneeling, they rub the hand over three heads which are cut in the stone, and which are much worn by reason of this hand-rubbing and kissing. Afterwards they pass the hand which has touched the stone over the part of the body which is afflicted, drink a large glass of the water, and wash their feet in the current. Children are sometimes plunged seven times into the cold water, and I have seen people, well clad and having the appearance of being in comfortable circumstances, perform these ceremonies just like the others. I have also seen a very pretty young girl kissing these ugly stones, and I could not help thinking that I would have been a much better restorer if she had paid the reverence to me.

This well is widely renowned in the country, and even the Protestants, who are not very numerous here, when they have tried other remedies in vain, will make up their minds to try the well and go through the usual performances like their Catholic friends. The greater part of these peasants, however, came in a rather careless spirit, seemingly more with a desire to meet their friends than to perform penitences. Speaking to one of the visitors I asked him what was the benefit to be derived from this water. His reply was that he could not tell, and when I asked him why he went through the usual performances, all he could say was 'to do what the others do and to see the women.' In effect, it is at these wells that a great number of marriages are arranged. It is in vain that the priest of the parish has often forbidden his people to go to such places; they have followed this custom so long before the establishment of Christianity that they cannot be broken off it.

In reality, there can hardly be anything more innocent than to go round one of these wells a number of times reciting prayers, and afterwards drinking a glass of water. I will go so far to say that it must be very good for the health of the poor women, since it forces them to take some exercise and to clean themselves. The only thing left to the priest is to see that order is observed in these gatherings, and by his exhortations to warn his people against any impropriety or indecency, and in this the priest of this parish has perfectly succeeded. The good folk come here on Saturday morning and finish their devotions by two o'clock. Then the young fellows make up to their girls and see them safe home to their mothers, chatting the while.

Nearly all the people in this part of the country are Catholics, but Catholic and Protestant agree here very well. The priest performs mass, and the minister preaches, and the two flocks seem not to trouble themselves about each other's religion for the rest of the week. I went on Sunday to the Catholic chapel. The women are always separated from the men here. I suppose this to be to avoid distraction. In the middle of the service the priest made a long discourse in Irish, afterwards translating the principal part into English. He consigned to all the devils (although in highly proper terms) all those infamous enough not to pay his dues.

The priests have great power over their people. They are, in fact, the judges of the country and settle everything connected with morals and manners. They excommunicate a peasant and oblige him to leave a parish. Great care, then, must be taken not to displease them, and especially care must be taken that they get their dues. The Government knows perfectly well that the priests have the people in the hollow of their hand, and, never-

Thomas Fitzmaurice, first Lord of Kerry, founded the Franciscan Friary at Ardfert in 1253.

theless, they make enemies of them and treat them badly. Can they make the peasants go whatever way they wish? Well, make them your friends and you have gained the people. I am convinced that a dozen benefices in favour of Catholic priests, at the disposition of the Viceroy, would make them all as flexible and courteous and as desirous to please as their dear brethren in God, the ministers and bishops of the Protestant Church.

The churches are all placed east and west – when the priest is at the altar he always looks towards the east. It is singular that this should be such a common practice over the whole of Europe, even in the case of the Lutheran churches, and perhaps there is not one person in a thousand who has noticed it. I remember perfectly that, in France, all the old churches are built in this manner, and I had not noticed it. It is true that the new were often placed indifferently, but even in the new the great number will have the door at the west and the altar at the east. It is a custom introduced into the world long before the establishment of Christianity, and which is yet followed by nearly all the people of the earth. The usual reason given is that the Christian religion took birth to the east of Europe, and that it is a mark of respect for the holy places where were manifested the first mysteries of religion. If that is so, Christians in Persia should look to the west, but I believe that this reason has been used simply to sanctify ancient custom, as Mohammedans look also to the east out of respect for the town of Mecca. Although I am not in a position to give the real reason, I cannot take the one mentioned as the true one. I would rather believe that the custom is simply a universal homage which men in old time rendered to the rising sun as the symbol of divinity.

The neighbourhood of the flat and sandy bay of Ballyheigh brings some visitors to Ardfert for sea-bathing. Following the line of the coast, and crossing a tongue of land infrequently visited, I arrived at last at Kerryhead, at the mouth of the Shannon. This river is the largest in Ireland; the inhabitants have for it a singular veneration of which it seems to be worthy. He is not truly an Irishman who has not yet plunged into it, and as I desired to do always in Rome as the Romans do, a plunge into the Shannon was my first operation here. The river is seven or eight miles wide at its mouth. Its shores are lined with high rocks, in which are deep caves, the waves breaking at their mouths with astonishing fury. At a little distance, on an isolated rock, are to be seen the remains of fortifications, and at another place the traces of a little town, among which can be distinguished lines of streets and the foundations of houses. These seem to have been no larger then ordinary cabins, although the fortified enclosure is very considerable.

Following the coast I passed the Cushin, which throws itself into the Shannon. It takes its source at the foot of some rising ground from the other side of which the Blackwater flows. There is no country in the world better situated than this for commerce, and there is none where with so little trouble communications with the interior could be made easy.

From *A Frenchman's Walk through Ireland*

George Holmes

1797

GEORGE HOLMES studied art and architecture at the Dublin Society's schools in the years 1783 to 1789, and won two medals for landscape drawing. In his artistic career he drew views for book illustrations, and exhibited at the Royal Academy. In August 1797 he set off from Kilkenny with two friends on a five-week tour through Tipperary, Limerick, Kerry, Cork and Waterford. Holmes drew some of the 'numerous remains of antiquity', and in 1801 he published an account of the tour, written as a series of letters. This was the year of legislative union between Great Britain and Ireland, and he hoped his book would be of topical interest for readers in England.

This morning we prepared for an excursion on the lakes. The boats are stationed at Ross Island, about a mile and a half from town; it is rather a peninsula, being separated from the main land only by a cut through a morass, over which there is a bridge.

Ross castle stands on this island, formerly the seat of O'Donoghoe Ross, one of the most ancient families in this county. It lies close to the water side, beautifully backed by wood, which covers almost the whole of the island; the banks, in most places, are hid by thick and hanging foliage. The castle is now in tolerable repair, having a garrison, with a governor appointed for it, upon the establishment . . . It was held by Lord Muskerry, against the English, commanded by Ludlow, with Lord Broghil and Sir Hardress Waller, who besieged it with four thousand infantry, and two hundred cavalry; it was surrendered upon capitulation. Having embarked, and taken on board two men with horns, and two small pieces of cannon, we stretched across the lower lake, to the base of Glenaá mountain, where we deposited our provisions in the cottage; and shaping our course towards the upper lake, we entered between the two mountains of Glenaá and Turc, a narrow canal, or river, which issues from the upper to the lower lake. Here the most wildly diversified scenery unfolds itself, that the enthusiastic imagination can conceive. The rugged and precipitate base of Turk, contrasted with the opposite richly wooded sides of Glenaá, whose romantic groves, falling to the waves, cast a deep and solemn shade around; whilst on the other side, rock piled on rock, flung in wild confusion along the banks, covered with crawling ivy, and from their interstices, bursting numerous shrubs, in flower, and bearing fruit; quickly the scene would change; the mountains retire suddenly and leave us in a plain, of perhaps three hundred yards in breadth; the green lawn spotted with groups of oak, holly, and wild ash; again the hills approach, and environ us with dark precipices and nodding woods; awhile the course seems lost, we are suspended in doubt; till turning short, we penetrate a deep and gloomy shade, hid from the blaze of day by the umbrageous arms of the trees, which, interwoven together, form an imperious canopy. Once more we are launched into an amphitheatre of lofty rocks, clad with countless shrubs and forest trees, which, shooting from their bare sides, send forth their twisting roots towards the earth. Arriving underneath the Eagle rock, we stopped, and, landing on the opposite bank, stood lost in admiration not unmixed with terror.

Its sublime height, girt with a waving forest, whose aspiring trees lift their tall shade high amongst the craggy eminences, the haunt of eagles and various birds of prey; at its base, the tremulous wave reflected all again with varied beauty. But how can I describe the wonders of its many echoes,

echoes, which, on the explosion of the cannon, burst with tenfold magnitude from its rugged cliffs, rolling with majestic horror round the neighbouring hills, each seeming to repel the thunder as it comes, till by reiterated peals, it sinks into hollow murmurs among the distant hills, and is for a few moments lost; but, from the silent pause, the distant sound again strikes faintly on the ear, and by degrees, with collected force, grows louder, till at last it faintly dies away to utter silence.

Just at this awful period, the bugle horn sounded, and there issued from the grots and steep recesses of the mountain, innumerable sounds, like celestial voices, diffusing inexpressible pleasure, each wood and rocky dell prolonging the notes, which, floating on the agitated air, fell behind the hills, and mingled into one grand chord of most angelic harmony, that like

A solemn breathing sound,
Rose like a stream of rich distilled perfumes, that stole upon the air,
That even silence was took ere she was aware,
And wish'd she might deny her nature, and be never more;
Still to be so displaced.

From this enchanting spot we proceeded on to the old Weir bridge, a rude and picturesque object where quitting the boat, we betook ourselves to the bank, whilst the boatmen prepared to drag the boat through a fall of water, which passes with great impetuosity under the arch; through it they conveyed ropes to the other side, and, with the most painful exertions, pulled it up through the fall into the higher stream, which is elevated about ten or fifteen feet. Thus continuing our course, we at length entered the upper lake through a narrow channel formed by two projecting cliffs, called Colman's Eye. This lake is surrounded by mountains of a fearful height, fringed with forests, which creep up their sides to various distances. From the glassy surface, emerge huge rocks, crowned with arbutus, displaying its bright green leaves of gayest verdure, blended with its scarlet fruit and snowy blossoms. Some immense islands lift their bare and craggy summits high above others, from whose fantastical shapes the boatmen have named them, one, the man of war, another, the church, and so on, according as there is an assimilation. The shores are mostly bold and steep, abounding with the most surprizing variety of shrubs and plants.

At the farthest extremity of the lake arose McGillycuddy's Rocks; its many pointed head immersed in mists and storms; along its prodigious furrows we could distinctly trace the cataracts, swollen by recent rains, tumbling with fury, and glistening like liquid silver. In a little time we observed its forky summit pierce through the clouds, and the grey mists

The Old Weir Bridge above the Meeting of the Waters on the Lakes of Killarney.

slow descending, like a great curtain, half way down, through which the Sun darted his rays, partially illumining its huge side and base. We landed on Romans' Island, where we found a small cabin, built by the person from whom the island takes its name: he was a singular character, and retired here to enjoy the pleasures of his rod and gun. It is finely situated, commanding a delightful prospect of the circumjacent hills, with the numerous islands scattered over the lake. Embarking again, we crossed to the shore, and wound round the woody promontories of those stupendous mountains, proceeding to the very extremity. We approached the rocks as near as the land would permit, but all was involved in shadows, clouds and darkness; we could scarce see upwards an hundred feet.

We now bent our course homeward; passing again through Colman's Eye, we entered the beautiful canal, or passage to the lower lake. When we arrived within a quarter of a mile of the old Weir bridge, we felt ourselves gently urged on by the current; the boatmen drew in their oars, and we committed ourselves to the guidance of the stream; trimming the boat well, and observing our balance, we found ourselves hurried on towards the arch with encreased velocity; till, with the torrent, we were swept through the arch and down the fall, with a force that must alarm any person looking at us from the bank. As we approached it, the boatmen mentioned an accident having happened to a boat, which was broken to atoms down the fall, by not having sufficient water to carry it clear over the rocks, which by no means tended to quiet my fears for our own fate; however, we had a fine sweep of water, and were launched pleasantly into the lower stream. On our arrival at Glenaá cottage, we found a comfortable dinner ready for us, attended by everything which could heighten enjoyment. About six o'clock we got on board, and winding round the fanciful shore which separates Mucruss lake from the lower, we returned to Ross Castle.

From *Sketches of Some of the Southern Counties of Ireland*

Isaac Weld

1800

BORN IN DUBLIN, Isaac Weld (1774–1856) was educated at the Samuel Whyte School on Grafton Street and in England. In 1795 he set out to explore North America. During his two years there he travelled extensively and even met George Washington. The book on his North American travels, with illustrations from Weld's own drawings, appeared in January 1799. A big success, it was translated into French and German. In 1800 Weld visited the southwest of Ireland. His account of his tour, again with his own drawings, further enhanced his reputation as a topographer.

Being in company with some friends, who, like myself, were desirous of ascending the most lofty mountain in the country, we procured guides for that purpose; and, under their direction, crossed the lower lake to Benson's point, where we landed. From this place we proceeded to Dunloh gap, and, having advanced into it to the distance of half a mile, began to ascend the mountain on our right hand. It proved extremely difficult of access, and in many parts so steep, that, without the aid of the sapling oaks which spring from their fissures, it would have been impossible to scale the rocks. On the summit of this mountain we found an extensive tract of ground, less encumbered with rocks than the valley below, and covered, as far as the eye could see, with heath and coarse grass, on which innumerable herds of cattle were fed. Beyond it appeared another mountain extremely rugged, which we reached at the end of two hours. The ascent was not steep; but it was laborious and tedious, owing to the immense heaps of loose stones in some places, and the deep rents in the rocks in others; which last could not be passed without the utmost caution. Along this part of the route the only animals we observed were eagles, of which numbers hovered above us, as if alarmed at the invasion of their lofty solitudes: at one moment we counted no less than twelve of them within gun-shot.

The craggy tops of the reeks appeared on reaching the summit of this latter mountain; and after walking for about an hour over a rugged way, nearly similar to that which we had already traversed, we gained one of their loftiest pinnacles, which our guides told us was Gheraun-tuel.

It is scarcely possible to convey an idea of the sublime view which was now unfolded to our eyes. On each side lay a vast precipice, beyond which arose other immense mountains: still further on we saw the Atlantic ocean bounding the horizon for a great distance; and, in the opposite direction, a wide expanse of the inland country, watered by innumerable rivers and lakes, amongst which that of Killarney was only conspicuous for its superior extent. One of the peaks before us seemed to be considerably more lofty that that which we had ascended; but the guides persisted in assuring us that the appearance was deceptive; and that if from any third station we could compare its elevation with that of the point on which we then stood, the superior height of the latter would be obvious. The intervening precipices were impassable; as it was out of our power, therefore, to make the trial, we were satisfied to receive this intelligence as conviction; and perhaps none of us, after so much fatigue, were willing to entertain a doubt of having attained the object of our laborious undertaking.

The mountain which we had ascended resembled the shape of a wedge; and, at the summit, presented a long craggy ridge, so narrow, that, whilst we stood upon it, we could look into the depths of the precipices at either side, or drop pebbles into them from each hand at the same moment. The ridge consisted, for the most part, of sharp siliceous rocks, seated on sloping layers or strata of soft argillaceous schistus and sandstone, which are both very liable to decomposition; and as these latter substances are mouldered away by the incessant action of the mists and vapours which prevail in these high regions of the air, the siliceous rocks become undermined: we found several of them apparently ready to fall on the first shock. Fortunately there are no habitations within their reach, or the mischief to be apprehended from their descent would be truly alarming. From the guides who accompanied us we learned that large masses of rocks frequently rolled down the mountain after the snow began to dissolve. Their effect was described as extremely awful; whole herds of cattle being sometimes overwhelmed by their fall. From these circumstances it is obvious that the height of the reeks must be gradually decreasing.

During our progress we overturned several loose stones on the edge of the precipice, where no danger was to be apprehended from their fall. In their course downwards they carried with them many of larger size; and presently we could distinguish a huge heap in motion at a vast distance below us. It was at first a source of surprise that no noise was heard from the mutual concussions of these ponderous masses, when they could so plainly be perceived tumbling down the sides of the mountain; but in a few seconds it was dispelled by a sudden and tremendous crash like the roar of thunder, which was echoed for a long time from mountain to mountain; and, after the sound had gradually died away in the upper regions, it a second time burst from the depths of the abyss.

The large rocks of this mountain are formed of a grauwacke, similar to that found on the banks of the lake; and they are commonly intersected by thick veins of quartz: in the interstices we found some beautiful groups of small rock crystals. Large and brilliant pieces of the same substance are found in other parts of Kerry, particularly, as I am informed, on the mountains near Tralee: coarse amethysts also abound there.

Puffin

We descended the reeks by a different route from that by which we went up; and, having arrived at the base, found ourselves in a valley at the head of the upper lake. Soon afterwards we joined a party who awaited our arrival, at a cottage situated at Carriguline, on the banks of a river which affords the chief supply of water to the lake.

From *Illustrations of the Scenery of Killarney*

John Carr

1805

JOHN CARR (1772–1832), a native of Devonshire, started out as a lawyer but, for reasons of health, soon abandoned this profession for travel. In 1803 he published *The Stranger in France*, which sold very well. It was followed two years later by *A Northern Summer*, about his journeys in Denmark, Sweden, Russia and Poland. In 1805 Carr toured throughout Ireland, and *The Stranger in Ireland* recounts his experiences. On a visit to Spain he met Lord Byron who, in his poem *Childe Harold*, refers to him as 'green Erin's knight and Europe's wandering star.'

I found Castle Island a large town, in a state of rapid decay, owing, as I was informed, to a dispute amongst the proprietors regarding the division of their respective interests. The place was formerly called the Castle of the Island of Kerry. The Castle was erected in 1226; but the ruins want wood and verdure to make them interesting. Immense masses of this building broken off, as solid and compact as rock, lie in the field in which it stands. Only the shell of the Market-house and Assembly-rooms remains. The Charter-school established here, I was informed, was wholly neglected: upon this subject I shall remark hereafter. It being cold, whilst the horses were feeding, I went into the kitchen to drink some wine and water; here I met with two old women who were smoking a single and very short

John Carr

The noddy, a light two-wheeled hackney carriage used in Ireland and Scotland during the 18th and 19th centuries.

pipe between them, each alternately taking a social puff. Upon my asking one of them whether the rebellion had raged here much, she replied: 'No, your honour, we had only a *little blast* of it:' this figurative strength of expression is very common amongst the low Irish. Upon the rain having fallen after a severe frost, and the weather becoming softer, a fellow said that 'the rain had taken the *venom* out of it.' Another said to a magistrate, before whom he brought a complaint against one of his neighbours, after describing what malice the latter bore him: 'By my shoul, your honour, he would *poison the very earth* under me if he could.'

One of my old ladies, with natural politeness, offered to extinguish their joint pipe, if smoking were unpleasant to me. At the Castle Island, the innkeeper insisted upon it that all my shillings were bad, for the purpose of forcing upon me his shilling and sixpenny notes. Such perfect strangers are the people of this county (Kerry) to coin, that when the new penny-pieces were first circulated, the following singular and whimsical circumstance occurred: a militia soldier offered one of them in market to a salesman for a pair of stockings, the latter returned a tester in exchange with the stockings.

Turning round the road as I left this town, which I did with infinite pleasure, I met an Irish funeral: the corpse was in a plain deal coffin, and the population of two or three villages followed it, amongst whom about four or five men and women kept up a constant mournful cry, without any other indication of affliction: not one of them was in mourning, and I found my approach encreased the chorus of the funeral yell. The country still continued very wild and dreary. In these mountainous regions, a stranger, moving in a *pair of breeches*, attracts even the attention of the dogs, the constant inmates of the cabins, who, upon seeing so great a novelty approach, naturally regard it as a phenomenon portending no good, and accordingly set up the faithful howl of alarm. One of these vigilant guardians, after contemplating me for some time as I walked forward, gave the usual public notice of my arrival; upon which one of these mountaineers threw, *not a stone*, but a bit of turf, at him, and pulling off his hat, apologized for his dog wanting better manners. In one cabin I saw a pretty obstinate contest between a pig and his mistress; the latter wanted him to go out, and the former was resolved to stay in, and gained his point. The low Irish are very fond of giving fine names to these animals. A woman was overheard to say to a great sow: 'Ah, Juliana! Get out, what do you do here?' This reminds me of a celebrated pig feeder and agriculturist in England, who, after dinner, at a shew of cattle meeting, gave as a toast, Virginia his sow, and Horatio his boar.

A few miles before we reached Killarney, the face of the country very rapidly changed to fertility and beauty. The blue and purple sides of those vast mountains which inclose the lakes appeared full in my view: they rose majestically from a sea of vapour, and their heads were lost in the clouds. As we descended into the vale which led to the town, my driver, who by this time was quite intelligible to me, and who I found had impregnated me with a little of his stuttering, the natural effect of sympathy and association, observed: 'Ah, your honour! Here are glens and mountains! If you had them in your country, what a fine thing it would be for the robbers and murderers there: by my shoul, they are here of no use.' I could not help smiling at his opinion of England: in vain did I tell him, that we had glens and mountains too, which were not infested with robbers and murderers. He shook his head to all I said. In many parts of Ireland I found the same unfortunate and unpleasant prejudice.

Instead of finding Killarney a little romantic place, as I previously penciled it in my imagination, I entered a large town resembling Newport in the Isle of Wight; its streets were crowded with people: it is the principal town in the county of Kerry. To my great disgust, I found the quarter-sessions were holding. Every Irishman thinks himself somewhat of a lawyer, and is, from the little vanity of displaying his logical skill, more than from a spirit of litigation, uncommonly fond of being a party to a cause, or forming one of the auditory of a court of justice; hence in Ireland the quarter-sessions never fail to bring an uncommon number of people together.

I arrived late, and found a very respectable hotel so crowded, that I could scarcely make my way to the landlord to learn that he had not even a vacant chair in his house; so I drove, by his recommendation, to an inn kept by a Mrs. Murphy, which I found to be more quiet and very comfortable, and with which I had no fault to find, but that I was obliged at night to fasten my room door with a pair of old snuffers. After a late dinner the weather cleared up, and the lustre of a new moon, occasionally obscured by light clouds, induced me to walk to Ross Castle, about two miles distant, to the shores of the lower lake. As I stood by this hoary pile, the stupendous mountains and dusky islands finely reflected in the water, which resembled a dark mirror, the soft brightness of the lunar light, the sound of distant cascades, and of a boat moving as if by magic to the shore, formed a sublime and solemn scene too powerful and impressive for the pen to convey. Before breakfast the next day, I strolled through the town, which contains several handsome houses. Behind a screen of arbutus, laurels, and jessamines, raised upon the external wall of the Roman catholic chapel, a monument attracted my notice; it was a marble urn, half covered with a pall, resting upon a sarcophagus, under which the following elegant and affecting epitaph was written.

'Entombed near this Monument, lie the remains of the Right Reverend Gerald Trahan, Doctor of the Sorbonne, and R.C. Bishop of Kerry. His doctrine and his life reflected credit on each other. In him were blended the easy politeness of a gentleman with the purest principles of a Christian. Given to hospitality, gentle, sober, just, holy, continent, his charity was diffusive and exemplary; the patron and protector of honourable merit. He was learned without ostentation, and religious without intolerance: his affable manners and instructive conversation charmed every ear, and vanquished every heart. To perpetuate the memory of so beloved a character, his mourning friends have erected this monument, a frail memorial of their veneration for his virtues, and a faint testimony of their grief for a misfortune, alas! indelibly engraved on their hearts. He died on the 4th day of July, 1797, aged 54 years.'

If I were charmed with the epitaph, I was doubly so upon finding that it was the composition of a *protestant clergyman*. Whilst I was puzzling myself to think how I should reach Major Mahony, of Dunlow castle, six miles distant, to whom I had a letter of introduction, he was pointed out to me in the street; and, after a very kind reception, he introduced me to Major, now Lieutenant Heyland, the commanding officer of the Londonderry militia, who, with the characteristic politeness and warmth of an Irish gentleman, improved by having visited the most polished courts of Europe, made an immediate arrangement for my seeing every thing worthy of attention at Killarney. In half an hour after this introduction, I was on my road to Mucruss, well mounted, with my Killarney friend. We passed by the house and grounds of Lord Kenmare: the former is large and somewhat aged, and possesses nothing worthy of notice; the latter are very beautiful. As we turned into Mucruss, the estate of H.A. Herbert, Esq., the richest scenery opened upon us: the ground, gently undulating, clothed with vivid green verdure, the effect of the great humidity of the climate here, was adorned with almost every variety of shrubs, flourishing in the highest beauty and perfection.

From *The Stranger in Ireland*

Edward Dubois

1807

EDWARD DUBOIS (1774–1850) was born in London, the son of a French merchant. Renowned as a wit, he contributed regularly to several periodicals, particularly the *Morning Chronicle*. Until the end of his life he worked as art critic for the *Observer*. For at least twenty years Dubois was deputy to the judge of the court of requests, and also for many years filled a position on the Metropolitan Lunacy Commission. Most of his eight books appeared when he was a young man. *My Pocket Book* (1807) was a satirical response to the recently published *A Stranger in Ireland* by Sir John Carr.

'A travelling Hint,' 'There are no stages or regular posting to Killarney,' therefore it is good to have this hint, lest you should get into one of the stages, or begin a regular sort of posting! Hire a chaise to 'go all the way for four guineas, and change your notes, on the day you start,' for those of Roches, bankers in this place, or you'll find that you'll not be able, as the song has it, to 'change your notes to-morrow.' At Limerick, Kerry, and Cork, a banker is as common as a potatoe. I saw one who had 'failed for five guineas.' The failure produced great consternation, and credit no doubt suffered a violent injury. 'These Musquito bankers have shocking temptations to fraud.'

About seven o'clock, A.M. when the blanket of the morning was as wet as heart could wish it not to be, 'I bade adieu to Limerick, so famous for pretty women and pork.' I say bade adieu, but the fact is, after the stinging epithet, Musquito, applied to the bankers, who were as numerous as potatoes, I was afraid to stay . . .

You cannot leave Adair, the first place you come to, 'without heaving a sigh for poor mortality.' It does not cost much, it's true, but it would be as well if one could know why.

'My driver was a very good humoured fellow.' I obtained all my information respecting the monastery from him – he 'stuttered most unintelligibly.' Upon the road I met 'pigs checked in their erratic disposition,' by tying one fore and hind leg together. I am glad they don't serve men of erratic dispositions in any such manner!

'I ascended those great mountains which rise between Rathkeale and Abbeyfeale.' These mountains are very awkwardly situated. A mountain's top here is not its own top, but the bottom of another. 'The summit of one mountain proved, when we reached it, to be only the base of another' – it was not so before we reached it!

The evening was 'shrouded in black clouds,' and I had a scene of 'universally deep-embrowned sterility.' There is the true curious felicity of language.

At Abbeyfeale, for supper, they gave me 'a fowl who had lost his head.' I did not half like this; and looked, as the French say, 'serieux comme un pot de chambre;' but thinking they were too simple to mean anything personal, I proceeded to dissect it, when I certainly found that it had not 'more tenderness than doth become' a chicken – I therefore spared his body, as well as my own teeth, and had recourse to 'a pyramid of fried pork, and a pint of excellent port wine.'

In Ireland smoking is a more affectionate amusement than in England. There two smoke a single pipe. It is improved upon by the Dutch, who, at tea, suck the same piece of sugar candy, suspended over the tea-table by a string from the ceiling. This is one of their social sweets. It is said that when the new penny-pieces first appeared, a soldier offered one to a salesman, for a pair of stockings, who 'returned a tester in exchange with the stockings:' this must have been a pretty penny.

On leaving Castle Island, which I did 'with infinite pleasure' (I must not always regret the beauties I quit) I made some very valuable discoveries; such as will be found worthy of my immortal page! I have often observed in life that there is much laughter without mirth, but, I believe that such an abundance of crying, as you hear in Ireland, without sorrow, is peculiar to that country. The perpetual yelling at an Irish funeral is merely pro-forma, or sham Abraham – no sign of grief, but a method

Edward Dubois turned his satirical eye on himself when he sketched himself making an illustration for his book.

of making themselves dry, as I imagine, that they may be able to drink the more whisky. But to matters more serious. 'In these mountainous regions,' if a dog catches you with a pair of breeches on, he barks at you – it is supposed that the dogs have been taught this by the women! A dog, 'contemplated me, for some time, as I walked forward.' I never was more flattered in my life, for I have no doubt that he took me for a cynic philosopher. However, my breeches were on, and, spite of his teeth, he could not help giving 'the faithful howl of alarm.' His master came immediately, and 'threw, not a stone, but a bit of turf at him.' Query, beef instead of turf, since the dog was quiet afterwards, though I still kept on my breeches? Here I saw a match of obstinacy, between two animals well pitted for a tough fight. It was a contest in a cabin, between a pig and a man's wife. In Ireland, in opposition to our custom, the mistress always likes to be master of the house – hence perhaps the novelty of seeing a man in these parts with breeches! I witnessed this contest with vast satisfaction, but much I trembled for poor pigee, seeing the nature of the dispute, and the antagonist a woman: however, to my great surprise, the pig beat her hollow, and kept possession of the cabin in defiance of her.

This sow was named 'Juliana,' probably by the husband, out of kind respect for her prowess, and as a sort of subsidy to secure her alliance against the common enemy.

As you approach Killarney, the sides of the mountains appear 'blue and purple.' These do not 'rise from the earth,' like some I mentioned before, but 'from a sea of vapour,' and, as usual, pop their 'heads in the clouds.' I must here notice a most singular fact, and well deserving the deep consideration of Mr. Thelwall, who cures defects in the organs of speech. 'As we descended into the vale,' I found, 'that my stuttering driver was quite intelligible.' What was gone with his stutter I could not guess, till, attempting to speak, egad, I found I had got it myself – he 'had impregnated me with his stuttering.' How I became pregnant with such a hop step and a jump family of words is worthy of investigation. My sentiment is, that it was the 'natural effect of sympathy and association' with the post-boy. Recovering his voice, it was his turn to speak, and mine to hear. So, said he, 'here are glens and mountains!' Had his stuttering remained, he could not have made such a plain observation. He then kindly wished that they were in England, for our robbers and murderers to hide themselves in, for 'by my shoul,' added he, 'they are of no use here.' Not being able to speak, I smiled – 'He shook his head.' I could not but think that his opinion of our being infested with murderers was an 'unpleasant prejudice.'

I had 'penciled in my imagination,' which is a spacious blank, 'a little romantic place,' and called it Killarney, but I discovered my mistake when I saw it, and am happy to confess this my single error. 'I entered a large town.'

From *My Pocket Book*

James Bell

c.1807

JAMES BELL was born in 1765 near Ballyshannon in County Donegal, the son of an Anglican father and Presbyterian mother. In June 1815, when his sons Thomas and John sailed from Belfast for America, he presented them with a hand-written history of his life that is now in the library of the New-York Historical Society. This account focuses on his spiritual odyssey: after experiencing an evangelical conversion at the age of twenty, Bell became a Methodist minister. From 1790 onwards he preached the gospel, sometimes in Irish, throughout the country. He served on a different circuit every year, apart from the three years – 1807 to 1809 – when he and his family were based in Cork.

During the three years Br. Taylor and I laboured in Cork and Kerry Counties we saw much of the power of God in the conviction & conversion of souls. In Milltown County Kerry we Mr. Taylor and I went to a place called Castleisland in County Kerry about 8 miles East of Tralee, and about 2 Oclock in the evening we stood upon the Street. numbers assembled and as a detachment of the Longford Militia commanded by Captn Armstrong were in Town, and many of them very friendly to the Gospel, they attended – A Clergymans servant of the Established Church was resolved to stone us when a private of the Longford, a Romanist Batn, Reynolds struck the person with his fist. I saw a Corporal Smith drawing his bayonet as the crowd encreased & requested he would not. he said it was only to intimidate them. A Soldier ran off to the Barrack and I soon observed Captn Armstrong coming out. He met Dennis McCarthy the young Priest and told him to call his flock to order. if not said I will bring them to order by calling the soldiers out of the Barrack.

Mr. John Williams, a respectable Local Preacher from Blennerville – being present – told the Priest, Sir said he, I am informed you said you would soon silence all the Methodist Preachers.I am one of them, and now Sir, I will answer you. the other said he would scorn to reason with him, although the other was a gentleman of property and he was a Carmans son 14 Miles from Cork on Kerry Road – The mob ceased shouting. – But about 10 Oclock at night we were informed 21 Men prepared themselves with Arms for the purpose of attacking us, about One Oclock at night in our lodging so one of our friends in the Army got a gun prepared which was to be fired if we were attacked. this signal was in order to call out the Guard at the Barrack – However it was very remarkable it blew a Tempest. The rain fell in torrents, about that time of night the Centinels box was blown down by the wind. Indeed we slept little that night – But above all Our Shepherd had his providential over and his Everlasting Arms underneath!!!!

From A Sketch of the Life and Experience of James Bell

Doorway at Aghadoe Church, near Killarney.

Lewis Dillwyn

1809

BORN IN SUFFOLK AT Ipswich, Lewis Dillwyn (1778–1855) attended the Society of Friends school at Folkestone. In 1798 he went to Dover and began his study of botany. The first of his botanical works appeared in 1802. The following year he moved to Swansea to manage a pottery his father had bought there. In July 1809 Dillwyn, accompanied by his friend Joseph Woods and another companion, visited Killarney. The journal he kept of his trip is preserved in Trinity College Library, Dublin. In 1832 Dillwyn was elected as Member of Parliament for Glamorganshire and later as mayor of Swansea.

The Priests Leap divides the Counties of Cork & Kerry into the latter of which we entered when we passed its Summit. About 100 yards from the top of the Mountain we crossed a small Bridge on which three months ago the Revd Mr. Tisdall, Protestant Vicar of Kenmare was waylaid, robbed, & inhumanly murdered by two Ruffians one of whom named Murphy now lies in Tralee Jail with the clearest Evidence against him. The manner in which he was taken is singular. Mr. Tisdall's Body was not found or his dreadful fate known till nine days after the Murder & in the Interim Murphy had escaped to the opposite side of the Kingdom where some Persons seeing such an ill looking Fellow well stocked with Bank Notes suspected they were forged & stopped him at Kilkenny. Before he could clear himself from the charge of Forgery, the murder was detected & printed descriptions of Murphy's Person were circulated by Mr. Hutchins, one of which reached Kilkenny just as the Magistrate was going to discharge him. He is accused of numerous other Crimes of the very blackest die, & is said to have hired himself for two Guineas, & assassinated a Person whom he never saw till pointed out for the bloody purpose. His accomplice was also taken but contrived to murder the Constable who had him in Custody & thereby effected his escape.

It is the custom of this Country when any person has been murdered to form a heap of stones on the Spot, to which every Passerby adds one or it is supposed that he would otherwise be haunted by the Ghost of the Deceased. The heap, or Cairne as it is here called, was in the present instance so small, that I should hardly have noticed it, if I had not been previously informed of its situation.

The Priests Leap is said to be more than 2,000 feet above the level of the Sea, and the prospect from its Summit is very grand and extensive. To the Southward the smooth & glassy surface of Bantry Bay with its numerous creeks & Inlets formed a fine contrast to the dark line of its surrounding Mountains, & a large tract of Country with the Atlantic Ocean beyond as if spread in a Map beneath us. To the North immediately below us appeared a Tract of dreary Peat without either a House or Tree in view, & beyond it the numerous vast Mountains of Kerry, many of which have no connection with each other, but rise separately from their own Bases, & in this respect the view differs from any other that I have ever seen.

At half past six having all met together and found our Carriage at the foot of the Mountain we proceeded towards Kenmare where however we did not arrive till half past eight tho' its distance from Bantry is said to be *only* 12 Irish Miles. We had sent a message to the Inn desiring that some Dinner might be prepared against our arrival, but it was not ready till an hour after, & a long hour it seemed for we had not eaten a Mouthfull since Breakfast. I had a violent Cold and felt so much indisposed that tho' I was not at all over fatigued I fell fast asleep immediately after Dinner and was unable even to journalise or preserve my Specimens that Evening.

Wednesday, July 19th. We had taken up our Quarters at a comfortable Inn, which is kept by a Mrs. Sullivan & has been recently built by Lord Henry Petty who possesses a large property in this Neighbourhood. After Breakfast we strolled for about 1 1/2 hours on the Banks of Kenmare Bay, which is a very fine winding Haven of the same kind as that at Bantry. It is, however, still larger, the length being about 30 and the breath from 3 to 9 miles but it's Banks are less mountainous & altogether the effect it produces is less striking & picturesque. Kenmare or Nedeen by which name it is most commonly known in this Country is a small & straggling Town. Close by the Inn a handsome Chapel has been built & is now nearly finished at the expence of Lord Henry Petty for the use of the Catholicks. On the Banks of the Bay I collected Venus Paphia and several other Shells.

There are two Roads from Kenmare to Killarney, by one of which the distance is 12 & by the other 20 or 24 miles. The former, however, is extremely mountainous & the latter is flat, & as we were told that it also passes thro' a far more beautiful country, we gave it the preference & set out accordingly at 1/2 past 10.

As near as it is possible to judge of distances where the Roads have never been measured & where they are reckoned differently by every Person you meet, the Country thro' which we passed for the first six Miles was not at all particularly picturesque. It then however became romantic & we soon afterwards entered a very extensive wood of Oak & Birch

Stag hunt at Derrycunihy Cascade near the Upper Lake of Killarney.

which is the first we had seen in Ireland except such as had been planted about the seats of the Gentry. On the opposite side of the Valley the Mountains rose to a great height & were in some places almost perpendicular, but they derived their principal beauty from the numerous deep Gullies which were well wooded whilst the more prominent points were bare. Our Horses were baited at a wretched Pot House & we availed ourselves of the opportunity it afforded to stroll among the neighbouring Woods, but without being able to make any botanical or entomological Discoveries. *Saxifraga umbrosa* by the road sides in almost every situation was the commonest of weeds.

About a mile or two from this place our course suddenly changed from Northward to Westward & we then passed the much and deservedly admired Flesk Rocks which take their name from the River that winds along their Feet. They are in many places nearly perpendicular & notwithstanding their apparent want of Soil, are beautifully scattered over with Oak, Birch & Ash Trees many of which have attained a large size. My idea is that their height is not less than 600 feet. From thence as we approached

Killarney, the view with the cloud capt Summits of Magillycuddy's Reeks in our front, became more & more mountainous & more sublime.

This entrance into the Town thro' Lord Kenmare's Plantation is handsome but we have yet had no good view of the Lake, Killarney being near two English Miles from it's Banks. We drove to Coffees Hotel which tho' very large for a County Inn was so full that we were shoved about from one Room to another, & were obliged to sleep in different houses over the way, which, however, were provided with good Beds.

From a manuscript at Trinity College, Dublin

Thomas Moore

1823

THE SON OF A GROCER from County Kerry, Thomas Moore (1779–1852) was born in Dublin. He entered Trinity College in 1779, just one year after the restrictions against Catholics were lifted. While still in Dublin he became friends with Robert Emmet but avoided being drawn into the United Irishmen movement. In 1799 Moore moved to London, and the first of his *Irish Melodies* was published there in 1807. These were so popular that he was paid the phenomenal sum of £3,000 for his next work, *Lallah Rookh*. A frequent guest at the houses of the aristocracy, Moore went to Killarney in June 1823 to stay with Lord and Lady Kenmare. During this visit he was inspired to write 'Inisfallen Fare Thee Well.'

Thomas Moore

7th. Started in the gig with Nick Beecher at eleven, in order to be time enough to catch the Killarney coach at Mill Street. Arrived at Lord Kenmare's at four. The dinner very good, and Lady Kenmare very pleasing.

8th. The weather rather favourable. Drove down to

Ross Island, and embarked on the Lake at eleven. Lady Kenmare's first time of being on her own lakes, having been but ten days here, and reserving her debut (as she says) for my coming. Landed on Inisfallen, and enjoyed thoroughly its loveliness. Never was anything more beautiful. Went afterwards to Sullivan's Cascade, which was in high beauty. Curious effect of a child on high, crossing the glen; seemed as if it was flitting across the waterfall. The peasants that live on the opposite banks come over with fruit when strangers appear, and their appearance, with their infants, stepping from rock to rock, across the cascade, highly picturesque. Mr. Galway (Lord Kenmare's agent) and his wife at dinner. Instance of the hospitality of the poor cotters, that it is the practice with many of their families to lay by, each individual, every day, one potatoe and a sup of milk for the stranger that may come.

12th. A beautiful day at last. Went with Lord Kenmare to see the Upper Lake. The whole scene exquisite. *Loveliness* is the word that suits it best. The grand is less grand than what may be found among the Alps, but the softness, the luxuriance, the variety of colouring, the little gardens that every small rock exhibits, the romantic disposition of the islands, and graceful sweep of the shores; – all this is unequalled anywhere else. The waterlilies in the river, both white and yellow, such worthy inhabitants of such a region! Pulled some heath on Roman's Island to send to my dear Bessy.

13th. A fine day for the hunt, but preferred the Lansdownes. Started after breakfast. At Lixnaw visited the ruins which the Kerry family inhabited; a spacious and formal dwelling. Lady L. wished to sketch it, but could make nothing of such a wilderness of chimneys. A pretty summerhouse, however, which she took, is the monument of the Earl of Kerry, to preserve which Lord L. has been left the farm around it, about forty acres, being all that he inherited with the title; the Earl of Kerry having sold all his estates for a life-annuity. The family lived here in feudal state; the old Earl and Countess dining by themselves, and when in company being the only persons sitting on chairs, the rest having tabourets. Had their Board of Green Cloth like royal personages; the shutters of the windows inlaid with silver.

From *The Journal of Thomas Moore*

A tunnel on the road from Kenmare to Killarney, part of the route designed by Alexander Nimmo.

Alexander Nimmo

1824

ALEXANDER NIMMO (1783–1832) was born at Kirkcaldy and educated at the universities of St. Andrews and Edinburgh. He first worked as a schoolteacher, and when he was recommended to the parliamentary commission fixing the boundaries of the Scottish counties, he did the work during his vacations. He soon gave up teaching and obtained an appointment as surveyor to the commission for reclaiming the bogs of Ireland. In 1822 Nimmo was appointed engineer of the western district. Under his direction thirty piers and harbours were built on the Irish coast, as was the Prince of Wales Route, the road that connects Bantry and Killarney.

The county of Kerry is particularly celebrated for the fondness of the peasantry for education; most of them can read and write; a great many of them understand Latin; and I believe there are more students in Trinity College from Kerry than from any other county in Ireland; nay, more, – I have had several people working on the roads who had children in the College of Dublin.

From *Minutes of evidence taken from select committee appointed to inquire into the disturbances in Ireland*

Innisfallen in Lough Leane, Killarney, where medieval monastic scribes wrote part of the famous Annals.

Walter Scott

1825

EDINBURGH-BORN Walter Scott (1771–1832) achieved popularity and wealth through his ballads, after publication of *Ministrelsy of the Scottish Border* (1802). A prolific author, he wrote romances, including *The Lady of the Lake* (1810), and the *Waverley*, *Ivanhoe* and *Woodstock* series of historical novels. Unfortunately, with the collapse of his publishing ventures in 1826, he spent his last years in immense writing labours, striving to clear his debts. In 1825 he had came to Ireland with family members, first visiting Maria Edgeworth in Longford and she accompanied them to Killarney. There he called on the historian Henry Hallam, mentioned in this letter to the poet Thomas Moore.

August 5. I return to England, yet, I am afraid, with little chance of seeing you, which I should wish to do, were it but for half an hour. I have come thus far on my way to Killarney, where Hallam is lying with a broken leg. So much for middle-aged gentlemen climbing precipices. I,

Walter Scott

who have been regularly inducted into the bed of St Kevin at the Seven Churches, trust I shall bear charmed limbs upon this occasion.

From a letter to Thomas Moore

John Lockhart

1825

JOHN GIBSON LOCKHART (1794–1854) came from Lanarkshire. He began his career as a lawyer, but took up literary journalism, contributing to *Blackwood's Magazine* in Edinburgh. He later settled in London as editor of the *Quarterly Review*. Lockhart married Sir Walter Scott's eldest daughter, Sophia, in 1820 and wrote four novels in four years. His masterpiece was a 7–volume biography of Scott, published in 1837–38, and he also wrote lives of Robert Burns and Napoleon Bonaparte. Lockhart visited Killarney with his famous father-in-law in August 1825, when they stayed at the Kenmare Arms Hotel. In letters to his wife at home he narrated the events of their tour.

Killarney, 7th August. . . . We sleep miserably at Listowel where is a ruined castle of singular architecture in some respects. Sad, wet weather, and Walter and I quite soaked. Next morning (Friday) we breakfast at Tralee, the capital of Kerry, and reach this about two in the day; and being favoured with a divine afternoon, we go to Mucruss Abbey, and ride along the shores of Mr. Herbert's demesne. The abbey is small and without ornamental architecture, but the most perfect, and I think, *by far* the most impressive specimen I have ever seen. It is absolutely clothed with ivy, and mantled with giant trees, and being the holiest burying-ground in Ireland among the Papists, there is an air of mortality and misery heaped upon the original wildness and gloom of the place, the like of which I have never imagined. The resort for burial is so great that they decompose the bodies by means of lime, and then after but a year or two (*on dit*) take out the bones and pile them up to make room within the small vaults for more Tybalts green in earth. The whole place is strewn with skulls and bones, and some Cockneys have written Hamlet's address to Yorick's headpiece on half-a-dozen of them.

John Lockhart

We were much gratified by this, and with the fine scenery of the lower Lake; and yesterday all but Jane (who took fright at starting) visited in a boat the whole, both of the upper and the lower Lakes, dining on one of the islands. . . .

Dublin, 14th August. . . . Sunday we spent in rowing again on the Lake, and the weather being quite calm, Jane was of the party. Innisfallen, a charming island, where of yore was a great abbey. Holly-trees here larger than anywhere I have seen – quite like moderate sized oaks. We saw the rock entitled, the 'bed of honour,' in scrambling near which Hallam fell t'other day and broke his thigh. Sir W. went to call on the invalid, who is doing well, and we had much ado to parry reiterated assaults of M. Alexandre, the ventriloquist. On the whole, Killarney disappointed us all. So much the greater should be the damnation of the road-book and tour-makers. O'Donoghue, the boatman, a character. A Catholic gentleman had died the day before, and we observed that men in mourning scarfs, etc., kept watch at his door. Miss E. said this was new even to her, probably the custom of one county or district only. The widow, who was acquainted with Mr. Wm. Edgeworth, sent him a note inviting him to the funeral, and remarking that she was *the more* in distress as the circumstances prevented her the honour of seeing Miss E. and Sir W. S. Killarney Club-rooms very poor affair.

From letters to Sophia Lockhart

Hermann von Pückler-Muskau

1828

PRINCE HERMANN VON PÜCKLER-MUSKAU (1798–1854) was so impressed with English gardens that he bankrupted himself creating a magnificent one around his home in Muskau. In an effort to acquire a fortune, he married Lucie Hardenburg, the daughter of the Prussian chancellor. Unfortunately Lucie's father cut them off without a penny, so the impoverished newlyweds hatched up an ingenious plan: they divorced and Hermann set off to find a wealthy wife who could support all three of them. With this goal he set out for England and Ireland. During this adventure he wrote long letters home to Lucie, calling her 'Julia' – like this one from County Kerry.

Tralee, September 23rd. This morning I was again received with cries of 'Long life to Napoleon and your Honour!' And while my servant, who was seated in my carriage and passed for Napoleon's son, drove off in the midst of cheers and acclamations, I slipped out at a back-door, with a lad who carried my travelling bag, and took my place in the stage which was to convey me to the lake of Killarney. My people had orders to wait for me in Cashel, where I shall probably rejoin them in a fortnight.

With my present simple exterior, no human being thought of assailing me with homage.

In a quarter of an hour I was comfortably established in the stage-coach. The passengers inside consisted of three women, one fat and jovial, another extremely lean and a third pretty and well-proportioned. I sat entrenched between the two slender ladies and conversed with the corpulent one, who was very talkative. On my letting down a window she told us that she had lately been nearly *sea-sick* in this very coach, because an ailing lady who sat opposite her would not allow a window to be opened on any account. That *she*, however, did not give it up and after a quarter of an hour's persuasion had succeeded in prevailing on the lady to admit one inch of air, a quarter of an hour after, another inch, and so on, till she manoeuvred the whole window open. 'Excellent,' I said; 'that is exactly the way in which women manage to get all they desire: first *one* inch and then – as much as they want. How differently do men act under similar circumstances,' I continued. 'An English writer in his directions to travellers says, that if anybody in the mail should insist on keeping all the windows closed, you should not enter into any 'pourparler' with him, but immediately thrust your elbow through the window as if by accident, beg his pardon and quietly enjoy the cool air.'

Killarney, September 24th. In the course of to-day I saw twelve rainbows, a bad omen for the steadiness of the weather; but I receive it as a good one for me. It promises me a many-coloured journey. The company had dropped off, one by one, like ripe fruit and I found myself alone with an Irish gentleman, a manufacturer from the north, when I entered the pretty cheerful town of Killarney, where the incessant resort of English tourists has almost introduced into the inns English elegance and English prices. We immediately inquired for boats and for the best way of seeing the lake, but were told that it was impossible to go on in such a storm; no boat could 'live on the lake,' as the fisherman expressed it. An English dandy, who had joined us during breakfast, ridiculed these assurances, and as I, you know, am also rather incredulous about *impossibilities*, we outvoted the manufacturer, who showed very little ardour for the undertaking, and embarked, 'malgré vent et marée,' near Ross Castle, an old ruin not far from Killarney.

We had a capital boat, an old, characteristic-looking, grey-headed steersman and four sturdy rowers. The heavens were as if torn open, in some places blue, in others various shades of gray, but for the most part raven-black. Clouds of all forms rolled in wild disorder, now and then tinged by a rainbow or lighted by a pale sunbeam. The high mountains scarcely appeared through their gloomy veil and on the lake all was like night.

Our boat, which was the only one on the lake (for even the fisherman would not venture out), danced so fearfully up and down without making the smallest way, in spite of all the efforts of the rowers, that the manufacturer began to think of wife, children and manufactory, and peremptorily insisted on returning, as he had no intention of sacrificing his life to a party of pleasure. The dandy on the other hand was ready to burst with laughter; he protested that he was a member of the Yacht Club and had seen very different sort of danger from this, and promised the rowers, who would rather have been at home, money without end if they would but hold out.

For some time we struggled with the waves, on which we floated like sea-birds in storm and darkness, till at last such a violent wind came upon us from a gorge in the mountains opposite to which we lay, that it grew rather too serious even for the member of the Yacht Club and he acceded to the request of the steersman, to row back with the wind and land on an island till the storm abated a little, which was generally the case about noon.

This happened as he predicted, and after encamping for some hours on Innisfallen, a lovely little islet with beautiful groups of trees and ruins, we were able to continue our voyage. All the islands of this little lake, even to the smallest, called the Mouse, which is only a few yards long, are thickly clothed with arbutus and other evergreens. They grow wild and both in summer and in winter enliven the scene with the bright colours of their flowers and fruit. The forms of many of these islets are as curious as their names. They are generally called after O'Donaghue. Here is O'Donaghue's 'White Horse,' on whose rocky hoofs the surf breaks, there, his 'Library,' further on, his 'Pigeon-house,' or his 'Flower-garden' and so on.

O'Donaghue was the powerful chieftain of a clan inhabiting a great and opulent city, which stood where the lake now rolls its waters. It had everything in abundance except water, and the legend says, that the only little spring which it possessed was the gift of a mighty sorcerer, who called it up at the prayer of a beautiful virgin adding a solemn warning, that they should never forget to close it every evening with a large silver cover which he left for that purpose.

But O'Donaghue, a mighty and dauntless warrior only made merry at this story and one day, being heated with more wine than usual, he commanded, to the terror of all present, the silver cover to be carried into his house, where, as he jestingly said, it would make him an excellent bath. All remonstrances were vain; O'Donaghue was accustomed to make himself obeyed, as his terrified vassals at length dragged in their ponderous burthen, he exclaimed laughing, 'Never fear, the cool night air will do the water good and in the morning you will all find it fresher than ever.' But those who stood nearest to the silver cover turned away shuddering, for it seemed to them as if the strange intricate characters upon it moved and wreathed like a knot of twisted snakes, and an awful sound appeared to come forth mournfully from it. Fearful and anxious, they retired to rest; one alone fled to the adjoining mountains. And now when morning broke and this man looked down into the valley, he thought he was in a dream; city and land had disappeared, the rich meadows were no more to be seen and the little spring bursting forth from the clefts of the earth had swelled into a measureless lake. What O'Donaghue prophesied was true; the water had become cooler for them all and the new vessel had prepared for him his last bath.

In very clear bright weather, as the fishermen assured us, some have seen at the lowest bottom of the lake, palaces and towers glimmering as through glass; but many have beheld, at the approach of a storm, O'Donaghue's giant figure riding over the waves on a snorting white horse or gliding along the waters with the quickness of lightning in his unearthly bark.

A fresh-caught salmon broiled on arbutus-sticks over the fire was an admirable specimen of Irish fare.

We rowed slowly back by moonlight, while the bugleman's horn started echo after echo from her repose.

Before we landed, a curious ceremony took place. The boat's crew asked permission to lie-to at a little island and to christen this after me, which could only be done by moonlight. I was therefore told to stand on a projecting rock; the six boatmen leaning on their oars formed a circle around me, while the old man solemnly pronounced a sort of incantation in a wild measure, which sounded awfully in this romantic scenery and the night. A young boy then broke off a large arbutus branch and, giving a twig of it first to me and then to the gentlemen in the boat, we fixed them in our hats; the rest he divided among his comrades. He then asked me with respectful earnestness what name the island – with O'Donaghue's permission – was in future to bear? 'Julia!' said I with a loud voice, on which this name was repeated, not very accurately, three times with thundering hurrahs. A third man now took a bottle filled with water, delivered a long addressing verse to O'Donaghue and threw the bottle with all his might against a piece of rock, so that it broke into a thousand pieces. A second bottle filled with whisky was then drunk to my health and a threefold cheer again given to Julia Island. The boatman, to whom the name was strange, took it for mine and henceforth called me nothing but Mr. Julia, which I heard with a melancholy satisfaction.

Your domains are thus increased by an island on the romantic lake of Killarney; it is only a pity that the next company that lands on the same spot will probably rob you of it, for doubtless such christenings take place as often as godfathers are to be found. The real child, the whisky-bottle, is always at hand. Nevertheless, I inclose an arbutus leaf from the identical sprig which flourished on my hat, that you may at least retain undisputed possession of something from your island.

From *Tour in England, Ireland and France*

William Wordsworth

1829

THE POET WILLIAM WORDSWORTH (1770–1850) was born in Cumberland. After leaving Cambridge University he went to France and met Annette Vallon, with whom he had a daughter. He returned to England and set up house with his sister Dorothy, first in Dorset and later at Grasmere in the Lake District. In 1798 the collaborative volume *Lyrical Ballads* appeared, with Wordsworth's 'Tintern Abbey' and Samuel Taylor Coleridge's 'Rime of the Ancient Mariner.' He spent a year in Germany and, on his return to England, married a childhood friend, Mary Hutchinson. In 1829, Wordsworth travelled to Kerry and, although nearly sixty years of age, he rode for long hours every day to see the sights, as recounted in the following letter to his family.

William Wordsworth

Limerick, September 17th

. . . Of the manner in which Mr. James Marshall and I exerted ourselves in the County of Kerry (look at the map) I will give you a specimen – We left Kenmare each on a vile Irish Hack horse at five in the morning, rode 3 hours, breakfasted and sailed on the bay of Glengariff upwards of two hours and called on Mr. White . . . returned to Kenmare on the Hacks in three hours over vile roads; reached the place by eight – were up next morning between 4 and five – off on our hacks after a poor breakfast about half past six, rode 11 Irish miles (about 15 English) took to our feet, clomb and clomb till we reached the summit of a ridge, descended something less than 1,500 feet, mounted another ridge as high, descended and then took the mountain of Carranthuouel the highest in Ireland, 3–4,000 feet above the level of the sea – descended walked two hours – then two hours more – mounted our horses which we had sent round the mountain, and rode 4 Irish miles to Killarney which we reached at ten – having taken nothing all day but a bad breakfast – one crust of bread, and two basins of milk, and glass of whiskey. When we reached Killarney we found Mr. Marshall, Mr. Dawes' Pupil, sitting with our Mr. M – they had dined together and were astonished at the performance especially for one in his 60th year. And to say the truth I was neither stiff nor fatigued, though my horse had the vilest paces that ever plagued a Rider. We left Killarney at six next morning, not so – I am mistaken, we rose at half past five but did not get off for an hour – Carranthouel as a mountain is a much sublimer object than any we have; and Killarney's three lakes with the navigable passage between the upper and lower lake, take the lead I think of any one of our lakes, perhaps of any *one* of our vales, but that may be questioned – but of all this you shall hear when we meet. Suffice it at present to say that we spared no pains in seeing everything; though one day was almost useless; it rained all day. – But upon the whole I reckon the weather has favoured us though it is raining hard now, and has done so all day.

From a letter to the Wordsworth family

Jonathan Binns

1835

JONATHAN BINNS (1785–1871) was born in Liverpool, the son of a Quaker doctor. Educated at Ackworth School in Yorkshire, he settled at Lancaster and took up farming. He was also a land surveyor and lithographer. Binns actively promoted agricultural improvements and wrote several works on farming topics. In 1835 he spent six months travelling throughout Ireland as an assistant commissioner on the Irish Poor Law Inquiry The account of this journey is *The Miseries and Beauties of Ireland* (1837), which includes his own illustrations. In it he hoped to promote an awareness of conditions in Ireland and to encourage practical help from England.

The only company I found at the Kenmare Arms, a very comfortable inn, was an elderly gentleman, whom I took for a clergyman, and a young gentleman from London. The latter, bound on the same errand as myself, agreed to accompany me on the following day in exploring the beauties of the neighbourhood. We accordingly devised a plan of operations for the morrow, and adopting the advice of Mr. Finn, the landlord, engaged a boat and four rowers to convey us round the lakes, with which a day, we were told, was sufficient to make us acquainted. The ensuing morning was cloudy and rainy, and I had some difficulty, first in getting my fellow-traveller out of bed, and afterwards in persuading him that the weather was not too stormy to admit of our venturing on the lake.

The lakes are more than a mile from Killarney. We were to embark at Ross Castle; and as my companion, who promised to follow, had not arrived, I beguiled the time by ascending the staircase of the ancient building, and had a view of the lake and several of its islands from the battlements. The castle is a lofty square building, and was formerly the royal residence of the Lords of the Lake, who bore the title of Kings. In 1652 it was defended by Lord Muskerry against an English force commanded by General Ludlow. This castle was the last place that held out against the English Parliament. In sailing by the shores of Ross Island, we passed near the lead and copper mines, supposed to have been worked at a very early period. They have been abandoned – probably for want of spirit and capital. Dr. Smith states that the copper mines were very productive, and that the adjacent mountains abound with iron: he also picked up specimens of ore containing some tin. On this island some of the rude stone implements, called Danish hammers, have been found.

My young friend and I were now seated comfortably in a swift-sailing boat, with four muscular rowers and a helms-man, and abundance of excellent provisions, supplied by our attentive landlord. The waves were somewhat larger, and the motion of the boat was somewhat less steady than we had expected, but our conductors assured us of safety, and we relied upon their experience and veracity. The day, though probably not such a one as we should have selected, was exactly the sort of day to set off the captivating scenery to the best advantage. The sun shone occasionally through showers of rain (and this, of itself, is one of the loveliest of sights, the small drops turning to gold as he smiles upon them) and at other times, and even *during* the showers, lighted up, not only the distance, but near objects also, with his brightest and most splendid beams. The day was an alternation of sun and shower – a succession of delicious lights and shadows. Every rock, and lawn, and shrub, glittered with rain-drops, and their minute but perfect mirrors reflected and heightened every variety of colour in the landscape, from the extreme verdure of the arbutus, to the bright red of the boughs of the birch. Our course lay between Ross Island and Ennisfallen, across the lower lake; the Tomies and Glena Mountains, in this course, were seen in perfection. The sides of these mountains, which form the west and south-west banks of the lake, are completely clothed with arbutus, mingled with birch, for several hundred yards from the shore; and this was the season in which the colour of the arbutus, contrasted strongly with the red stems of the birch, is most vivid and beautiful. The profusion of the arbutus surprised me; it is as common as the furze or hazel in England, and reaches the size, and assumes the character, of a large tree, girthing as much as from seven to nine feet. I measured one of seven feet. They who have not seen the lakes of Killarney, can form no adequate idea of the abundance and exquisite loveliness of this plant.

From *The Miseries and Beauties of Ireland*

Georgiana Chatterton

1838

BORN IN LONDON, Henrietta Georgiana Iremonger (1806–1876) married Sir William Abraham Chatterton of Castle Mahon, County Cork when she was eighteen. Her first book, *Aunt Dorothy's Tales*, was published anonymously. For her second she travelled throughout Kerry and Cork – by every conveyance from boat to horsecart. The account of this tour, *Rambles in the South of Ireland*, sold out in a week, to become the most successful nineteenth-century travel book on Ireland. After her husband died Georgiana married Edward Dering. She converted to Catholicism shortly before her death at Malvern Wells.

This morning I felt too much fatigued by our long expedition of yesterday to venture over the same road again. My companions wished to take some more accurate sketches of the Ogham inscriptions, &c. So, as I heard from a local antiquarian, that many interesting antiquities were to be found within a very short distance of Dingle, I thought I would venture alone on this short excursion.

That I might have plenty of time to make drawings of the objects and inscriptions, I started off at half-past eight. My conveyance was a little jingling nondescript vehicle, drawn by a rough pony, whose solemn pace, and philosophical contempt for the whip, shewed that he was little accustomed to convey parties of pleasure to view antiquities. We, or rather he, (the horse) was driven by our grave friend the waiter, a sort of matter-of-fact, yet good-humoured man of all-work, to the Inn; who clambered up the little dickey, and perched himself on its narrow summit, with a degree of trembling caution which made me apprehend he would find as much difficulty in keeping his own seat, as in driving the horse. I expected this the more surely, from having seen our experienced and able gingle-man from Tralee, pitched off his box, and deposited under the wheels of

Bridge across the River Inny, a short distance north of Waterville on the way to Cahirciveen.

the jaunting car, by one of those tremendous jolts, which are of such common occurrence in these roads.

However, to-day, our route for the first two miles was along the high road to Tralee, and by dint of sage advice, which I suddenly felt competent to give relative to the noble art of driving – by often telling my charioteer not to hold himself so tight on by the reins, just at the moment of administering a sharp whipping to the horse, &c., &c., we got on three miles the first hour without accident.

But beyond this the good road did not last; we came to a narrow stony track, with a deep ditch, full of black water, on either side, in one or other of which the pony seemed much inclined to take refuge. We then came to a broad, but apparently shallow river, over which there was no bridge.

'Are you sure this is the way to Kinard?' I enquired of the trembling waiter, who looked with great dismay upon the rushing stream that barred our passage.

At this moment of dilemma, when I saw by the grave, blank visage of our waiter-coachman that he knew nothing about the matter, a countryman came galloping along the river side. I enquired of him, whether we must pass the river to get to Kinard; he did not understand a word of English, but the waiter made him comprehend in Irish what we used to know.

The countryman was evidently much surprised, and wondered what could induce a lady to visit such a remote place as Kinard. He pointed to a little village half-way up the rugged mountain before us, and gave our driver to understand that we must cross the river to get there.

Now, though I was willing to be jolted or to walk any distance, on dry land, to see my favourite Ogham stones, I did not relish the idea of encountering that rough stream, and being upset in the water. The countryman, who like most Irish peasants, was both good-natured and quick of apprehension, soon divined my fears; and to shew that the water was not so deep as to float the carriage, he rode over and back again, at the same time making me a sign that there was no danger. But the water appeared deep, and full of large stones, and I therefore enquired if there were no foot-bridge over any part of the stream. Of course there was none, for what would this primitive, barefooted population want of a dry passage over a river!

The poor countryman, who saw that in spite of all his representations I still feared to cross the stream, made the driver ask me if I would like to ride over on his horse, which he would lead through for me. I gladly accepted the poor man's offer, and mounted up into one of the empty panniers, which were slung over the horse's back. But what was now to become of my man and maid servant, whom I had brought with me in the gingle? – and then, unless the vehicle could get over the river too, I despaired of being able to walk all that way up the mountain to Kinard.

However, I went, feeling confident that my energetic friend would devise some means to get the whole party across. I was not wrong; he first led the gingle over empty, to prove it would not upset and then took it back for its terrified driver and my servants. For this service, and the long delay it caused him, the tattered peasant would accept no money! With a proud and respectful bow, and a smile which would not have ill suited a gallant of the court of Louis the Fourteenth, he mounted his horse and galloped off.

On we jolted, over a narrow road, which in about half an hour brought us to a village – but not Kinard; that was still far above us, and at the one we had reached, the road ended!

The whole population of this little hamlet, pigs, dogs, and all, turned out to stare at the strangers, and formed a long cortège behind me all the way up to Kinard.

We had a long and dirty walk, across potato fields, and over stone walls, which my civil attendants were most anxious to pull down for me.

Not one of them spoke English, and as the waiter was left with the gingle in the village, I had no interpreter.

When at last we reached Kinard, the same wondering greeting awaited me. The two village populations joined together in noisy surprise. The girls stared; the old women and men chattered; the rival sets of dogs quarrelled and barked; pigs, fowls, and geese, disturbed by this vast concourse of visitors, grunted and cackled with furious vehemence. But fortunately, in the midst of all this uproar, we, who were the cause of it, were left unescorted; the people were so busy talking and wondering, that I proceeded with my servant alone towards the churchyard, which was still further up the mountain.

In this little remote village, all the cottages were well built, with real windows, and comfortable-looking chimneys; each being surrounded with a little sort of paved trottoir. I observed here, as at Ballyheigh, that the doors were so low as to oblige the inhabitants to stoop on entering, and so narrow that a fat person would find great difficulty to pass.

At last, I reached the ruined church of Kinard; and I found, among a thick growth of nettles and thistles, a curious stone, a drawing of which is here inserted; the marks upon it have been engraved with care, and resemble some of the inscriptions at Persepolis; indeed the Ogham character itself bears a striking similitude to the arrow-headed inscriptions found among the Persian ruins.

I was so tired after this long walk, that I gladly mounted the rough vehicle, and remained in it over roads which a few days before I should have looked on as utterly impassable; I even jolted through the river with tolerable composure, though we had not the assistance of our civil friend; and the driver trembled so much as to be totally unable to guide the horse.

However, we got through the river, and reached the high road again in safety. At the little village of Ballyristan, I got out to hunt for an inscription I had heard of, and a copy of which is here given.

One of these stones stood amid a heap of dirt, near a cottage door; the other formed the corner stone of a wretched hovel.

An old woman told our driver that she remembered when they had formed a single high stone, or rather pillar (for, unlike most other Ogham stones, they seemed to have been chiselled into an exact round). Why it had been broken, I could not ascertain.

I was now so exhausted that I felt delighted to turn homewards, and to hear that Garfinny Bridge, another piece of antiquity I wished to visit, was not far out of our road. But, alas! as usual, the 'not far' turned out to be a long, a weary long way, and the most fatiguing part of our expedition was still to come.

Again we had to leave the high road, and proceed along a rocky track which gradually became too narrow for the gingle, so that I was obliged to have recourse to my tired feet.

Here there was no village, nor any one to shew us the way; so we proceeded up and down, and over ditches and stone walls, in a sort of steeple-chase fashion, after a ruined church which I saw in the distance, and concluded to be Garfinny. We reached it at last, without meeting a human being, nor was there any sign of habitations near. I despatched the servant to search for the bridge, while I remained to examine the tombstones, in hopes of finding some Ogham inscriptions.

This old churchyard was indeed gloomy: and I never saw a place which impressed me with such utter loneliness. It was in a narrow deserted valley, or rather glen, between two rugged mountains, whose summits were now covered with dreary drooping clouds.

A drizzling rain fell, but in such quiet silence, that, like the touch of time, it was scarcely felt. It did not move the rank grass and nettles which overshadowed the graves; nor even, by pattering against the tombstones, interrupt the death-like stillness which reigned.

As I walked up the lonely aisle of the ruined church, I started at the sound of my own footstep on the grave-stones. All was so shadowy, remote, and unconnected with the haunts of living creatures – I was so surrounded with images of death, that the spirits of departed ages seemed hovering in the dull, heavy air.

The rocks and distant tombstones appeared through the dark misty atmosphere, like shadows of strange beings condemned to remain eternally in this gloomy spot; immoveable and silent, chained to the abodes where

Georgiana Chatterton climbed Ballyferriter Hill with the local curate to view this ancient structure, whose origins are lost in antiquity.

their mouldering bodies lay. Though shuddering at all I saw, I felt rivetted to the spot, almost spell-bound; yet feeling that if I remained much longer in this land of shadows, I should become a shadow myself.

At last, I heard the sound of a living human footstep. It was that of the servant, coming to tell me, that after considerable difficulty, he had found the old bridge. The silent spell of death seemed broken, and I joyfully quitted the old churchyard. Proceeding some way further up the solitary glen, I traversed Garfinny bridge, which I then sat down to sketch. It appears to have been built (like the stone-roofed chapels and ancient cells we have seen), with flat horizontal stones, which form the arch, nearly as far as the summit. At the top, they are placed edgeways, but I should think this part has been repaired in modern times.

From *Rambles in the South of Ireland*

Michael Condon

1839

MICHAEL CONDON, who was born in Coolcappa, County Limerick in 1817, had a hedge-school education. Although he felt he had a vocation for the priesthood from childhood, he had difficulties gaining admittance to a seminary. For this purpose he set out in 1839 to enlist the support of Daniel O'Connell, and to add his signature to his 'Memorial,' which had already been signed by other people of influence. Condon did eventually achieve his goal: he completed his studies at All Hallows College in Dublin and was ordained priest in Glasgow in 1845. His diaries are a useful source on conditions in Ireland and the Catholic church in the west of Scotland.

Thus provided, I set off, in bleak Thursday October 24, for the far-famed Derrynane, with seven shillings and 6d in my pocket. The distance thereto and back was 160 miles.

On I journied, thro' frost, sleet and snow in cold and hunger, for three days, by Newcastle (where I slept on 24th), Abbeyfeale, Kilorglan and Caherciveen, I travelled all on foot. On reaching Caherciveen, I thought myself fully compensated for my chill and cheerless journey, by one glance at the little cottage where the great O'Connell was born. Nor was I much less delighted by the wild and wintry cascades which leaped so sublimely, from their high and heathery hills, to the foaming waves that rushed and lashed them on the beach below. On reaching Cahir, I met a man, and having asked him earnestly, had he a lodging or a fire? I learned he had, and I agreed to put up with him.

So beaten up had I been with the storm and so drenched was I with the rain, that even a Turk would pity me; and my host, a Mr. Connor, was far kinder than a Turk. He forced me to go to bed in a cold garret and induced me to give up my clothes to be dried by him at the blazing fire. I tendered them to him, after having extracted my Memorial and my 5/- which I carefully deposited under the pillow beneath my head. As my teeth were chattering at a terrible rate, he brought me in a glass of brandy to nullify the effects of the fatigue and cold.

Perspiration soon succeeded to the gnashing of cold teeth; and I was about to sink into a delightful, tho' reluctant, slumber, when I heard the following conversation, carried on in the native tongue.

'Arrah! What can he be?'

'Arrah! Sure, I don't know. When I met him, I thought he was drunk, or mad, to be out on such a day as this; and when I asked him 'did he want a lodging?' sure, my heart was like to burst, when he only said: Have you a fire? – and when I said: Yes; he shook his head and followed me, like a lamb.'

'Is he a poor scholar, may be?' asked another.

'Is it him?' cried the whole of them. 'Faith, he has a voice that would shame all the Masters of Kerry.'

'Believe me,' added another, 'that's a gentleman in disguise.'

He had conjectured this, because I had taken and worn my father's coat which I thought better than my own, and it misfitted me.

Next morning I rose refreshed, and having thanked my host for his kindness and paid a few pence over his very moderate bill, I proceeded on to Derrynane. Derrynane was fourteen miles from Caherciveen; and for near half that distance, that is to say, from Miltown of the salmons, to O'Connell's mansion, there was not so much as the shadow of a road. With the mouth of the Kenmare and its rocky islets on my right, and mist-clad mountains on my left; with cone-peaked hills before, and chasms and cascades behind, I groped my way as best I could.

Twas now noon; and never will I forget the terror that brooded over me, as I ascended the farther side of the mountain that overhangs O'Connell's house. The sun, which two minutes previously had shot its radiance thro' the clouds and on me, became suddenly red as blood, then black as pitch and instantly disappeared. A more than midnight gloom shrouded everything. Finding myself thus benighted at noonday, within a mile or so, almost within view of O'Connell's house, and knowing nothing of the transient nature of such obscuration, I groped wildly about for some solid rock, and having felt one, I sat down and wept aloud.

After an interval, the thick mist sailed away and the sun once more appeared; but lest it may treat me to a similar eclipse, I ran like a maniac, over every opposing ledge of rugged rock until, at length, I espied O'Connell's mansion, in sheltered anchorage, at the base of a thousand circling hills. Like the eagle of those mountains, I dashed down to that promised land and breathed, I thought, the air of Paradise.

O'Connell, as was his custom, was chasing the hare, on yon red mountains and I anxiously awaited his return. He returned, but he had no time for any conference with me that night.

There was an O'Connell who kept a bed or two for strangers, about a mile or more from the Liberator's. Thither I proceeded on Saturday night; and, having with difficulty induced him by an offer of half what I now possessed, viz. 2/- to shelter me for the night, he did so and shared his own bed with me.

The next morning being that of Sunday, I heard Mass in O'Connell's domestic chapel, presented my Memorial thro' his son Morgan, and had it returned, inscribed: 'Mr. O'Connell, being a Repealer, can ask nothing of the Government.'

Tho' asked to breakfast at O'Connell's, I declined. I had breakfasted already at my entertainer's, and I was in no mood to feast on dainties, now that I must starve or luxuriate as best I could on 2/6 for 80 miles of road. Having asked for a draught of water, I got and quaffed a cup of cider; and off I started, with a heavy heart, and shoes worn to shammy, for Caherciveen which I reached late the same night.

From Michael Condon's diaries

William Makepeace Thackeray

1842

WILLIAM MAKEPEACE THACKERAY (1811–1863) was born Calcutta and at the age of five moved to England after his father died. He studied at Cambridge but left without taking a degree. Anticipating a large fortune, Thackeray turned to journalism and bought a newspaper, but he lost his fortune within a year. He first attracted attention as a writer with his work in *Punch*. Most of his major novels, including *Vanity Fair*, were published in monthly serials. He travelled widely as a lecturer in Europe and in 1860 became the first editor of the *Cornhill Magazine*. In the following extract he describes his visit to Killarney.

On his tour of Ireland in 1842, William Makepeace Thackeray sketched this pious scene in Tralee.

The races were as gay as races could be, in spite of one or two untoward accidents that arrived at the close of the day's sport. Where all the people came from that thronged out of the town was a wonder; where all the vehicles, the cars, barouches and shandrydans, the carts, the horse- and donkey-men could have found stable and shelter, who can tell? Of all these equipages and donkeypages I had a fine view from Mrs. Macgillcuddy's window, and it was pleasant to see the happy faces shining under the blue cloaks as the carts rattled by.

A very handsome young lady – I presume Miss MacG. – who gives a hand to the drawing-room and comes smiling in with the teapot – Miss MacG., I say, appeared to-day in a silk bonnet and stiff silk dress, with a brooch and a black mantle, as smart as any lady in the land, and looking as if she was accustomed to her dress too, which the housemaid on banks of Thames does not. Indeed, I have not met a more ladylike young person in Ireland than Miss MacG; and when I saw her in a handsome car on the course, I was quite proud of a bow.

Tramping thither, too, as hard as they could walk, and as happy and smiling as possible, were Mary the coachman's wife of the day before, and Johanna with the child, and presently the other young lady: the man with the stick, you may be sure: he would toil a year for that day's pleasure. They are all mad for it: people walk for miles and miles round to the race; they come without a penny in their pockets often, trusting to chance and charity, and that some worthy gentleman may fling them a sixpence. A gentleman told me that he saw on the course persons from his part of the country, who must have walked eighty miles for the sport.

For a mile and a half to the racecourse there could be no pleasanter occupation than looking at the happy multitudes who were thronging thither; and I am bound to say that on rich or poor shoulders I never saw so many handsome faces in my life. In the carriages, among the ladies of Kerry, every second woman was handsome: and there is something peculiarly tender and pleasing in the looks of the young female peasantry that is perhaps even better than beauty. Beggars had taken their stations along the road in no great numbers, for I suspect they were most of them on the ground, and those who remained were consequently of the oldest and ugliest. It is a shame that such horrible figures are allowed to appear in public as some of the loathsome ones which belong to these unhappy people. On went the crowd, however, laughing and as gay as possible; all sorts of fun passing from car- to foot-passengers as the pretty girls came clattering by, and the 'boys' had a word for each. One lady, with long flowing auburn hair, who was turning away her head from some 'boys' very demurely, I actually saw, at a pause of the cart, kissed by one of them. She gave the fellow a huge box on the ear and he roared out, 'O murther!' and she frowned for some time as hard as she could, whilst the ladies in the blue cloaks at the back of the car uttered a shrill rebuke in Irish. But in a minute the whole party was grinning, and the young fellow who had administered the salute may, for what I know, have taken another without the slap on the face by way of exchange.

And here, lest the fair public may have a bad opinion of the personage who talks of kissing with such awful levity, let it be said that with all this laughing, romping, kissing and the like, there are no more innocent girls in the world than the Irish girls; and that the women of our own more squeamish country are far more liable to err. One has but to walk through an English and Irish town, and see how much superior is the morality of the latter. That great terror-striker, the Confessional, is before the Irish girl, and sooner or later her sins must be told there.

By this time we are got upon the course, which is really one of the most beautiful spots that ever was seen: the lake and mountains lying along two sides of it, and of course visible from all. They were busy putting up the hurdles when we arrived: stiff bars and poles, four feet from the ground, with furze-bushes over them. The grand stand was already full; along the hedges sat thousands of the people, sitting at their ease doing nothing, and happy as kings. A daguerreotype would have been of great service to have taken their portraits, and I never saw a vast multitude of heads and attitudes so picturesque and lively. The sun lighted up the whole course and the lakes with amazing brightness, though behind the former lay a huge rack of the darkest clouds, against which the cornfields and meadows shone in the brightest green and gold, and a row of white tents was quite dazzling.

There was a brightness and intelligence about this immense Irish crowd, which I don't remember to have seen in an English one. The women in their blue cloaks, with red smiling faces peering from one end, and bare feet from the other, had seated themselves in all sorts of pretty attitudes of cheerful contemplation; and the men, who are accustomed to lie about, were doing so now with all their might – sprawling on the banks, with as much ease and variety as club-room loungers on their soft cushions, – or squatted leisurely among the green potatoes. The sight of so much happy laziness did one good to look on. Nor did the honest fellows seem to weary of this amusement. Hours passed on, and the gentlefolks (judging from our party) began to grow somewhat weary; but the finest peasantry in Europe never budged from their posts, and continued to indulge in greetings, indolence, and conversation.

When we came to the row of white tents, as usual it did not look so brilliant or imposing as it appeared from a little distance, though the scene around them was animating enough. The tents were long humble booths stretched on hoops, each with its humble streamer or ensign without, and containing, of course, articles of refreshment within. But Father Mathew has been busy among the publicans, and the consequence is that the poor fellows are now condemned for the most part to sell 'tay' in place of whisky; for the concoction of which beverage huge cauldrons were smoking, in front of each hut-door, in round graves dug for the purpose and piled up with black smoking sod.

Behind this camp were the carts of the poor people, which were not allowed to penetrate into the quarter where the quality cars stood. And a little way from the huts, again, you might see (for you could scarcely hear) certain pipers executing their melodies and inviting people to dance.

Anything more lugubrious than the drone of the pipe, or the jig danced to it, or the countenances of the dancers and musicians, I never saw. Round each set of dancers the people formed a ring, in the which the figurantes and coryphées went through their operations. The toes went in and the toes went out; then there came certain mystic figures of hands across, and so forth. I never saw less grace or seemingly less enjoyment – no, not even in a quadrille. The people, however, took a great interest, and it was 'Well done, Tim!' 'Step out, Miss Brady!' and so forth during the dance.

Thimble-rig too obtained somewhat, though in a humble way. A ragged scoundrel – the image of Hogarth's Bad Apprentice – went bustling and shouting through the crowd with his dirty tray and thimble, and as soon as he had taken his post, stated that this was the 'royal game of thimble' and called upon 'gintlemin' to come forward. And then a ragged fellow would be seen to approach, with as innocent an air as he could assume, and the bystanders might remark that the second ragged fellow almost always won. Nay, he was so benevolent in many instances, as to point out to various people who had a mind to bet, under which thimble the pea actually was. Meanwhile, the first fellow was sure to be looking away and talking to some one in the crowd; but somehow it generally happened – and how of course I can't tell – that any man who listened to the advice of rascal No. 2, lost his money. I believe it is so even in England.

Then you would see gentlemen with halfpenny roulette-tables, and, again, here were a pair who came forward disinterestedly with a table and a pack of cards, and began playing against each other for ten shillings a game, betting crowns as freely as possible.

Gambling, however, must have been fatal to both of these gentlemen, else might not one have supposed that, if they were in the habit of winning much, they would have treated themselves to better clothes? This, however, is the way with all gamblers, as the reader has no doubt remarked for, look at a game of loo or *vingt-et-un* played in a friendly way, and where you, and three or four others, have certainly lost three or four pounds, – well, ask at the end of the game who has won, and you invariably find that nobody has. Hopkins has only covered himself; Snooks has neither lost nor won; Smith has won four shillings; and so on. Who gets the money? The devil gets it, I dare say; and so, no doubt, he has laid hold of the money of yonder gentleman in the handsome great-coat.

But, to the shame of the stewards, be it spoken, they are extremely averse to this kind of sport; and presently comes up one, a stout old gentleman on a bay horse, wielding a huge hunting-whip, at the sight of which all fly, amateurs, idlers, professional men, and all. He is a rude customer to deal with, that gentleman with the whip: just now he was clearing the course, and cleared it with such a vengeance, that a whole troop on a hedge retreated backwards into a ditch opposite, where was rare kicking, and sprawling, and disarrangement of petticoats, and cries of

'O murther!' 'Mother of God!' 'I'm kilt!' and so on. But as soon as the horsewhip was gone, the people clambered out of their ditch again, and were as thick as ever on the bank.

The last instance of the exercise of the whip shall be this. A groom rode insolently after a gentleman, calling him names, and inviting him to fight. This the great flagellator hearing, rode up to the groom, lifted him gracefully off his horse into the air, and on to the ground, and when there administered to him a severe and merited fustigation; after which he told the course-keepers to drive the fellow off the course, and enjoined the latter not to appear again at his peril.

As for the races themselves, I won't pretend to say that they were better or worse than other such amusements; or to quarrel with gentlemen who choose to risk their lives in manly exercise. In the first race there was a fall; one of the gentlemen was carried off the ground, and it was said *he was dead*. In the second race, a horse and man went over and over each other, and the fine young man (we had seen him five minutes before, full of life and triumph, clearing the hurdles on his grey horse, at the head of the race): – in the second heat of the second race the poor fellow missed his leap, was carried away stunned and dying, and the bay horse won.

I was standing, during the first heat of this race (this is the second man the grey has killed – they ought to call him the Pale Horse,) by half a dozen young girls from the gentleman's village, and hundreds more of them were there, anxious for the honour of their village, the young squire, and the grey horse. Oh, how they hurrah'd as he rode ahead! I saw these girls – they might be fourteen years old – after the catastrophe. 'Well,' says I, 'this is a sad end to the race.' '*And is it the pink jacket or the blue has won this time?*' says one of the girls. It was poor Mr. C.'s only epitaph: and wasn't it a sporting answer? That girl ought to be a hurdle-racer's wife; and I would like, for my part, to bestow her upon the groom who won the race.

I don't care to confess that the accident to the poor young gentleman so thoroughly disgusted my feeling as a man and a cockney, that I turned off the racecourse short, and hired a horse for sixpence to carry me back to Miss Macgillicuddy. In the evening at the inn (let no man who values comfort go to an Irish inn in race-time), a blind old piper, with silvery hair and of a most respectable, bard-like appearance, played a great deal too much for us after dinner. He played very well, and with very much feeling, ornamenting the airs with flourishes and variations that were very pretty indeed, and his pipe was by far the most melodious I have heard; but honest truth compels me to say, that the bad pipes are execrable, and the good inferior to a clarionet.

From *The Irish Sketch Book*

Johann Georg Kohl

1842

JOHANN GEORG KOHL (1808–1878) was born in Bremen, and studied at the universities of Heidelberg and Munich. He travelled widely throughout the world, visiting Hungary, Russia, the Ukraine, Canada, the United States, Great Britain and Ireland. He was a prolific writer and his books *Travels in Canada*, *Russia and the Russians* and *Austria* were as popular in their English translations as they were in German. After starting his Irish tour in Dublin, he went to Edgeworthstown, then south and across the Shannon to Tarbert.

From Tarbert I proceeded on my journey on one of those remarkable cars which are still used in some parts of Ireland as means of public conveyance from one town to another. These diligence cars are built upon the same principle as the jaunting cars, except that they run on four wheels, and are often drawn by four horses. The seat on each side is long enough to accommodate eight persons, and between the two seats is a kind of abyss called the 'pit,' in which the luggage is deposited. This pit is generally too small for all the boxes and trunks which it is intended to contain, and the remainder are piled up into a high wall that forms an effectual partition between the two divisions of passengers. Each traveller, therefore, sees only one side of the road; and when the vehicle stops to change horses or to rest them, the one party is sure to have a deal to tell to those to those who have been looking only into the opposite half of the world. The number of passengers by one of these cars is very undefined; for when all the seats are occupied, it is nothing uncommon to see people sit in each other's laps, or place themselves upon the luggage, or hang on to the carriage in a variety of ways. Such was the mode in which we were ourselves packed on the day on which I started from Tarbert.

When the horses got into motion, the crowd of beggars by whom we had been surrounded divided in front, and those who were nimble of foot ran along by the side of us for some distance. One ran off in front of us like an *avant-courrier*, and continued to do so for nearly two miles. When he saw that all the others had dropped off, he came to the side of the car, and received a few pence as a reward for his perseverance.

Though our view was confined to one side of the road, I saw enough to amuse and instruct me. In one village we saw the national process of house-building. A house of some length had fallen in, probably without any volcanic agency, but simply by the effect of its own weight, and the proprietor was repairing the injury sustained by his mansion; but being

As Johann Georg Kohl was to discover on his 1842 trip, Irish cars offered few comforts.

either too poor or too indolent to re-establish the tenement in its former extent, he had contented himself with cutting away as much of the broken wall as was necessary to make it smooth, and was running up a new wall at the place where the old one remained. In this way, he was abandoning one half of his old house, and was about to reduce his family, his pigs, his dogs, and his poultry, to one half of their previous accommodation. The manner of building the wall, too, was characteristic. The father brought the mould to the spot in a wheelbarrow, the eldest son with a shovel fashioned the material into the shape of a wall, and a younger boy stood upon the top to stamp it into something like consistency. A pair of swallows would have expended more care and skill upon the construction of their nest.

All the people I met with spoke English, though Kerry is considered to be one of the counties where the Irish language has been best preserved. Only in very out-of-the-way places, they told me, would I find people that understood no English. Of this I had seen instances in Clare, where children would run by the side of the car, crying 'Burnocks, halfpenny!' 'Burnocks' being an appellation applied to every stranger, and 'halfpenny' the only English word that the little rogues seemed to know. 'Our English,' said one Kerry farmer to me, 'is a sort of home-English. We don't learn it correctly. But we have high-bred men among us, even among the farmers, and some of the shepherds among the mountains know as much Latin as so many priests.'

I had heard a good deal of these Kerry scholars, and was anxious to satisfy myself, by the evidence of my own senses, of the extent to which their scholarship was carried. I heard everywhere a great deal of shepherds and labourers who could read and speak Latin; but the only instances in which I was able to come into contact with any of these learned personages, were not calculated to impress me with much respect for the extent of their classical lore. On two occasions I saw a few men who told me they understood Latin, but when I came to examine them more closely, I found they knew nothing beyond a few sentences that they had retained from the Missal. One young peasant I found, who really knew something of the classics, and was tolerably well acquainted with Horace; he told me, however, he had been brought up for a priest, but, not liking the church, had returned to the plough on his father's farm. I met subsequently a young man whose story was nearly the same, and I am, therefore, disposed to believe, that Kerry scholarship, where it really exists, is always more or less connected with the church, and that, at all events, these mountain peasants have no notion of studying Latin with a view to anything like aesthetic enjoyment.

'It's not even English they can speak,' said my neighbour on the car.

In the western parts of Scotland, Ireland, and Wales, to say of people that they cannot even speak English, is intended to mark the extreme barbarism in which they live. The English language is the only medium of cultivation, and all endeavour to learn it, as without it they are quite helpless the moment they leave their native hills. In the same way the French express their contempt for the Basques among the Pyrenees, and for the Germans among the Vosges, by saying that they cannot even speak French; and so, in Bohemia, Galicia, Courland, and Livonia, the knowledge of German is deemed inseparable from even a rude education.

I had an opportunity, by the road side, of seeing a genuine Irish hedge school, and truly an interesting and affecting spectacle it was. The school-house was a clay cabin, roofed with sods, and without so much as a window. The smaller of the ragged scholars sat as close as they could to the entrance, towards which they turned their books to catch as much as possible of the light from without. Some were lying on the ground, behind these were a few seated on a board, and behind these were the taller boys, leaning over those in front, likewise to catch the light. The teacher was seated in the middle of the group, and was clad in what I have already described as the national costume of the country. In a book of Irish sketches this picture would have been invaluable, and I was sorry I had not a daguerreotype apparatus with me, to perpetuate the impression. In front of the school-house lay as many pieces of turf as there were students within, each boy having brought one as a tribute to his teacher.

As I entered through the narrow entrance, the dominie rose from an inverted butter-cask, on which he had sat enthroned. 'Indeed, I am very sorry, your honour,' said he, 'that I have not the opportunity of offering you a chair.' He was teaching his pupils the English alphabet, and they all looked fresh and cheerful, notwithstanding their poverty, as indeed most Irish children do, in the country at least, despite of their ragged attire and their scanty food.

Both children and teacher lived some miles away from the school-house, which stood by the side of the road. When the hours of study are over, the boys thrust their spelling-books into their pockets, and the master, after having fastened the door of his college, collects the tributary turf into a sack, throws the burden over his shoulder, and having grasped his staff, trudges away to his cabin on the other side of the bog.

Our diligence car was not to carry us farther than Listowel, and I was obliged to look out for some other conveyance to Tralee, where I proposed to sleep. Some gentlemen who had been my fellow passengers thus far, and who, like myself, were on a pilgrimage to the far-famed beauties of Killarney, joined me in the hire of a one-horse car. We were standing at the door of our inn, in expectation of our equipage. Some of us had been smoking and threw the ends into the street. Two of the poor that were loitering about, rushed forward to fight and scramble for the prize, and each carried away a portion of the booty, carefully concealed among his rags. 'These are all temperance men,' said our host, 'and very strict ones too. Indeed they're all very strict in this part of the country, and there are very few here who have broken their pledge.' My host went on to speak of Father Mathew as an old acquaintance, and told us many anecdotes about him. Among other things, he told us that the apostle of temperance, when young, had been expelled from his college, on the ground of habitual drunkenness, the whiskey bottle having several times been found concealed about his bed. The anecdote, if true, is not, in my opinion, at all to Father Mathew's discredit.

We had got but a short way from Listowel, when there happened to us an accident which, harnessed as they are, is by no means an uncommon one for Irish cars to meet with. Our merry driver, to show the mettle of his horse, began to stimulate him to increased speed. The gallant courser,

Torc Waterfall, in a wooded glen near Killarney, was one of the attractions that drew lovers of the picturesque to Kerry.

Built of unmortared stone, Gallarus Oratory on the Dingle Peninsula remains completely watertight after nearly a thousand years.

however, disapproving of the manner of Paddy's persuasion, began to kick, and then fairly ran away with us. As he was going the right way, we, at first, reconciled ourselves to the rapidity of his pace, but in a little while, the girth, on which the whole economy of these primitive vehicles generally depends, gave way, and the car, according to its usual practice on such occasions, tipped over and deposited us and our baggage in the high road. It was the first time it had happened to me to be overturned in a carriage, and it was of some interest to me to follow the course of my thoughts, which succeeded each other with the rapidity of lightning. When I became perfectly conscious of what had happened, and while the shaft of the car was still describing its semi-circle in the air, I thought to myself: 'This may be a serious accident. The car and all the luggage may fall on my head, and put an end at once to all my observations on Irish peculiarities. If I come off with a bruise or two, or a broken finger, how thankful I ought to be.' When, however, we all got upon our legs again, and found we were none of us hurt, though all well bedaubed with mud, and with a rent here and there in our garments, all our gratitude to Providence seemed to be gone, and to have given way to a general feeling of indignation against the clumsiness of our driver. Such is man. Fainthearted in the hour of need, and ready to make any pact with Providence; but in prosperity insolent, and grumbling against Fate at the most trifling annoyance.

We left our baggage under guard, and proceeded on foot, while the driver went in search of cords and thongs to repair the consequences of his awkwardness. A little way from Listowel the country will repay a pedestrian, but farther on, let no man trust to the treacherous shadowings which he may discover on his map. All these beautiful linings, intended to mark hills and mountains, are extremely inviting, and in Germany keep the promise they hold out, by delighting the wanderer with the most romantic and picturesque landscapes. This, in Ireland, is not, by any means, always the case. The mountains we were now passing were naked from the base to the summit, and of a gloomy monotonous colour, for they were covered with bog, and so was the lower part of the country, all the way from the Shannon to Tralee Bay. And yet I saw villages of which the inhabitants were complaining of a scarcity of turf! In the county of Cork, I was told, the scarcity of turf had already become a subject of general complaint.

From *Ireland, Scotland and England*

Asenath Nicholson

1845

ASENATH NICHOLSON (1792–1855) first became acquainted with the Irish while working among the poor in New York. In 1844, recently widowed, she set off for Ireland with two suitcases of Irish-language Bibles which she hoped to distribute. Dressed in a polka-dot coat, bonnet and rubber boots, she tramped the countryside but she had little success with the Bibles, finding the poor illiterate in any language. When the Famine struck, Nicholson stayed on to help, and started a relief operation from her own funds. Before returning to America in 1852, she spent time in Cork with her friend, Father Theobald Mathew, the apostle of temperance.

Monday (24 March). I walked this morning to the coast opposite Valentia. Here both men and women go out in boats, to gather from the rocks seaweed, which is used for manure. They take a long pole with hooks upon the end, wade in, standing often to the armpits in water, and scrape the weed from the rocks, put it in the boats, and the men take it ashore; the women remaining in the sea often through the day. At night they take a basketful upon their backs, and bend to their wretched cabins, to boil their potatoes, and lie down upon the straw; and in the morning awake to the same hopes, and go to the same employment. Woman is here worse than a beast of burden, because she is often made to do what the beast never does.

We crossed in a ferry-boat to the rock-bound island of Valentia. A slate quarry, of great extent upon the coast and upon the mountain, was in excavation; two hundred men, and sometimes more, here found employment, and this has been in operation for nearly thirty years. An English nobleman, much beloved by the islanders, owns the quarry, stays continually upon the island, and spends his money there; his wife likewise is a pattern of goodness.

As I went on, a resolute man interrupted me by 'Are you a foreigner? I am likewise a stranger here, a coastguard; and did you ever see or hear anything like Kerry? The people jabbering like blackbirds, and wild rocks and mountains, the most frightful, ma'am. I'm from the north; and where are you going?' 'To O'Connell's sir.' 'And there you'll find the hospitality; and I wish I was going, too; but I'm stationed here to guard the coast against smugglers, do ye understand?' There was something peculiar in this man's appearance; he seemed to have caught the wildness of the scenery around him, or his occupation had given him that watchful restlessness that made me feel uneasy in his presence.

Seeing a hole in the wall, and a hut upon the other side, I crept through, and found a widow sitting in a corner, with a pig on the skirt of her dress, asleep, and three little children beside. I saw no bed, table, or cupboard, but a niche in the wall, in which were a couple of plates, and asked her where

Ruined 12th-century oratory on Innisfallen.

she slept. 'Here, ma'am,' pointing to a pile of straw by her side. 'I wish I had something to give you to eat, but I have not a bit of bread, nor a potato.' 'I wish I had something to give *you*,' I answered, 'for I see no way how you can live.'

This was a fair specimen of all the mountaineers around the residence of O'Connell. But when I inquired the price of ground, and found they were giving but a shilling an acre, for the same kind of mountain land I had seen elsewhere rented for twenty and twenty-four shillings, and no ejectments allowed, I wondered less that they were loud in their praises of him, and that I heard the voice of singing and of laughter from cabin and rock, from potato-ridge and bog, wherever a peasant was using his spade or hunting the hare. From the top of the mountain here may be seen the celebrated lighthouse, on what is called Skellig-rock; a dangerous place to approach where the adventurer must sometimes pass a week before he finds it safe to leave. The people of Kerry and Cork, on Shrove-tide eve, amuse themselves by hunting out the old maids and widows, putting them into carts, on asses, and all kinds of ludicrous vehicles, to send them to Skellig-rock. The streets of Cork were alive with people pursuing such as they deemed worthy a residence there, and often is the joke carried so far, that some are conveyed miles out of town, and set down, and left to make their way back as they can.

When I reached the summit of the mountain, and the sea with its wild shore, islands, and dashing waves broke upon my view, I knew the abode of the wonderful man O'Connell was near. Here no walls or surly porter, demanding a pass, hedge up the entrance; but a path like that to a New England farmhouse leads you on, and you may take your choice of entrance into the heterogeneous abode, by kitchen, chapel, or hall. I rang the hall bell, and was told that all were from home but Maurice O'Connell and the housekeeper. The countenance of the latter was to me better fitted to drive away an enemy than to invite a friend. She showed me into the library, which presented a tolerable assortment of encyclopaedias, lives of saints, Waverley Novels, law books, etc. In the drawing-room were portraits of O'Connell, engraved to the life, taken while in the penitentiary, and one taken some years before. In a family group are a brother and sister, the sister in the act of swinging, sitting in a rope; the little brother with a roguish smile, holding the rope, and a little dog looking on, enjoying the sport. It is the happiest touch of nature, in portrait-painting, I ever saw. A well-fed priest was walking about, ready at notice to perform any religious duty, within the pale of his conscience, for the good of the family.

A lunch was before me at my return into the house; the long table was in the dining-room, around which are seated, when O'Connell is at home, a goodly number of his children; and sometimes thirty-six grandchildren have been seated together there, with priests and guests, partaking the bounties of this hospitable board.

While enjoying my bread and cheese, it began to rain; it was now twenty minutes past four. I had a wild mountainous walk of five miles before me, and the wind was howling tremendously among the bleak mountains. I said, 'I dread the walk, my feet are blistered, and should the storm increase upon the mountain, as there is no place to lodge, what shall I do?' 'It will be bad for you,' replied the housekeeper, a fixture in female form, as she showed me out of the house. I said, 'Should you ever visit New York, I will do as much for you, if you will call on me.' But I was outside and the door was shut, and never did the bolting of the prison gate of a condemned culprit grate more harshly upon the ear than did the closing of this door of the 'Agitator,' when its last echo died on my ear. The rain and wind were in my face, and the wild mountain before me. When I could face the storm no longer, I turned my back, and endeavoured to walk in that way. A poor woman and her basket were sheltered under the wall, and she cried out, 'And why, ma'am, are ye out in this stawrm? And sure why didn't ye lodge at Derrynane?' 'Because they did not ask me,' I replied. 'And sure they wouldn't turn a stranger out on the wild mountains in such a stawrm as this?' 'And sure they did,' was all I could say.

At the top of the mountain the wind was at my back, and I soon had trouble to keep my feet; for some perches there was actual danger of being dashed against the rock on one side, or thrown over the wall into the sea, upon the other. Two men upon a horse were blown aside from the path, and I in the same direction. One hat fell from a rider's head, and was blown a good distance, when my parasol held it fast, till a footman could carry it to the owner; and we were all going zig-zag as best we could. I was once forced against a rock, and saved myself from being lost by clinging to a shelving part of it, till the gust passed over. It was a night which cannot soon be forgotten, and while my despairing grasp held me to the slippery crag, my soliloquy was, 'And is it from the house of Daniel O'Connell that a female stranger has been driven this perilous night? Is it from the house which, above all others, I had been told, in my own country, was the welcome resort and tarrying-place for every stranger of every clime, that I had been virtually turned out to perish, if not saved by little else than a miracle?' Though I dealt out no anathemas, yet I did say, that the hospitable abode of such a man should have a sentinel with a common share of common hospitality. Again I ventured on amid pelting rain and furious blasts, till night overtook me, and a company of mountain peasantry met me. 'And where have ye been, this bleak evening

In 1825 Daniel O'Connell inherited Derrynane House from his uncle 'Hunting Cap' O'Connell.

– not to Derrynane?' 'Yes, to Derrynane.' 'But I'm sorry I didn't know it. I live a mile from the Abbey, and would have made ye quite comfortable in my cabin; and why didn't ye stay? I've been lookin' for ye. I wanted to talk of New York.' At ten I reached an inn. 'Welcome, welcome to our house, and stay as long as ye will, without any charges.' Never was a salute more pleasant or more timely.

Next morning the tempest was still high, and venturing upon the strand, I there saw, as at Valentia, crowds of females busied; and speaking to one, she replied, 'These stawrmy nights, ma'am, blow good luck to the poor; they wash up the say-weed, and that's why ye see so many now at work.'

The company increased, till I counted more than sixty; and busy, merry work they made of it; running with heavy loads upon their heads, dripping with wet, exultingly throwing them down, and bounding away in glee. Truly, 'A merry heart doeth good like a medicine.' 'And are you not cold?' 'Oh no, ma'am, the salt say keeps us warm; the salt say, ma'am never lets us take cold.' 'And how many days must you work in this way, before you get a supply?' 'Aw, sometimes not fawrty, but scores of days.' 'And all you have for your labour is the potato?' 'That's all, ma'am, that's all; and it's many of us that can't get the sup of milk with 'em, no, nor the salt; but we can't help it, we must be content with what the good God sends us.'

She hitched her basket over her shoulder, and in company with one older than herself, skipped upon the sand made wet with rain, and turning suddenly about, gave me a pretty specimen of Kerry dancing, as practised by the peasantry. 'The sand is too wet, ma'am, to dance right well on,' and again shouldering her basket, with a 'God speed ye on yer journey,' leaped away.

I looked after them among the rocks, more with admiration for the moment, than with pity; for what hearts, amid splendour and ease, lighter than these? And what heads and stomachs, faring sumptuously every day, freer from aches than theirs, with the potato and sup of milk? This woman, who danced before me, was more than fifty, and I do not believe that the daughter of Herodias herself was more graceful in her movements, more beautiful in complexion or symmetry, than was this dark-haired matron of the mountains of Kerry.

It was three o'clock, and a walk of eleven Irish miles, covered with broken stones, fresh from the hammer, was before me. Killoyra was my destination, and Maurice Raheley's house, which I was assured was 'nate and tidy.' The hospitable inn-keeper would take no pay for lodging or board. Blessed inn!

A comely well-dressed young man, on a good horse, accosted me. 'And wouldn't ye get up, and let me give ye a lift of a couple of miles?' I looked at the lively steed, the sprightliness of the young man, and had I been in my teens, might have been strongly prompted to accept the offer. But I declined, and he walked his horse to keep me company, giving me intelligent answers to my inquiries of the state of the country, presenting the same dark picture of its hapless condition as others had done, till a different road turned him away; I saw the grey courser galloping off, and heard the last sound of his hoofs upon the path, and all was again solitude.

The sun had sunk behind a black mountain, twilight was letting down her soft curtain upon the healthy landscape, and not the buzz of an insect fell upon my ear. Not the smoke of a cabin curled in the air, and neither man nor beast met my admiring eye. From a far distant mountain, a mournful sound fell on my ear. It was the wail for the dead. It swelled in heavy tones, and then died away, as they who chanted it descended a valley; thus alternately rising and falling, for five long miles, did this lamentation float on the air. The solitude, the lateness of the hour, my distance from the land of my fathers, among so primitive a people, whose Bible customs have been retained since the mourning for Jacob in the 'threshing-floor of Atad,' made this lamentation a pleasant mournful accompaniment over the barren waste I was walking. The rustics afterwards told me it was a lone old woman who had died in her cabin on the mountain, and she must be brought 'to lie with her kin in the valley.'

The shadows of night were now heavy on the out-stretched bog before me. The road, long and dreary, was covered with coarse gravel, without the smoke of a cabin to tell me that I was not alone in the world. The stillness of death reigned; and not a sound broke upon my ear. Suddenly the barking of a dog from a far-distant mountain told me that I was in the precincts of man's abode. The Irish peasant dogs, like their masters, are patient and kind; many a one has met me at the door of a cabin, and instead of barking as a surly dog would, by the wagging of his tail and inviting look of the eye, said, 'Walk in, walk in; my master will make ye welcome to our fire and our potato.'

From *The Bible in Ireland*

William Bennett

1847

ON 6 MARCH 1847, William Bennett, a Quaker, accompanied by his eldest son, set off to investigate the conditions in Ireland during the Famine. His *Narrative of a recent journey of six weeks in Ireland in connection with the subject of supplying small seed to some of the remoter districts* is an account of that journey. The book consists of memoranda, and letters written mainly to his sister, who was one of the working members of the Ladies Irish Clothing Committee in London.

Ioth–17th April 1847. Killarney, Kenmare, Glengariff, are names which have long been associated with all that is lovely and beautiful in the Sister Isle. The first named I had visited on a former occasion; the two latter were new ground to me, but an investigation of the scenery was not now the object.

It was late in the evening when we arrived at Kenmare – tired, and a good deal exhausted. I had looked upon our painful mission as now completed, not having any idea of the awfully wretched condition of this town and neighbourhood, until accounts had begun to reach us, the last day or two, on approaching its vicinity. We were beset immediately with the most terrific details of the want and sufferings of the people: indeed it could not be concealed. The sounds of woe and wailing resounded in the streets throughout the night. I felt extremely ill, and was almost overcome.

In the morning I was credibly informed that NINE DEATHS had taken place during the night, *in the open streets*, from sheer want and exhaustion. The poor people came in from the rural districts in such numbers, in the hopes of getting some relief, that it was utterly impossible to meet their most urgent exigencies, and therefore they came in literally *to die*; and I might see several families lying about in the open streets, actually dying of starvation and fever, within a stone's throw of the inn. I went out accordingly. In the corner of an old inclosure, to which my steps were directed, on the bare ground, under the open heaven, was a *remnant of three*. One had just been carted away who had died in the night; the father had died before; the rest could not long survive. A little further, in a cask, placed like a dog-kennel, was a poor boy, who had lain there some time, in high fever, without friends or relatives. I proceeded down the main street. In the middle of it, on a little straw, under an open erection, made by placing two uprights and a board across them, were two women, horrible to behold, in the last stages of consumptive fever, brought on by evident starvation. The town itself is overwhelmed with poverty; and the swollen limbs, emaciated countenances, and other hideous forms of disease to be seen about, were innumerable. In no other part of Ireland had I seen people falling on their knees to beg. It was difficult to sit over breakfast after this. Two clergymen, hearing of our being there, came in, along with Captain Herbert, the Government Inspector, who had just come down under the new relief measures. With one of the former, I immediately went to visit a family he had just come from. The house itself was not so completely wretched; but the scene within was the counterpart of what we had witnessed in Erris. He could have shown me many such. At his earnest request and representations, I engaged to visit his additional parish of Tuosist, lying along the southern shore of the Kenmare estuary, which I had previously heard described as in the most awfully destitute condition. The other clergyman, who officiated in Tuosist and Kilcatterin, still further down, was returning home. We all started together, the first-mentioned clergyman accompanying us about two miles.

A handsome suspension-bridge leads out of the town, and is a work of great public utility. The passage was often difficult, and liable to much detension, especially to the poor, before its erection – to which the Marquis of Lansdowne, the principal owner of the town, and of the property in the neighbourhood, contributed liberally. But his influence does not extend to the welfare of the peasantry on his estates in the parish of Tuosist. We took the car as far as Kilmichalog, about ten miles along the coast. It is a wild alpine region; the inhabitants being mostly self-dependent, and in ordinary times holding very little communication with the rest of the world. The clergyman depicted their present state and condition in the most affecting terms. He could think of but two persons at all in the condition of gentlemen residing in the whole district. He declared it to be his belief, that out of a population of upwards of 30,000, there were 10,000 who had no other means of subsistence, at the present moment, than seaweed and shell-fish from the rocks. There existed considerable remains of clanship among these mountaineers. He described them as highly moral, a careless, but a peaceable and contented race, with great kindness and simple hospitality, and strong family attachments; but now the bonds of natural affection were fearfully broken and destroyed, under the pressure and sufferings of their present calamity. Their cattle, as in other places, had almost wholly disappeared. Cows had been parted with for 20*s.* to 25*s.*; sheep 3*s.* 6d. to 5*s.*, being brought in by the poor people to sell for anything they would fetch. At parting I handed him £5 for immediate urgency; and ordered to Kenmare two small bales of clothing I had remaining in Dublin. The Central Committee have since responded to an application on behalf of this district.

From *Narrative of a recent journey of six weeks in Ireland . . .*

Thomas Carlyle

1849

ESSAYIST AND HISTORIAN Thomas Carlyle (1795–1881) was born in Dumfries, the son of a stone mason. He went to Edinburgh University at the age of fifteen to study to be a clergyman. Religious doubts ended this ambition, and he worked instead as a schoolmaster and tutor for several years. Carlyle's first works were a biography of Friedrich Schiller and a translation of Goethe's *Wilhelm Meister*. In 1826 he married Jane Welsh and they moved to Cheyne Row, Chelsea. He had almost finished his most famous work, *The History of the French Revolution*, when disaster struck: the manuscript was accidentally burned at the home of his friend John Stuart Mill. In the summer of 1849 Carlyle toured Ireland for five weeks.

Wednesday 18 July . . . Mangerton, streak of Killarney evening smoke, and Macgillicuddy's serrated ridge, front of the mountain-country, handsomely fringed too with some wood, were now getting very visible; the moor changes itself into drained cultivated land, with gentlemen's seats, and human, or *more* human farmhouses: – decidedly rather beautiful, by contrast especially. Rain gone, wind tolerably fallen; western sky

Thomas Carlyle

clear as *silver*, but mostly still overhung with dark waving sheets of cloud. 'Inn, and a cup of hot tea;' that is the grand outlook! Big mills (I think?) at crossing of some stream; we are near some *castellated* modern house up on the left, – name forgotten, proprietor (useful, slightly squinting young man, connected with Peoble O'Keefe's territory) dined with us next day. High avenues, Lord Kenmare's; steepish descent; paved street at last, and square-built open street (town of 6,000 you would have said, 12,000 I was *told*); chaos of hungry porters, inn agents, lodging-agents, – beggars, storming round you, like ravenous dogs round carrion; this is Killarney. Swift, O swift into the car for 'Roche's,' for anybody's; and let us off! Roche's, I find is a mile-and-a half distant; at the lake side or near it; fine avenues all the way, and we go fast – the inn itself, a kind of general lodging house rather, did, in my experience, by no means correspond to our hope. Funeral overtaken by us; the 'Irish howl;' – totally disappointing, there was no sorrow whatever in the tone of it. A pack of idle women, mounted on the hearse as many as could, and the rest walking; were hoh-hoh-ing with a grief quite evidently hired and not worth hiring. Swift, thro' it! Here is 'Roche's,' a long row of half-cottage looking buildings; in the middle part is the inn proper and we get admitted *taliter qualiter*. Bedrooms of the smallest ever seen 'no private sitting room;' bread bad, tea luke-warm, &c: public room (which happily is nearly empty) has no window that will come down in it, and to shove any up (or support it up) you must have a stick: evidently not the best ventilated or the best in any respect of terrestrial inns. I walked out, to be free of the hot foul air; would fain have seen the lake or Mucruss Abbey at night without any guide, – but couldn't, no admittance anywhere. Rain beginning, I came in; wrote a letter; went to bed.

Thursday 19 July. Bedroom reminds me of being tied up in a sack; clean quiet little cell, however; smoke out of the window, and look at the early sun and moon. – Moon turned away from Killarney. Shine Lawlor appears at breakfast: polite, quick, well-bred-looking, intelligent little fellow, with Irish-English air, with little bead-eyes and features, and *repale* feelings, Irish altogether. We are to come after breakfast, he will 'show us the lake,' regrets to have no bed &c. – polite little man; – and we are to bring the *inn* car for ourselves and him. Poor S.L., perhaps he *had* no car of his own in these distressed times! The evident poverty of many an Irish gentleman and the struggle of his hospitality with that, was one of the most touching sights; – inviting, and even commanding respectful *silence* from the guest surely; Shine Lawlor's 'Castle-Lough' (I think he calls it) is a beautiful little place, in thick woods, close to 'Roche's,' and looking over the very lake, – though not from this parlour where we now were. *Shea* Lawlor there too, a kinsman from Bantry; tallow-complexioned, big, erect man, with sharp-croaking Irish voice, small cock-nose, stereotype glitter of smile, and small, hard blue eyes, – explodes in talking about Duffy; ex-repaler, talks *much*, half-wisely, whole-foolishly (I find) in that vein. 'Revd. Dr. Moor, Principal of Oscot,' high heavy man in black (catholic) gaiters; Catholic Harmonious Blacksmith, – really very like Whewell. Young Shine Lawlor's brother a *medicus* from Edinburgh; pleasant idle youth with cavendish tobacco: these are the party; Shine, Duffy, and I, off in car for 'Gap of Dunloe,' the others, all but Shea, – are to meet us in boat. Killarney workhouse; 3000 strong, the old *abominable* aspect of 'human swinery' – managed as handsomely as they could. Rain has begun; Duffy turns, prefers to talk all day with Shea at Castle Lough: Shine and I alone; swift pleasant-enough colloquy; sensible, shifty man, has done his best in famine-time, with wretched tenants; still above water, thanks to 'lying money' he had. Farm of his, 'will you enter?' Yes. *Bare*, very bare, new cottage; built by farmer himself, who has a long lease; docks, puddles, with rubbish all round; kitchen place empty of furniture, except a stool or two, and some vestige of perhaps one table by the back-wall; sod roof visible from within; bearded, dirty, big farmer there, who stutters and is civil; worn little old wife; who is reluctant 'to shew me her milk-house'. How she keeps her milk? 'I kape it in *keelers*!'; – with a haggard glance from the corner of her old black eyes. Daughter and she conduct us nevertheless; over wet cowhouse spaces from stepping stone to stepping stone; an ancient *cowhouse*, windows walled up with mortarless stones, no cows in *it*, milk in 'keelers' (wooden *coolers*, shallow pails), standing two rows on the floor; sod-roof visible above has once had some smear of lime-wash, transient rat had rained down clay into some of the dishes; alas, alas! They supply the Killarney workhouse with milk; have 40 cows (they say – perhaps 40 *head*): that is their farm industry. Fat stuttering farmer escorts us through spongy dock-field civilly to the road; and we mount again, and roll. 'National School here, walk in?' A most somnolent dusty establishment: perhaps some sixteen little scholars; unshaven sleepy schoolmaster, '*has* no best class,' he says; – and indeed it is all a shrine of dusty sleep, among the worst of 'National Schools;' not at all without rivals and even surpassers (victors in that bad race) as I found. 'Outdoor relief' next; at a wretched little country shop; Shine's frank swift talk to the squalid crowd: dusty squalor, full of a noisy hum, expressing greed, suspicion and *incarnated nonsense* of various kinds. Ragged wet hedges, weedy ditches; nasty ragged, spongy-looking flat country hereabouts; – like a *drunk* country fallen to sleep amid the mud.

To left, up narrow hard moor-road here, hard like Craigenputtock country; beggars waiting at solitary corners, start with us, run sometimes miles, – get nothing, Lawlor doesn't mind them in the least. We are mounting fast into the stony hills; Macgillicuddy, not always very conspicuous, lies still further to the west (I think); this route is wholly westward of the lake. One beggar ran for 2 or perhaps 3 miles; he, on the dismissal of our car, does get coats &c. to carry, and a shilling I suppose. Ex-*repale* Shine does agree with me that a Parliament, – any Parliament in these times, is a mere talking-machine; that 'Parliament in College-green,' even if it could be had, is moonshine. Pass is getting straiter, high rocky brows on left hand; We dismiss our car, take to walking; mount now thro' the 'Gap' itself; high rugged black cliffs, of slaty or *flag* structure lower overhead on both hands; with tumbled masses of the same below, and bright fat grass bordering them, – 'grass with *kills* cattle' (when they get too *much* of it suddenly, I suppose!). – Melancholy small farm (with clean straw-roof however), where the gap *opens* into a kind of craggy wide-pit, and we are now at the summit of the place; wild grey damp sky, and showers still scudding about. In front of the farmhouse is 'Dunloe hotel,' so Shine laughingly names it. Squalid, dark, empty cottage, where with a dirty table and bench, without fire visible, food, or industry of any kind, sit two women to press upon you the 'dainty of the country' 'whisky and goat's-milk.' Taste it; a greasy abomination; gave the wretches sixpence; and get away. Poor wretches, after all; but human *pity* dies away into stony misery and disgust in the excess of such scenes. One of these women is the farmer's sister; 'he won't let me enter *his* house,' she said or hinted; the other *mistress* of the vendible dainty, I learned afterwards, (at least if Irish carman's observation could teach) was 'Kate Kearney's' niece; 'Kearney' she too, but not of the song, – tho,' if lifted from her squalor, she might be a handsome woman. Step along out of rocky circuit (amphitheatre would have *sloped* more); Shine talking of deer-hunts here; no other *stock* (heard of), unless it were that farmer's 2 or 3 small *kews* (cows). Other face of the wild, too, haggard misty glen (to right of us), and glens and hills; *boggy* looking; air of Galloway and Puttock. Path, for which we have left the road, is craggy; sharp showers fall; descend, descend; near the bottom we meet young Lawlor, find Catholic Harmonious Blacksmith waiting for us under the shelter of a little bridge: forward now to – boathouse (it proves), with gay boat, four dressed handsome native boatmen; and sherry &c.; lunch in it (as the oars go), of which I cannot eat, much preferring to smoke instead.

Lake clear, blue, – almost black; slaty precipitous islets rise frequently; rocky dark hills, somewhat fringed with native arbutus (very frequent all about Killarney), mount skyward on every hand. Well enough; – but don't bother me with *audibly* admiring it: Oh! if you but wouldn't! Come once or twice aground with our boat, in muddy creeks seeking the picturesque too eagerly; otherwise a pleasant sail. 'Ornamental cottages,' deep shrouded in arbutus wood, with clearest cascades, and a depth of *silence* very inviting, abound on the shores of these lakes; but *something* of dilapidation, beggary, human fatuity in one or other form, is painfully visible in nearly all. 'Ornamental Cottage' first; woman had gone out to gain a half-penny by opening a gate for us (but missed that somehow); within one window of the place, a grey fat *savant* is busy sticking dead beetles into his Natural History pocket-book with pins; rolls a big minatory eye on us as we pass; Kitchen next to him, where we enter, is squalling infant (mother out to gain halfpenny), rubbishy fireless floor with two other children; – ugly upon my honour! Stag-hunts have been; *yonder* (west side of the lake); most silent, solitary, with a wild beauty looking thro' the squalor of one's thoughts; that is the impression of the scene; moist, soft weather too harmonized. Boatman sings us, by order, two 'repale songs;' deep bass voice, and business tone, songs obscurely *emblematic*, clearly of most ignorant character; a fine roman-nosed steel-complexioned fellow, the singer; who also awoke *echoes*, worth not much. I remember a most rapid

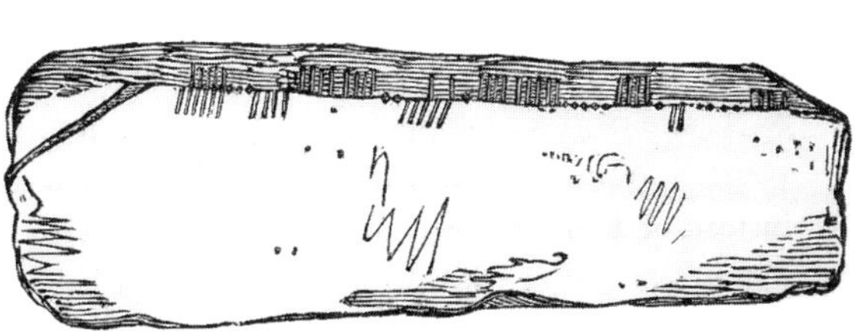

One of the Ogham stones that Georgiana Chatterton found and sketched during her 1838 visit to Kerry.

strait, between black rocks, sometimes reckoned dangerous; item, an old black bridge (beggar-girls at it, 'we been waiting for ye all day!'). Boatman steered – (song-boatman chiefly) and *shot* the lightened boat, we passing on foot, along the rapid rock-walled channel here. Dangerous this truly; especially in floods; gentleman (young Lawlor's acquaintance) drowned there, in spite of best swimming skill. We waited, in rain, below some other bridge (I remember till boat came up); passed also below a wooden bridge (woody, wild, but pleasant country all this); and now we are in the *lower* lake, bigger but not so interesting. Land at some ornamental cottage called —, where the people being understood to be at dinner we do not call; go onto 'Lady Kenmare's cottage;' and return. Beautiful little cottage, 'which her Ladyship never inhabits;' in the sweetest little woody bay or cove; mosaic pavement down to the water edge; grand *Swiss* projecting eaves; bay windows &c.; All the floors and sofas *pealed*, if we look within; and for a finale a big stone has been hoisted through one of the glass-panes, which gapes there, wide as your hat, as if in sorrowful anger and surprise; 'her Ladyship never visits it.' Alas, the futilities of man! Big lake is rather windy, even rough; some religious island with edifice (name forgotten) is visible in it to left or *north-west*. Mucross House (Herbert's) indistinctly, Mucross Abbey hardly at all, with woods and those bare Mangertons and mountains in front; pale brassy sky glitters cold on us, boat pitches, wind blows; one is hungry, and glad enough to reach Castle-Lough. Confused toilette; confused drawing room; dinner at last; squires, two doctors, two poor English ladies (Mrs. Lawlor and sister), quite '*subdued* to what they work in,' not interesting, tho' really sad to me (what interest there was); – Harmonious (Catholic) Blacksmith was on one side (eupeptic, tolerably thirsty too), then Peoble O'Keefe (let us call him the *castellated* squire slightly squinting), Duffy and one or both doctors; I was on the other side, 2nd English lady (knows 'Bayswater' if nothing else) was mine, then Shea Lawlor, and perhaps another or two others. Dinner was noisy-Irish, not unpleasant, not anywhere unpolite; nor was intelligence or candour (partly got up me it might be, yet I think was not) amid the roughish but genial mirth a quite missing element. Shea talked largely, wanted *me* to open on O'Connell that he might hear him well denounced; but I wouldn't; Shine talked, workhouse labour &c., and Peoble O'Keefe talked; bad tea in fireless parlour; finally we emerge in pitch-dark night, with escort thro' the woods; and bid our kind Irish entertainers a kind adieu. Good be with them, good struggling people; that is my hearty feeling for them now.

From *Reminiscences of My Irish Journey in 1849*

Thomas Babington Macaulay

1849

THE HISTORIAN, POET and statesman Thomas Babington Macaulay (1800–1859) was born in Leicestershire. He was educated privately and at Cambridge University. Called to the Bar in 1826, he soon abandoned law for literature and politics. Macaulay became a Member of Parliament in 1830 and established his reputation as an orator during the Reform Bill debates. After a period in India, he became Secretary of War. He is best known for his *History of England*, which appeared between 1848 and 1861, a fifth volume being unfinished at the time of his death.

August 24. Killarney. A busy day. I found that I must either forego the finest part of the sight or mount a pony. Ponies are not much in my way. However, I was ashamed to flinch, and rode twelve miles, with a guide, to the head of the Upper Lake, where we met the boat which had been sent forward with four rowers. One of the boatmen gloried in having rowed Sir Walter Scott and Miss Edgeworth, twenty-four years ago. It was, he said, a compensation to him for having missed a hanging which took place that very day. Nothing can exceed the beauty of the Upper Lake. I got home after a seven hours' ramble, during which I went twelve miles on horseback, and about twenty by boat. I had not crossed a horse since in June 1834 I rode with Captain Smith through the Mango Garden near Arcot. I was pleased to find that I had a good seat; and my guide, whom I had apprised of my unskilfulness, professed himself quite an admirer of the way in which I trotted and cantered. His flattery pleased me more than many fine compliments which have been paid to my History.

From *The Life and Letters of Lord Macaulay*

Thomas B. Macaulay

John Windele

1851

JOHN WINDELE (1801–1865) was born in Cork and developed his interest in Irish antiquities at an early age. He had an especial interest in searching for the primitive records recorded on Ogham stones. A Gaelic speaker, he made a large collection of manuscripts in that language which was later purchased by the Royal Irish Academy. In 1839 Windele published *Historical and Descriptive Notices of the City of Cork and Its Vicinity*, later abridged and published as *A Guide to Cork*. He also wrote a *Guide to Killarney* and was a frequent contributor to the *Dublin Penny Journal*. Windele visited Skellig Michael with a Cork friend, Edward Fitzgerald, on 23 June 1851.

At 25m after 7 o'clock we reached the hooker which was still lying torpid in front of the Abbey at Ballinskellig. We made our acquaintance now with her well seasoned and tanned captain, Michael Mahony by name. His hopes of a prosperous voyage were not high; he had in fact no wind. Waiting our arrival were a curious native or two who chose to have a call to Skellig; they were accompanied by a fiddler who plied his instrument with much diligence during and after navigation. I endeavoured to obtain some local native airs from him, but his collection were the ordinary airs in general circulation. Slowly and sluggishly we proceeded to the seaward round Ballinskellig island, and a most tedious process our attempt at sailing proved; for hours we kept beating about and tacking between Bolus head and Scarriff island but could make no progress to the westward. The Skelligs being all the while most provokingly near in view. At length our Ancient Mariner, the captain, declared his conviction that we could not reach the rock before night, if then. This was a fatal blow to my hopes . . .

At 10m after 3 o'clock we made the landing place at the greater Skellig. We found other boats there before us, some engaged in fishing and one with a party of visitors there like ourselves. They consisted of the Knight of Kerry, his mother and one or two friends. We found but little difficulty in landing; the place for so doing is near a dark recess backed by enormous precipices. Steps have been formed at the little quay and these attained an easy road way cut out of the solid rock and fenced by a strong parapet, – on which by the way workmen were employed making repairs after the past winter – led up towards the light houses. High above our heads butting on the edge of a crag we caught a view of the 'Yellow Cross,' a rude weather eaten dark stone bearing but a poor resemblance to

John Windele sketched the ancient chapel and beehive huts when he visited Skellig Michael in 1852.

its intended object. This stands at an elevation of about 150 (feet) above the little road way near the path leading to the oratories but in such a situation that en passant I felt little inclination to try and approach it. Our road proceeds by an easy slope, sinuously and at a breadth of about 4 feet along the Eastern side of the island, beetled over by lofty precipices to the two light houses at the last of which it ceases. The first or lower light house stands on a projection of rock at the S.E. angle of the island at a height of about ( ).

The second is at a considerable distance and on a much more elevated point at the S. West side under the great rocky spire or spit. Both are placed on the edges of precipices of almost perpendicular steepness and profound depth. The seal cove an open bay edged with fearful precipices lying between. The water here is of immense depth; the sea being, according to Smith 90 fathoms deep. . . .

The lights were first exhibited on this island on the 4th of December 1826. They are a bright colour. The two are placed one on the south and the other on a higher site on the SW side of the island. They stand 650 feet apart.

On the way up I picked out specimens of the stone which compose the rock forming the island. It is of a soft blue slaty character. I do not think Smith's description – 'a coarse kind of brown grit' correct.

Having taken a running glance at the light houses at which I saw evidences of society and population which I hardly had expected where I was only prepared for 'deep solitude and silent cells,' we speedily retraced our steps downward towards the point where the Yellow cross impended over head. Here a ladder leads up the cliff to where a gigantic stair case – gigantic in its length but not its breadth, has been formed by the Trinity board, it winds on the external face of the precipice with no protection at the outer side, the sheer wall like a rock at the inner. It was by no means a comfortable ascent for me, little accustomed as I am to ascend elevations. I soon learned to sympathize with the poet and mentally exclaimed 'Ah who can tell how hard it is to climb.' I gradually became alarmed and nervous as I looked down upon the vast and frightful depths below and the total want of protection, and I found my best course was to shut out the view in that quarter by closing my seaward eye and looking only at the rock inside me and the steps before. After a continuous ascent of some duration I was at length extremely rejoiced when I found myself entered upon 'Christ's Valley' upon whose short green sward I threw myself with great satisfaction, a pleasure which my half faded companion Murthy O'Sullivan freely participated in.

From a manuscript at the Royal Irish Academy

Harriet Martineau

1852

BORN IN NORWICH, Harriet Martineau (1802–1876) was a sickly child. She was educated at home and started writing at an early age. At first she concentrated on articles and short stories, but when forced to earn a living, she turned to social, economic and historical writing and wrote twenty-five volumes in the series *Illustrations of Political Economy*. In 1834 she set off for America, where she attended abolitionist meetings and met the abolitionist leaders. Her *Society in America* appeared in 1837. In 1852 she visited Ireland and travelled through Kerry. Although it was only five years after the Famine, she had little sympathy for the conditions she encountered.

September 29, 1852. There are various reasons why Valentia is interesting. Its Spanish name catches the ear, and reminds one of the

Harriet Martineau

Spanish legends which exist all down the coast from Galway hither; and of the wrecking of two vessels of the Armada in Malbay; and of the friendly intercourse which existed between the continental pirates and the Irish, in the time of war, in consequence of the representations of a Catholic bishop that the value of all depredations was levied on the Catholics by the English. Valentia is interesting from its position – so favourable to smuggling, invasion, and other sea tricks (from its enabling such tricksters to slip out on one side while their pursuers came in at the other), that Cromwell erected forts at both its north and south entrances. It is interesting as overlooking O'Connell's town of Cahirciveen, yet being never visited by him. It is interesting as being a sort of little kingdom of the Knights of Kerry – the Fitzgeralds – who would not exchange that old title of Knight of Kerry for any that the Queen could bestow. It is interesting as being one of the places named for a packet-station – its port being the westernmost in Europe; and 'the next parish,' for which an official gentleman was one day inquiring, being in America. A packet-station however it is not to be. Passing over other causes of interest, we come to that which is, at the present moment, of the deepest significance in our eyes. Valentia affords the broadest hints of any place we have visited of the importance of the settlement of the English in Ireland. And the present moment is the time to point this out, as the island is in the Incumbered Estates Court, and is to be sold (the inhabitants believe) in October.

The island is five miles long, by two and a half broad. Of its noble scenery, this is not the place to speak. Before the famine, its population was 3000. Now, in spite of the highly favourable circumstances we shall speak of, the population is only 2500. The Knight of Kerry has a house there, in a fine situation, with some woods about it, and a capital dairy of Kerry cows. A good deal of butter is made for exportation, and the cattle, a small and pretty breed, are an ornament to the hills and fields. The cabins of the rural population are wretched. The thatched roofs are rounded, and have no eaves; and the dwellings are usually set down one before another; so that a hamlet has the appearance, from a little distance, that we noticed in the fishing villages in Achill, of a cluster of Hottentot kraals. In our eyes they are less respectable than Indian wigwams, because of their darkness, and the infamous filth surrounding them, in the hollows in which they are sunk. The squaws in Wisconsin throw skins and fish-bones about; but their wigwams are pitched on dry sand or the wholesome grass of the prairie, and are shifted when the stench begins. Throughout the rural districts – elsewhere as well as here – we have been struck with the laziness of the people about beginning the day. Daylight is precious now, and we are abroad early. After a couple of hours' travelling, we see the housewife sitting down to milk her cow (by her own fireside, literally), and the donkey putting his head out of the cottage door, going forth for his morning meal: he has waited till the dew is off the grass. The children, still hot and heavy with sleep, in their rags (the same that they have slept in), are a disgusting sight to the traveller who is some miles on his road. This is not digression, though it looks like it.

You ask somebody at Valentia whether there is no fishing going on. The answer is that you may get any fish you please. 'But *does* anybody get it?' Two or three nets may be seen drying on the grass in the space of five miles, and a man on the road wanders about with two crabs to sell. You are told that there is a fishing station about a mile and a half from the port; a curing-house, where there were to have been boats and nets and employment for many people; but, from one thing or another happening, the place has never been opened. You find that one of the Fitzgeralds designed this fishery; and then it was sold – not yet in operation – to a gentleman who hoped great things for it; that he, in his turn, parted with it to the Irish Fishing Company, who talk about opening it; but that it is still only talk. If you look in upon the people, you find them at dinner, perhaps; or rather, you find them eating; for regular meals seem not to be liked. They prefer salt fish to fresh, and sour milk to sweet: so you find them turning out their potatoes and salt fish (dried on the roof or the fence) upon the floor, – or a board, if they happen to have one, – there being no utensil whatever in the house but the big pot the potatoes are boiled in, and the bogwood keeler or beaker that the cow is milked into; for this discomfort is not from poverty, but occurs in a dwelling where the man possesses a cow, pigs, geese, and chickens, as readily as where he is worth nothing. The doctor cannot find any sort of utensil in which to administer medicine in cabins which shelter as many farm beasts as children, and where the owner farms twenty acres! This is enough. It will show you one

Valentia Island, where the first transatlantic telegraph cable was laid in 1866, is now linked to the mainland by a bridge. (Lawrence Collection R10577)

aspect of life at Valentia, – which is much like that life at Caherciveen with which everybody has been made familiar. Now for the other.

At the little port there is a preventive station, a station of constabulary, a little inn renowned for its 'fragrant cleanliness,' and a large establishment of slate-works, in connection with the splendid slate-quarries up in the hills. These slate-works have been in operation five-and-thirty years, sustained by English capital, and conducted by English skill and care. The work-people however are Irish, every man of them, except the overlooker, who is Welsh. At present there are 120 men employed at the quarries and works; and the difference between this part of the population and the rest is so striking that the blind might be aware of it. It is not only that the men and boys, even those at the roughest work, can scarcely be called ragged at all; there is a look and tone of decent composure and independence about them which seems at once to set one down among a company of well-paid English artisans. These people are well-paid: and, by good training, they get to work very well in time. Their ideas rise with their position: and then occurs the difficulty – what to do for wives; for men thus improved in their tastes do not exactly like to pick up wives out of the stench of the cabins.

From *Letters from Ireland*

Isabella Beeton

1860

ISABELLA MAYSON (1836–1865) was born in London, grew up at Epsom, and married women's magazine publisher Samuel Beeton in 1856. After the death of their first child she began writing her *Book of Household Management*: this first appeared in parts in *The Englishwoman's Domestic Magazine*. In 1860 the Beetons visited Killarney, staying at the Railway Hotel. The following year her book was published and was an immediate success. Beeton achieved renown for *The Englishwoman's Cookery Book* (1863) and *Mrs. Beeton's Dictionary of Every-day Cookery* (1865).

Isabella Beeton

Wednesday 11 July . . . Landed and made our way up the mountain to the Gap of Dunloe. Girls with bare feet carrying goat's milk tormented us to buy of them. Very be-ringed handsome girls with smart shawls over their heads. Danced on the Lady's Rest to a very peculiar wild air.

Did not have a very good view of the Gap.

Returned home, on our way fell in with a large party from our hotel headed by Mr. Spillane, who looked a veritable captain of his party. Heard him play on his bugle; he wakened the echoes from the Eagle's Nest. The effect was charming. You merely heard the echoes and not the bugle.

They fired off 3 or 4 shots which reverberated through the

mountain and sounded like thunder. Altogether one of the pleasantest days of our trip. . . .

Wednesday 18 July. Took the boat to Ross Castle. Rowed round a point of the island into Castlelough Bay. Got into a quiet corner. Patrick pulled off his shoes and stockings; met with no success, went further up the Lake to the River Flesk . . . succeeded in catching 6 perch between us.

Pat went to the Lake Hotel for bread and butter. Rowed over to Innisfallen. Then we kindled a fire and Pat cooked the fish in the most artistic manner in the ashes. Eat particularly sweet. . . .

Very windy, stormy and cold. Sam and Pat dropped me at the pier of Ross Island as it was by now blowing a great gale. They had a very rough journey home, put up umbrellas for sails coming down Ross Bay. Took tea and went to bed.

Friday 19 July. . . . Wrote some letters and then both started with Pat for Coleman's Castle. Very much pleased with the buildings, nicely kept, good garden, beautiful view.

Fed some young turkeys. Took luncheon underneath the trees and returned to the hotel.

After dinner walked to Ross Castle to bid farewell to the Lakes. This was the first and last place visited at Killarney.

From Isabella Beeton's diary

Daniel Gooch

1865

RAILWAY PIONEER AND inventor Daniel Gooch (1816–1889) was born at Bedlington, Northumberland. As a child he acquired his first knowledge of engineering at Birkinshaw's ironworks in his home village. At the age of twenty-one he was appointed locomotive superintendent of the Great Western Railway, and he designed engines that attained speed and safety records not seen before. In 1864 Gooch resigned the post to inaugurate telegraphic communication with the laying of a cable between Valentia, County Kerry and Newfoundland. His efforts were successful, and he dispatched the first cable message across the Atlantic in 1866.

Berehaven, July 19th. We arrived off Valencia this morning at 6 a.m. The night up to about 4 had continued very stormy. At that time the two ropes of the *Caroline* chafed through, and she was left to her own

Daniel Gooch

resources. Fortunately the weather moderated, and we had the great pleasure of seeing her get into harbour. The two war steamers, the *Sphinx* and *Terrible*, were also lying off near Valencia waiting for us. As it will take a couple of days at least (even if the weather is fine enough to do the work at all) to lay the shore-end, the captain has determined to run into this bay and wait. It is a long way from our work, being about eight hours' steaming. We therefore, as soon as the *Caroline* was safe, turned round and retraced our steps. The day turned out beautifully fine, and it was a delightful sail along the wild and beautiful coast of Kerry. The Skellig rocks are very fine, one being 740 feet high. There are also two beautiful rocks called the Bull and the Cow; they have fine natural arches through them . . .

Atlantic, July 23rd. I had just fallen asleep last night when a loud knock at my cabin door awoke me, and, after spending some seconds in trying to recollect where I was, and endeavouring to get out of bed on the side next the cabin partition, I got up and found a messenger had come from Valencia Bay to say they were laying the shore-end. The fires were at once lighted, and we left Bantry Bay at 2 a.m., reaching the *Caroline* at 10 a.m. Steps were immediately taken to make the splice, which was completed at 5.30, and we got fairly away on our voyage. A glorious day, nothing could have been finer, and our cable is now running out at the rate of nearly six knots per hour, the *Terrible* being on our port and the *Sphinx* on our starboard bows, about a half-mile from us. It was a beautiful and interesting scene all day as we lay together on the waters of the Atlantic, about twenty-five miles from the land, the two war-steamers, the *Caroline* and the *Great Eastern*. Mid-day, the *Hawk* came off to us with Canning, Sir Robert Peel, the Knight of Kerry, and others, amongst them friend Barber. About four o'clock matters were so near ready that the ship was cleared of visitors, and, as we started, every one on board the ship thought it necessary to cheer until I think their lungs must have ached. It was an exciting scene. All our machinery works admirably, and I see no human reason why we should not in twelve days land it safely in Trinity Bay. Fine weather is predicted by all, and we are now satisfied it must be bad weather indeed which will seriously impede our work.

From *Diaries of Sir Daniel Gooch, Baronet*

William W. Barry

1865

WILLIAM WHITTAKER BARRY (1830–1875) was born at Draycot Cerne, Wiltshire, the son of a rector. He won the first law scholarship awarded by the Inns of Court, and was called to the Bar in 1853. He practised as an equity draftsman and conveyancer at Lincoln's Inn and wrote several legal books. He also reviewed British Academy publications. In 1865 Barry embarked on a walking tour in Ireland, recording his experiences in a book published in 1867 under the pseudonym 'An Englishman.'. *A Walking Tour in Normandy.* (1868) followed after a similar journey in France. He was on a walking tour when he died in a snow storm in the Tyrolean Alps.

Thursday, September 21. Listowel is a nice town, with an ivy-covered tower and a fine market square, in which is the church. I left Listowel at half-past ten o'clock this morning for Tralee. The road winds round the grounds of Lord Listowel's residence, and then crosses by a bridge the river Feale, a broad stream here. It was a lovely morning, the cattle were standing about in the water refreshing themselves; the view is fine and the whole scene quite romantic. Two women, apparently farmers' wives, pass. I ask the name of the river. 'The Feale,' was the reply; 'but I perceive, sir, you are a stranger, not to know the name of this river.' 'Yes.' 'What are you travelling for?' 'On pleasure; I am come on a walking tour to see the country.' 'Oh! Indeed, sir, this is a long way to come to see Listowel.' Perceiving that the women had some foolish suspicion which I could not remove, I bade them good morning and walked on. Presently my questioner, who had left her companion, overtook me on the road, and after some conversation on ordinary topics she seemed to acquire confidence, and said voluntarily, 'You know, sir, when you joined us just now and had left, my neighbour said, "I should not wonder now if that man were come out to look after these 'ere Fanians, I shouldn't be surprised if he had a shot;" and I thought so too.' I had then some talk with her about the Fenians, but she knew or professed to know nothing

The busy market town of Listowel, which William Barry visited in 1865, has achieved renown as the literary centre of Kerry. (Lawrence Collection R8226)

about them. The good woman, however, was evidently sorry at having suspected me of being a spy, and at the cross-road where we parted she said, 'I suppose you will be coming this way again never-more?' 'Probably not.' 'But if so, that is my house yonder, and if you will pay me a visit there you shall be welcome.' I thanked her for this kind proffer of hospitality and went on my way, though not exactly rejoicing, for this new feature of travel somewhat alarmed me. I had little doubt that with the same opportunity for explanation I could easily remove any suspicion of this kind. But what if I should be taken for a spy as a matter of course, and shot at from behind a hedge. The idea certainly was not a pleasant one to entertain, and happily it obtained no practical hold on the mind.

The road then proceeds with the river to the right, and two or three good residences in the distance, and a fine view of Listowel in the rear. Then on through a well-cultivated country and a pretty valley, when after several miles you enter a beautifully wooded glen, and further on proceed through a valley with a waterfall. Then for two or three miles the road is dull, until you come in view of the Slieve Mish and Dingle Mountains with Macgillicuddy's Reeks above to the left. I then enter Tralee, which I presume has not many visitors, for the waiter or boots from two or three of the hotels, comes out to seek my custom. These are called by the uncharitable 'touters,' a word I do not adopt, because it is offensive. Indeed I do not dislike their assistance, for sometimes on entering a strange town, even if it be recognised by your guidebook and an hotel recommended, it is difficult to find the one indicated, and when the place is ignored then you are relieved of the tiresome process of enquiry and search. I invariably find these 'touters,' as they are called, civil and amenable to reason, and I by no means feel bound to follow their directions, unless they are supported by the merits of the case. After looking about me a little I put up at the Blennerhassett Arms, which I found clean and comfortable. The waiter tells me a story about the alarm created at Killarney by the Fenians. A musician from Dublin about to give a concert there, arrived a day or two ago at the Victoria Hotel, and meekly asked whether he could have a bed. 'A bed!' the master replied, 'why you can have any bed you like in the house, for all the visitors are leaving, on account of the Fenians.' I afterwards discovered that this story could not be true, and also that there is a perpetual feud kept up in the local papers of Tralee and Killarney, the one attempting to injure the other. The latter place at least might well rest on its far-famed lakes, and leave its less fortunate neighbour alone.

Before dinner I walked out to see the town of Tralee. It is a clean-looking place with some good streets, the most fashionable being Denny Street, leading to the grounds of Sir Edward Denny. These grounds are liberally thrown open to the public. I entered them and sat about there, but they are nothing in particular. In the middle of the town there is a fine town-hall, with some guns in front, in memory of officers and men who fell in India. Tralee is distant from Listowel about seventeen miles. It presents to the eye of the stranger the appearance of doing a good trade, and of being a mart for the supply of the surrounding country.

From *A Walking Tour round Ireland in 1865*

Tomb at Muckross Abbey.

Bernard H. Becker

1880

BERNARD HENRY BECKER (1833–1900) was born in London. A journalist by profession, he wrote sketches and stories for *All the Year Round*, and contributed regularly to the *Daily News*. In the winter of 1878–79 the *Daily News* sent him as special commissioner to investigate the distressing conditions of manufacturing workers in Manchester and Sheffield. Becker undertook a similar assignment in 1880 when he crossed to Ireland to report on the conditions of the people in Munster and Connacht. The letters he wrote on this visit provoked attention, and were discussed in the British parliament. Other works were *Scientific London*, *Adventurous Lives* and *Holiday Haunts.*

To reach Valentia Island it is necessary to leave the railway track from Mallow to Tralee, and at Killarney commence what in London parlance might be called a cruise in a 'growler'; for an unmistakable 'growler,' well built and comfortably lined, was the vehicle supplied to me as a 'carriage,' with a pair of excellent horses, by Spillane, the sometime guide and present postingmaster of Killarney. The postchaise assumes many forms in Ireland, but only once have I met the original *coupé* holding only two persons. It is a long drive to the ferry at the extremity of the peninsula between the bays of Kenmare and Dingle. Beyond, the Island of Valentia lies like a breakwater against the Atlantic, and the scene at nightfall is strange enough, with flashing lanterns, shouting ferrymen, and plashing oars. The ferryman is far from considering Valentia Harbour as a drawback to the island, and, like a fine old discontented retainer as he is, complains bitterly of the attempt made years ago by the late Knight of Kerry to establish a steam ferry. But ferrymen are always stern sticklers for vested rights. Doubtless Charon claimed heavy compensation when the Styx Ferry was disestablished. Apart from the ferryman, however, the Valentians are by no means enamoured of their insular position. 'That ould blackguard of a ferry' is in fact, just now a serious item of discontent.

It is urged by the islanders, nearly three thousand in number, including the villagers, the quarrymen and the staff of telegraphists, presided over by the skilful and courteous Mr. Graves, that the ferry is the cause of half their troubles. The peasants, who sell their stock at the thirteen fairs held yearly at Cahirciveen, declare that the cost of the ferry-boat for themselves and their beasts is a substantial reason for the reduction of the rent, inasmuch as they are put at a disadvantage with the people on the mainland. This is not the only grievance of that section transplanted to the hill side

Staigue Fort on the Iveragh Peninsula, one of the largest Iron Age stone forts in Ireland.

by Bray Head. They complain that they are afar off – a droll objection on an island six miles long – and have given their settlement the nickname of 'Paris,' in allusion to its remoteness from Knightstown and the ferry which leads to the grogshops and Fenian centres of Cahirciveen. I am told that the duty on the spirits sold in that cheerful townlet exceeds the whole annual value of the barony of Iveragh, and can bear witness to the convergence of the surrounding population on market day. . . .

Pursuing my cruise in a Growler round the coast I came past some magnificent scenery by Waterville, at the head of Ballinskelligs Bay to Derrynane, once the abode of the 'Liberator' and now occupied by Mr. Daniel O'Connell, his grandson, who gave me a curious instance of the profit to be realised on a dairy and grazing farm. He has leased the island of Scariff from Lord Dunraven for £60 per annum, has put a dairyman upon it, and sells off of it yearly produce, butter, cattle, sheep, wool, and pigs, to the value of £230, the valuation of the island, according to Griffith, being, including the dairyman's house £27 5s. Mr. O'Connell also gave me an odd proof of the retribution which appears likely to fall upon the landowners of the barony of Iveragh.

When the Government valuation was first made public it was protested against by Sir James O'Connell, who succeeded in getting it reduced by

30 per cent., an unfortunate circumstance for the present proprietors if the Land League continue to have it all their own way. The League, however, has not yet troubled Derrynane; the tenants, who since 1841 have been greatly reduced in number by emigration and the consolidation of holdings, have paid their rent fairly up to this, that is to say fairly according to the usage of that remote part of Kerry. They average 'the grass of six cows,' with the run of the mountain, 'for rather more' collops or young cows, not yet in milk.

Derrynane rejoices in many memorials of the Liberator, but the relic of 'Ould Dan' that all visitors, and especially Irishmen, are most anxious to see, is in the oblong mahogany box lying on the tall desk at which he was wont to stand and write. It is that article of furniture without which no Irish gentleman's equipment was more complete than his house without an avenue. 'My pistols which I shot Captain Marker,' as poor Rawdon Crawley put it. There reposes peacefully enough now by the side of its companion, the weapon with which the 'Liberator' shot Mr. D'Esterre. It is a flint lock pistol of very large bore, and with stock reaching to the muzzle. One peculiarity about this pistol is worthy of note. Beneath the trigger guard a piece of steel extends curving downwards and outwards towards the muzzle, a convenient device, as I find, for steadying the weapon by aid of the second finger. On the stock is cut rudely a capital D., for D'Esterre. There are no other marks, although the pistols have a pedigree and a story attached to them. . . .

Mr. O'Connell also showed me a brass blunderbuss once the property of Robert Emmet. It has a revolving chamber, which, instead of turning automatically, must be adjusted by hand after every shot, a curious forerunner of Colt's invention, adaptation, or revival. Derrynane is delightfully situated at a spot called appropriately 'White Strand,' from the silvery sand washed by the Atlantic waves. Above it stands the celebrated circular fort of Staigue, built of dry stone, and with an inclined plane inside like those at West Cove and Ballycarbery. Opposite is the magnificent rocky peninsula of Lamb Head, the road across which much resembles parts of St. Gothard, plus the magnificent sea shining in the sun.

The crag of Lamb Head, broken into a thousand jagged slopes, is here and there overgrown with short sweet herbage. Wherever grass grows there will a Kerry calf or 'collop' be found. How the pretty little black cattle cling like flies to those dizzy windy heights is marvellous; but there they are, night and day, for months at a stretch, giving no trouble to anybody, growing into condition ready for 'finishing' on richer pasture, and giving life and beauty to a scene which would, without them, be but grandly desolate. The little Kerries are greatly prized as 'milkers' and they yield good beef, but very little of it – not more than four hundredweight per beast. By the side of the superb shorthorns of the Ardfert herd, they look like goats; but such cattle as Mr. Crosbie's cream-coloured bull are only suited to richer pasture than the rocks of Lamb Head. It may also be added that for the purpose of dairy-farms the best commercial cows are all bred between the rough native cattle and shorthorns, or between Devon and Ayrshire, the latter cross being specially liked by Mr. Hegarty, of Mill Street, county Cork, referred to in a previous letter, and by many other good judges. This fact, however, by no means detracts from the value of such a magnificent herd as that of Mr. Crosbie. On the contrary it is held by many experts that first-class shorthorn bulls are a necessity for preventing the cross-bred animals from reverting to the original local type.

From *Disturbed Ireland*

E. de Mandat-Grancey

1887

French Baron Edmond de Mandat-Grancey (1842–1911) travelled extensively throughout his life and wrote many books about his journeys. He visited the western frontier of the United States and described the events in *Cow-Boys and Colonels: Narrative of a Journey across the Prairie and over the Black Hills of Dakota*. He also wrote books about his trips to the Rocky Mountains, and to New York and Chicago. Mandat-Grancey's travels took him to Africa, which he recounted in *Au Congo,* published in 1898, and to Madagascar, resulting in the book *Souvenirs de la Côte d'Afrique*.

We reached Kenmare about six o'clock. It is a pretty little port, situated on one of the deepest of the innumerable bays that the great Atlantic rollers have washed out of the west coast of Ireland; they form havens that would be invaluable for commerce – if there were any. There is a gate in the chief square of Kenmare, I may say the only square, through which we enter a beautiful park, and in the midst of it stands one of those small English villas, which look foolish when they are placed side by side in a row, but which, standing alone, are really charming. This one is hidden under a thick mantle of climbing plants, through which the large glass panes of the bow windows glitter brightly. This is Lansdowne Lodge, the residence provided by the Marquis of Lansdowne for the use of his agent.

The interior is not less delightful than the exterior. The hall is ornamented with a number of deer and elk horns, found in admirable preservation in the turf pits. I had already seen some superb specimens the other day at Sir Croker Barrington's. To the left opens a dining-room, where at eight o'clock some of the inhabitants of Kenmare assembled, to whom Mr. Trench wished to introduce me. The chief dish on the table was a splendid salmon that one of these gentlemen had killed two hours before. The conversation was most lively and interesting, but really whilst listening to it one feels in a dream. For instance, I discover that in compliment to me these gentlemen have consented to dine away from home, but that it is a very exceptional circumstance, and they are not sure that they may not regret it. No one dare go out at night for fear of being shot. One of them, who is employed on the estate, has just heard that he is to be boycotted, because of an eviction in which he was concerned. He expected that on the morrow the butcher would refuse to supply him with meat, but he consoled himself by the reflection that he had some biscuits and some tins of preserves in the house.

After dinner we went to Mr. Trench's study to smoke. I sat down by a small table on which stood a candlestick, and placed my coffee by it.

'Excuse me, dear sir,' said one of the guests, addressing me, half laughing, half serious, 'but you are wrong to sit there. You see, if any one fired at us through the window you might be hurt. There, allow me to move your chair a little. Now you are safe. And besides, hanging on the wall within reach of your hand you have a loaded revolver and a tomahawk – both excellent weapons. Try the edge of the tomahawk. Look, too, on the mantel-piece, there is a bowie knife; some people prefer a bowie knife, but I like the tomahawk best, and this one is extremely sharp.'

I effusively thanked this amiable gentleman. The conversation became general, and the guests discussed weapons. Each drew a revolver from his pocket and warmly defended his own theories. They all agreed that Mr. Trench's revolver was too small. He was sitting about five or six paces from me on the other side of the chimney.

'Ah!' said they, 'you may be the best shot in the country, but you are wrong to use such a short weapon, it cannot be relied on; you would miss a man at ten paces.'

'You say that I could not be sure of my aim!' cried Mr. Trench; 'you shall see.'

Instantly I heard a frightful noise, in which I distinguished three reports, a sound of broken glass, and then I felt on my back and head a succession of tiny pricks, as though all the archers of Lilliput were shooting at me. Thinking it was a Fenian attack I sprang to the tomahawk, seized the revolver in the other hand, and, entrenched behind my arm-chair, I awaited events.

It was only Mr. Trench who had fired at the candle within a foot of my head. The first two bullets had simply broken the sconce, the last had cut the candle in two, and one of the balls had struck a box of steel pens that had been placed on a what-not; the pens had flown into the air, and some had fallen into my collar and had produced the pricking.

After warmly congratulating the master of the house, the guests took leave of us, we conducting them to the door. There each one grasped his shillalah with the left hand and his revolver with the right, and we saw them passing all the clumps of trees carefully and at a respectful distance. For ourselves, after watching them for a minute we securely barricaded the door, and I was then shown to a capital room, where I slept in an excellent bed.

But what an extraordinary country!

From *Paddy at Home*

Marie-Anne de Bovet

1889

BORN AT METZ IN 1860, Marie-Anne de Bovet (later Marchioness Deschamps de Bois-Hébert) first worked as a translator. She travelled widely and wrote books about her journeys to Poland and Algeria. Under the pseudonym 'Mab,' de Bovet contributed to many French and English newspapers and periodicals. However, it is as a novelist that she was best known: her works include *Contre L'Impossible*, *Confessions d'une Fille de Trente*, *Court Folie*, and *Marionnettes*. In 1889 she embarked on a three-month tour of Ireland.

When Marie-Anne de Bovet visited Kerry in 1889 the Land War was raging and scenes like this one she witnessed were common.

When after a walk by the lake or among the hills you examine the agricultural environs of Killarney, the glamour quickly vanishes. By the wayside is a cabin, built of stones without mortar, and thatched with turf. The door is wide open day and night, because there is no window and nothing to steal; a small peat-fire burns under a conical opening in the roof, which does not prevent the atmosphere from being dense with smoke; for floor, there is nothing but trodden earth; a bench, a broken chair, a bed of moss and rushes, half-a-dozen pots and pans, and a few unrecognizable wrecks of garments hung on the walls, make up the furniture. This den is the dwelling of an old woman, who receives you with pious ejaculations and effusive blessings, delivered with great volubility and in a strong brogue. She is a widow, and how she lives is a mystery; but we are assured that she does very well in the tourist season, and her expenses cannot be great in the matter either of food or dress. Pursuing our melancholy way, we arrive in the open country, and are struck with the fact that half the houses are apparently in ruins. We are looking upon evicted farms, and they are barricaded or demolished to prevent the inmates from returning as soon as the police have gone. All around, the uncultivated soil is covered with thistles and weeds, to the extent of many square miles. We are on the land of Lord Kenmare, desolated by the agrarian war which the Land League encourages and maintains with all its might.

It is the same upon the neighbouring lands of Mucross, and still the same upon the estate of Lord Lansdowne; that is to say, over two-thirds of the county. The smaller proprietors are in no better case than the large ones. The more energetic part of the population has emigrated; many have gone to the towns to swell the ranks of poverty, and some remain as a Land League garrison. By the side of the ruined farms stand groups of the huts erected by the League for the accommodation of evicted tenants. The chief difficulty is to find sites, but there are frequently common lands available, or deserted roads. These wooden barracks are relatively comfortable, the outer walls being covered with felt or rush mats, and the interior decorated with pious images, caricatures of Mr. Balfour, and portraits of the Nationalist leaders – Mr. Gladstone holding the place of honour – cut out of popular journals. It is said that the evicted tenants make a better living out of the contributions of the League than they did by honest labour. Their cattle are in suspiciously good condition, but as they are never housed by day or night their owners naturally cannot hinder them from straying upon the meadows of the absent landlord; and though the police are not far off, they have plenty to do without running after cows. These evicted tenants laugh till the tears run down their cheeks at the tricks they play upon the landlords and the authorities. They make a living which, though poor enough, costs them no labour, and they complacently watch the thistles overspreading the fields, and the land going back to waste, so long as they can read the papers, attend meetings, and anticipate the time when they shall return to the houses now slowly falling into ruin.

Ordinary evictions are commonplace affairs, but those which are carried out at the price of a regular battle are worth going to see. The whole apparatus of the law is brought into play – police, infantry, and cavalry. Barricading themselves in their houses, the inhabitants launch from the windows stones, broken pots, hot oil, and boiling water. To break in the doors a sort of battering-ram is employed, the walls are demolished stone by stone, men, women and children are dragged forth by main force, the movables are turned out, the doors and windows closed with planks, and sometimes the roof itself taken off to render the tenement uninhabitable. All this goes on amid the execrations of a yelling crowd, which an agitator or the priest of the parish inflames with well understood exhortations to abstain from violence. Nothing can be more distressing than these scenes, though my pity cannot be entirely withheld from the officers and soldiers, who frequently suffer severely in the discharge of their unpleasant duty. It is related that Lord Kenmare once found himself by accident present at an eviction of this kind. Seizing a hatchet which lay among the miserable furniture on the road-side, he knocked away the planks with which they had closed the doorway, gave the evicted family a handful of money, and told them to re-enter. It was a natural movement of compassion; but after all he cannot allow hundreds of such families to appropriate his land without payment. It may be asked why these unfortunates allow things to proceed to such extremities. They had some excuse in the old days, when the mad competition for land forced rents up to an impossible figure; but these rents have been reduced again and again by legislation, which has placed the Irish tenant in a better position than any other in the world. But the old grudges remain, and are sedulously fostered by the League for political purposes, while the peasants cherish the ineradicable belief that the soil is theirs and not the landlords.

From *Three Months Tour in Ireland*

Bertha Beatty

*c.*1890

BORN IN LISTOWEL in 1879, Bertha Beatty was a daughter of Francis Creagh who, besides having a large practice as a solicitor, was a well-known racehorse owner and amateur rider. She was educated at home in the Square, Listowel. After her marriage to a County Wexford-born doctor Richard Beatty, she settled at Swindon in Wiltshire. This area prompted her first book, *Westcountry Thoughts*. In 1939 her recollections of her younger days, *Kerry Memories*, appeared.

Nine miles west of Listowel and opposite to Loop Head (Clare) stands the little town of Ballybunion. At the time of which I write, the Lartigue railway from Listowel connected Ballybunion with the world. . . . Stories were numerous of the difficulty in balancing the carriages, and one was that a very fat woman once took her seat on one side of a carriage. No one could be found to make the weight correct on the other side, so a cow was put on board! This is one of, it is said, 10,000 jokes about the Lartigue. For that alone it should be remembered! It really was necessary to get the balance even, otherwise there was a danger of the carriage turning over, also it was uncomfortable if it swayed. Once all was arranged, sitting facing the scenery side by side, two advantages are obvious. Firstly one didn't have to turn to look out of the window, and secondly one didn't have people sitting opposite! We frequently went in the summer for a day to Ballybunion, taking lunch to the sandhills where we picnicked.

Later the sandhills became golf-links. Now I hear enthusiastic praise of these. Wild pansies grew freely on these sandhills, a kind of berry – blueberry – abounded, and many other wild flowers. There was also a spot known as the 'shellpick' where masses of shells were to be found between the hills. On the sands were more shells in great variety, especially on the 'men's strand' and near the black rocks. These included many of the Cowrie variety formerly used as coin.

There is an old burial-ground in the sandhills, where some of the Creaghs are buried. This reminds me of a local story; a man walking past a milestone, marked '110 miles from Dublin' was heard to say, 'God rest his soul, a hundred and ten, and his name was Miles from Dublin!'

When we went to stay at Ballybunion, which we did every year, it was generally in September. We rented a house and the entire household went. A dray took luggage, which included a piano. Later we drove in a 'waggonette and pair' with servants and governess. My Father and Mother came by train to find everything ready. We used to take our two fox-terriers and one year, when we rented the Rectory, one of them came into the Church during a morning service.

One cow, known as the 'blue cow' was also driven over by road. On one occasion she didn't like it evidently, and was found next morning outside her own field at home – having 'walked by herself' nine miles! One of my brothers once took a pet duck known as the Yellow Duck, and used to take it into the sea.

The Rectory had one locked room, which excited our curiosity. One day the Rector arrived and went into the mysterious room. On coming out his coat showed that it was merely a store-room, flour gave 'the ghost' away!

The Rector suffered terribly from shyness. His manner was painfully nervous. When he called he brought his hat into the room, put it under the chair he sat on, and then forgot where he put it.

We once took one wing or lodge as it was called, of the Castle Hotel. There I remember sleeping in a room by myself and playing 'cats' cradle' in bed. My toes acted as the other party! I also remember taking a hammer to knock out a front tooth in that room.

Shopping in Ballybunion was a great thrill. We always bought 'surprise packets' which were a feature of those days and I feel sure are no longer procurable. In each 'packet' was a 'surprise' – something such as is found in crackers nowadays. Sweets of a doubtful kind were in every packet.

Food was good in Ballybunion. Fish was brought over from Co. Clare by boatmen. I remember seeing baskets of live lobsters brought to the door for sale. I liked putting a wooden spade into an open claw and feeling how tightly it closed on the spade. One food I did not like was a jelly made from Carrigeen-moss. I refused it once at lunch and it was kept for my supper. Did I eat it then? My memory doesn't tell me. Women used to sell dried seaweed called 'Dillisk'. It was eaten by country-people largely, being salt and 'good for one'. I only tasted it and never eat it.

Bathing we enjoyed very much. There were two so-called 'strands.' One, the men's strand and the other the ladies' strand, divided geographically only, by a headland, on which was the ruin of an old castle. Smugglers caves also were on this promontory – relics of past history. Bathing-boxes drawn by donkeys were brought over from the men's strand to the ladies' when needed, and when tide permitted. Countrywomen undressed in caves. The machines were owned and run by the Danahar family, the boys urging the donkeys along with the aid of sticks and shouts. Atlantic waves made bathing at times impossible. They were glorious to watch, breaking against the cliffs, the spray rising to a great height.

From *Kerry Memories*

John Millington Synge

1903

JOHN MILLINGTON SYNGE (1871–1909) was born in Rathfarnham, Dublin. While living in Paris, he met W.B. Yeats who persuaded him that the Irish peasantry were a worthy subject for a writer. On returning to Ireland, Synge made several visits to the Aran Islands to study the folk culture. He visited West Kerry for the first time in 1903 and returned in 1904 and 1905. His impressions and memories are recalled in his book *In Wicklow and West Kerry*. In 1907 the staging of his play *The Playboy of the Western World* at Dublin's Abbey Theatre caused riots: fifty policemen were needed to control the audience.

This evening a circus was advertised in Dingle, for one night only; so I made my way there towards the end of the afternoon, although the weather was windy and threatening. I reached the town an hour too soon, so I spent some time watching the wild-looking fishermen and fish-women who stand about the quays. Then I wandered up and saw the evening train coming in with the usual number of gaily-dressed young women and half-drunken jobbers and merchants; and at last, about eight o'clock, I went to the circus field, just above the town, in a heavy splash of rain. The tent was set up in the middle of the field, and a little to the side of it a large crowd was struggling for tickets at one of the wheeled houses in which the acrobats live. I went round the tent in the hope of getting in by some easier means, and found a door in the canvas, where a man was calling out: 'Tickets, or money, this way,' and I passed in through a long winding passage. It was some time after the hour named for the show, but although the tent was almost filled there was no sign of the performers; so I stood back in a corner and watched the crowd coming in wet and dripping from the rain, which had turned to a downpour. The tent was lighted by a few flaring gas-jets round the central pole, with an opening above them, through which the rain shot down in straight whistling lines. The top of the tent was dripping and saturated, and the gas, shining sideways across, made it glitter in many places with the brilliancy of golden silk. When a sudden squall came with a rush from the narrow valleys behind the town, the whole structure billowed, and flapped and strained, till one waited every moment to see the canvas fall upon our heads. The people, who looked strangely black and swarthy in the uncertain light, were seated all round on three or four rows of raised wooden seats, and many who were late were still crushing forward, and standing in dense masses wherever there was room. At the entrance a rather riotous crowd began to surge in so quickly that there was some danger of the place being rushed. Word was sent across the ring, and in a moment three or four of the women performers, with long streaming ulsters buttoned over their tights, ran out from behind the scenes and threw themselves into the crowd, forcing back the wild hill-side people, fishwomen and drunken sailors, in an extraordinary tumult of swearing, wrestling and laughter. These women

J.M. Synge

The Lartigue railway, a unique passenger-carrying monorail service, ran between Ballybunion and Listowel from 1888 to 1924. (Lawrence Collection R4275)

seemed to enjoy this part of their work, and shrieked with amusement when two or three of them fell on some enormous farmer or publican and nearly dragged him to the ground. Here and there among the people I could see a little party of squireens and their daughters, in the fashions of five years ago, trying, not always successfully, to reach the shilling seats. The crowd was now so thick I could see little more than the heads of the performers, who had at last come into the ring, and many of the shorter women who were near me must have seen nothing the whole evening, yet they showed no sign of impatience. The performance was begun by the usual dirty white horse, that was brought out and set to gallop round, with a gaudy horse-woman on his back, who jumped through a hoop and did the ordinary feats, the horse's hoofs splashing and possing all the time in the green slush of the ring. An old door-mat was laid down near the entrance for the performers, and as they came out in turn they wiped the mud from their feet before they got up on their horses. A little later the clown came out, to the great delight of the people. He was followed by some gymnasts, and then the horse-people came out again in different dress and make-up, and went through their old turns once more. After that there was prolonged fooling between the clown and the chief horseman, who made many mediaeval jokes, that reminded me of little circuses on the outer boulevards of Paris, and at last the horseman sang a song which won great applause:

Here's to the man who kisses his wife,
And kisses his wife alone;
For there's many a man kissed another man's wife
When he thought he kissed his own.

Here's to the man who rocks his child,
And rocks his child alone;
For there's many a man rocked another man's child
When he thought he rocked his own.

About ten o'clock there seemed to be a lull in the storm, so I went out into the open air with two young men who were going the road I had to travel. The rain had stopped for a moment, but a high wind was blowing as we made our way to a public-house to get a few biscuits and a glass of beer before we started. A sleepy barmaid, who was lolling behind the counter with a novel, pricked up her ears when she heard us talking of our journey.

'Surely you are not going to Ballydavid,' she said 'at such an hour of a night like this.'

We told her we were going to a place which was further away.

'Well,' she said, 'I wouldn't go to that place to-night if you had a coach-and-four to drive me in, and gave me twenty pounds into the bargain! How at all will you get on in the darkness when the roads will be running with water, and you'll be likely to slip down every place into some drain or ditch?'

When we went out, and began to make our way down the steep hill through the town, the night seemed darker that ever after the glare of the bar. Before we had gone many yards a woman's voice called out sharply from under the wall: 'Mind the horse.' I looked up and saw the black outline of a horse's head standing right above me. It was not plain in such darkness how we should get to the end of our ten-mile journey; but one of the young men borrowed a lantern from a chandler in the bottom of the town, and we made our way over the bridge and up the hill, going slowly and painfully with just light enough, when we kept close together, to avoid the sloughs of water and piles of stones on the roadway. By the time we reached the top of the ridge and began to work down carefully towards Smerwick, the rain stopped, and we reached the village without any mishap.

I go out often in the mornings to the site of Sybil Ferriter's Castle, on a little headland reached by a narrow strip of rocks. As I lie there I can watch whole flights of cormorants and choughs and seagulls that fly about under the cliffs, and beyond them a number of niavogues that are nearly always fishing in Ferriter's Cove. Further on there are Sybil Head and three rocky points, the Three Sisters; then Smerwick Harbour and Brandon far away, usually covered with white airy clouds. Between these headlands and the village there is a strip of sandhill grown over with sea-holly, and a low beach where scores of red bullocks lie close to the sea, or wade in above their knees. Further on one passes peculiar horseshoe coves, with contorted lines of sandstone on one side and slaty blue rocks on the other, and necks of transparent sea of wonderful blueness between them.

I walked up this morning along the slope from the east to the top of Sybil Head, where one comes out suddenly on the brow of a cliff with a straight fall of many hundred feet into the sea. It is a place of indescribable grandeur, where one can see Carrantuohill and the Skelligs and Loop Head and the full sweep of the Atlantic, and, over all, the wonderfully tender and searching light that is seen only in Kerry. Looking down the drop of five or six hundred feet, the height is so great that the gannets flying close over the sea look like white butterflies, and the choughs like flies fluttering behind them. One wonders in these places why anyone is left in Dublin, or London, or Paris, when it would be better, one would think, to live in a tent or hut with this magnificent sea and sky, and to breathe this wonderful air, which is like wine in one's teeth.

Here and there on this headland there are little villages of ten or twenty houses, closely packed together without any order or roadway. Usually there are one or two curious beehive-like structures in these villages, used here, it is said, as pigsties or storehouses. On my way down from Sybil Head I was joined by a tall young man, who told me he had been in the navy, but had bought himself out before his time was over.

'Twelve of us joined from this place,' he said, 'and I was the last of them that stayed in it, for it is a life that no one could put up with. It's not the work that would trouble you, but it's that they can't leave you alone, and that you must be ever and always fooling over something.'

He had been in South Africa during the war, and in Japan, and all over the world; but he was now dressed in homespuns, and had settled down here, he told me, for the rest of his life. Before we reached the village we met Maurice, the fisherman I have spoken of, and we sat down under a hedge to shelter from a shower. We began to talk of fevers and sicknesses and doctors – these little villages are often infested with typhus – and Maurice spoke about the traditional cures.

'There is a plant,' he said, 'which is the richest that is growing out of the ground, and in the old times the women used to be giving it to their children till they'd be growing up seven feet maybe in height. Then the priests and doctors began taking everything to themselves and destroyed the old knowledge, and that is a poor thing; for you know well it was the Holy Mother of God who cured her own Son with plants the like of that, and said after that no mother should be without a plant for ever to cure her child. Then she threw out the seeds of it over the whole world, so that it's growing every place from that day to this.'

I came out to-day, a holiday, to the Great Blasket Island with a schoolmaster and two young men from the village, who were coming for the afternoon only. The day was admirably clear, with a blue sea and sky, and the voyage in the long canoe – I had not been in one for two or three years – gave me indescribable enjoyment. We passed Dunmore Head, and then stood out nearly due west towards the Great Blasket itself, the height of the mountains round the bay and the sharpness of the rocks making the place singularly different from the sounds about Aran, where I had last travelled in a curragh. As usual, three men were rowing – the man I have come to stay with, his son, and a tall neighbour, all dressed in blue jerseys, homespun trousers and shirts, and taking in Irish only, though my host could speak good English when he chose to. As we came nearer the island, which seemed to rise like a mountain straight out of the sea, we could make out a crowd of people in their holiday clothes standing or sitting along the brow of the cliff watching our approach, and just beyond them a patch of cottages with roofs of tarred felt. A little later we doubled into a cove among the rocks, where I landed at a boat slip, and then scrambled up a steep zig-zag pathway to the head of the cliff, where the people crowded round us and shook hands with the men who had come with me.

Gannet

This cottage where I am to stay is one of the highest of the group, and as we passed up to it through little paths among the cottages many white,

Port Magee a century ago, when people of all ages in the coastal communities took part in fishing and fish processing activities. (Lawrence Collection R4582)

wolfish-looking dogs came out and barked furiously. My host had gone on in front with my bag, and when I reached his threshold he came forward and shook hands with me again, with a finished speech of welcome. His eldest daughter, a young married woman of about twenty, who manages the house, shook hands with me also, and then, without asking if we were hungry, began making us tea in a metal teapot and frying rashers of bacon. She is a small, beautifully-formed woman, with brown hair and eyes – instead of the black hair and blue eyes that are usually found with this type in Ireland – and delicate feet and ankles that are not common in these parts, where the woman's work is so hard. Her sister, who lives in the house also, is a bonny girl of about eighteen, full of humour and spirits.

The schoolmaster made many jokes in English and Irish while the little hostess served our tea; and then the kitchen filled up with young men and women – the men dressed like ordinary fishermen, the women wearing print bodices and coloured skirts, that had none of the distinction of the dress of Aran – and a polka was danced, with curious solemnity, in a whirl of dust. When it was over it was time for my companions to go back to the mainland. As soon as we came out and began to go down to the sea, a large crowd, made up of nearly all the men and women and children of the island, came down also, closely packed round us. At the edge of the cliff the young men and the schoolmaster bade me good-bye and went down the zig-zag path, leaving me alone with the islanders on the ledge of rock, where I had seen the people as we came in. I sat for a long time watching the sail of the canoe moving away to Dunquin, and talking to a young man who had spent some years in Ballyferriter, and had good English. The evening was peculiarly fine, and after a while, when the crowd had scattered, I passed up through the cottages, and walked through a boreen towards the north-west, between a few plots of potatoes and little fields of weeds that seemed to have gone out of cultivation not long ago.

Beyond these I turned up a sharp, green hill, and came out suddenly on the broken edge of a cliff. The effect was wonderful. The Atlantic was right underneath; then I could see the sharp rocks of several uninhabited islands, a mile or two off, the Tearaught further away, and, on my left, the whole northern edge of this island curving round towards the west, with a steep heathery face, a thousand feet high. The whole sight of wild islands and sea was as clear and cold and brilliant as what one sees in a dream, and alive with the singularly severe glory that is in the character of this place.

As I was wandering about I saw many of the younger islanders not far off, jumping and putting the weight – a heavy stone – or running races on the grass. Then four girls, walking arm-in-arm, came up and talked to me in Irish. Before long they began to laugh loudly at some signs I made to eke out my meaning, and by degrees the men wandered up also, till there was a crowd round us. The cold of the night was growing stronger, however, and we soon turned back to the village, and sat round the fire in the kitchen the rest of the evening.

At eleven o'clock the people got up as one man and went away, leaving me with the little hostess – the man of the house had gone to the mainland with the young men – her husband and sister. I told them I was sleepy, and ready to go to bed; so the little hostess lighted a candle, carried it into the room beyond the kitchen, and stuck it up on the end of the bed-post of one of the beds with a few drops of grease. Then she took off her apron, and fastened it up in the window as a blind, laid another apron on the wet earthen floor for me to stand on, and left me to myself. The room had two beds, running from wall to wall with a small space between them, a chair that the little hostess had brought in, an old hair-brush that was propping the window open, and no other article. When I had been in bed for some time, I heard the host's voice in the kitchen, and a moment or two later he came in with a candle in his hand, and made a long apology for having been away the whole of my first evening on the island, holding the candle while he talked very close to my face. I told him I had been well entertained by his family and neighbours, and had hardly missed him. He went away, and half an hour later opened the door again with the iron spoon which serves to lift the latch, and came in, in a suit of white homespuns, and said he must ask me to let him stretch out in the other bed, as there was no place else for him to lie. I told him he was welcome, and he got into the other bed and lit his pipe. Then we had a long talk about this place and America and the younger generations.

'There has been no one drowned on this island,' he said, 'for forty years, and that is a great wonder, for it is a dangerous life. There was a man – the brother of the man you were talking to when the girls were dancing – was married to a widow had a public-house away to the west of Ballydavid, and he was out fishing for mackerel, and he got a great haul of them; then he filled his canoe too full, so that she was down to the edge in the water, and a wave broke into her when they were near the shore, and she went down under them. Two men got ashore, but the man from this island was drowned, for his oilskins went down about his feet, and he sank where he was.'

Then we talked about the chances of the mackerel season. 'If the season is good,' he said, 'we get on well; but it is not certain at all. We do pay four pounds for a net, and sometimes the dogfish will get into it the first day and tear it into pieces as if you'd cut it with a knife. Sometimes the mackerel will die in the net, and then ten men would be hard set to pull them up into the canoe, so that if the wind rises on us we must cut loose, and let down the net to the bottom of the sea. When we get fish here in the night we go to Dunquin and sell them to buyers in the morning; and, believe me, it is a dangerous thing to cross that sound when you have too great a load taken into your canoe. When it is too bad to cross over we do salt the fish ourselves – we must salt them cleanly and put them in clean barrels – and then the day it is calm buyers will be out after them from the town of Dingle.'

Afterwards he spoke of the people who go away to America, and the younger generations that are growing up now in Ireland.

'The young people is no use,' he said. 'I am not as good a man as my father was, and my son is growing up worse than I am.' Then he put up his pipe on the end of the bed-post. 'You'll be tired now,' he went on, 'so it's time we were sleeping; and, I humbly beg your pardon, might I ask your name?' I told him.

'Well, good night so,' he said, 'and may you have a good sleep your first night in this island.'

Then he put out the candle and we settled to sleep. In a few minutes I could hear that he was in his dreams, and just as my own ideas were beginning to wander the house door opened, and the son of the place, a young man of about twenty, came in and walked into our room, close to my bed, with another candle in his hand. I lay with my eyes closed, and the young man did not seem pleased with my presence, though he looked at me with curiosity. When he was satisfied he went back to the kitchen and took a drink of whisky and said his prayers; then, after loitering about for some time and playing with a little mongrel greyhound that seemed to adore him, he took off his clothes, clambered over his father, and stretched out on the inner side of the bed.

From *In Wicklow and West Kerry*

Michael Myers Shoemaker

1908

MICHAEL MYERS SHOEMAKER (1853–1924) was born in Covington, Kentucky. As an adult he travelled far afield, visiting nearly every continent and many countries, especially in Asia, North Africa and Australasia. In the 1890s and early 1900s he produced ten travel books, among them *The Great Siberian Railway from St Petersburg to Pekin*, *The Heart of the Orient*, *Islands of the Southern Seas* and *Quaint Corner of Ancient Empires.* Shoemaker also wrote of his experiences in France and Ireland, and in this excerpt describes his visit to Kerry.

As night closes in the clouds lower and finally rain comes down heavily but fortunately not until we have reached our journey's end, and the lights from the quaint Hotel Victoria stream out a welcome. They really act glad to see us and from the proprietor down to 'Dinnis' the buttons each and all appear personally interested in our arrival. How different from the magnificent insolence of an American hotel clerk. But we are too tired for further comparisons and are soon off to bed.

To pass from the pomp and splendour of the army and the kaleidoscopic, unrestful, rushing life of the world to the peaceful shores of Killarney is a grateful change. It is so beautiful here to-day and the world seems so far away that one has no desire to do aught save sit under the waving boughs of the trees and watch the glittering waters of the lake. Off across its mirror-like surface the mountains rise abruptly and over them masses of white clouds hang broodingly, peacefully. Lazily I wander over the grass, and entering one of the many boats drifting in the water allow the boy to row me away upon the glassy surface.

Boyse is still in bed and so I have the boat to myself and also all the lake, for there is no sound or sign of life anywhere as we drift outward. The boy moves the oars lazily, scarcely touching the water with their tips, and we seem to drift half-way between the white clouds overhead and those far beneath us. Lily pads bearing their white and gold chalices wave gently to and fro and a stately white swan with her brood of little ones keeps us company for a space.

I have not told the boy where to go and he has not demanded to know, indeed he scarce seems conscious of my presence, but keeps his dreamy eyes fixed upon his beloved mountains brooding yonder under fleecy clouds. Ahead of us a fairy island floats waving green boughs in greeting and as our boat grounds on its gravelly beach, the boy rolls over and goes to sleep.

This is evidently the haven where we would be, this holy Isle of Innisfallen, but it is some time before I am willing to break the brooding silence by any movement. The long drooping boughs of the trees trail gently to and fro across the boat and parting now and then give glimpses of the chapel of St. Finian the leper, but it is so in ruins, and it and its saint belongs so to the very long ago, that to-day it is like a thought in a dream.

As I wander off through the underwood shaded by giant ash the spirits of the dead monks seem all around me. The path leads to the grave of the abbot, so long dead that a huge tree growing from his ashes has encircled his tombstone with its very roots. . . .

It is said that Innisfallen may not be put to profane uses, that early in the last century its owner commanded that it be cultivated, but when the work was begun the air at once became filled with millions of white birds, whose beating wings drove the men forth and away, leaving the isle sacred and unprofaned, and the abbot and his brethren to their dreamless slumbers, and so the years glide by.

As I pause to-day by the abbot's grave, its great tree rises above with arms extended, as though in final benediction, the grasses are spangled with millions of daisies, and the warm air is again, as in his day, full of the song of birds, and unless I desire a sleep of centuries it may be as well to return to the world of to-day.

The boy in the boat awakes with a yawn, and smilingly moves the boat off and away farther and farther until the Holy Isle seems to detach itself from the shimming waters and to float cloudlike slowly heavenward.

How little the casual tourist ever sees of any land, especially of Ireland, – a day or two at Killarney, an hour at Blarney, some time waiting to hear Shandon bells, then a rush to Dublin and the Causeway, and they leave

View near Dinis Island in Muckross Lake, drawn by Isaac Weld.

the island with a shrug of the shoulders and a belief that there is little to see. But wander into the byways, linger in the lost corners and talk to these people, and every moment will be of some sort of interest, – the tears and sadness will pull your very heartstrings one moment and laughter and fun will bubble all around you in a mad frolic an hour later. You may hear the wild songs of the mountains, or the wilder wailing for the dead, and the clouds will drift far overhead, as though in mourning for their sorrows, then the sunlight will follow after, sparkling, as though in laughter. Some of the inns will be neat and comfortable, whilst others will turn out like that horror of a hotel in Galway.

We are welcomed on our return to that at Killarney by 'Dinnis.' Now 'Dinnis' is the 'buttons' of the house and stands up to the magnificent altitude of four feet. He looks about fifteen and when I ask him if he goes to school I am about bowled over by his reply, – 'I'm a married man, sor.' Great heavens! I am told later that the fair bride is near twice Dinnis's height and that his wooing was of such an ardent nature that it nearly created a scandal. Ah, well – we don't live but once and Dinnis believes that if his life is to be as short as his stature, at least it shall be a merry one. I am told also that there are great expectations in his family and as our car glides away I lean out and implore him – if it's a boy – to name it 'Mike.' Dinnis's indignation at my intrusion upon his private life is vast but somewhat drowned out by a half-crown and the roars of laughter from the car boys around.

The poor car boys in Ireland, especially at Killarney, are so many that there is not work for all and they have to take certain days for each, that all may have a share. The drivers of jaunting-cars turn gloomy eyes at our auto as we roll by, well knowing that the advent of such means loss to them.

I was strongly tempted to essay the Gap of Dunloe in the motor. The result would probably have been a fight, as one of Cook's waggons was attacked not long since while trying the same thing. According to my recollection of that road, its passage would not be at all difficult for a good car, but once the legend of its impassability save by ponies is done away with the occupation of many hereabouts would be over for all time.

From *Wanderings in Ireland*

George Bernard Shaw

1910

BORN IN DUBLIN, George Bernard Shaw (1856–1950) moved to London in 1876. There he became a Socialist and joined the Fabian Society. In 1885 he began to write plays and endured for many years without success, until he succeeded with *Arms and the Man* and *Candida*. Shaw continued writing into his nineties, producing forty plays in all. He was awarded the Nobel Prize for Literature in 1935. Shaw and his wife often came to Ireland and spent several summers at Parknasilla in County Kerry. In 1910 he visited the Skelligs, and vividly depicts the excursion in a letter to Fredrick Jackson of Hindhead, Surrey.

Parknasilla Hotel, Sneem. 18th September . . . . We are both here – in the only place in the world that makes Tarn Moor a mere dust heap.

Yesterday I left the Kerry coast in an open boat 33 feet long, propelled by ten men at 5 oars. These men started at 49 strokes a minute, a rate which I did not believe they could keep up for five minutes. They kept it without slackening half a second for two hours, at the end of which they landed me on the most fantastic and impossible rock in the world: Skellig Michael, or the Great Skellig, where, in south west gales, the spray knocks stones out of the lighthouse keeper's house, 160 feet above calm sea level. There is a little Skellig covered with gannets – white with them

The Skellig Michael monastery continued until the twelfth or thirteenth century when the monks moved to Ballinskelligs on the mainland.

(and their guano) – covered with screaming crowds of them. The Bass rock is mere lump in comparison: both the Skelligs are pinnacled, crocketed, spired, arched, caverned, minaretted; and these Gothic extravagances are not curiosities of the islands: they *are* the islands: there is nothing else. The rest of the cathedral may be under the sea for all I know: there are 90 fathoms by the chart, out of which the Great Skellig rushes up 700 feet so suddenly that you have to go straight upstairs to the top – over 600 steps. And at the top amazing beehives of flat rubble stones, each overlapping the one below until the circles meet in a dome – cells, oratories, churches, and outside them cemeteries, wells, crosses, all clustering like shells on a prodigious rock pinnacle, with precipices sheer down on every hand, and, lodged on the projecting stones overhanging the deep, huge stone coffins made apparently by giants, and dropped there, God knows how. An incredible, impossible, mad place, which still tempts devotees to make 'stations' of every stair landing, and to creep through 'needle's eyes' at impossible altitudes, and kiss 'stones of pain' jutting out 700 feet above the Atlantic. Most incredible of all, the lighthouse keeper will not take a tip, but sits proud, melancholy and haunted in his kitchen after placing all his pantry at your disposal – will also accompany you down to the desperate little harbour to squeeze the last word out of you before you abandon him, and gives you letters to post like the Flying Dutchman – also his strange address to send newspapers and literature to; for these he will accept.

I tell you the thing does not belong to any world that you and I have ever lived and worked in: it is part of our dream world.

And you talk of your Hindhead! Skellig Michael, sir, is the Forehead.

Then back in the dark, without compass, and the moon invisible in the mist, 49 strokes to the minute striking patines of white fire from the Atlantic, spurting across threatening currents and furious tideraces, pursued by terrors, ghosts from Michael, possibilities of the sea rising making every fresh breeze a fresh fright, impossibilities of being quite sure whither we were heading, two hours and a half before us at best, all the rowers wildly imaginative, superstitious, excitable, and apparently superhuman in energy and endurance, two women sitting with the impenetrable dignity and quiet comeliness of Italian saints and Irish peasant women silent in their shawls with their hands on the quietest part of the oars (next the gunwale) like spirit rappers, keeping the pride of the men at the utmost tension, so that every interval of dogged exhaustion and drooping into sleep (the stroke never slackening, though) would be broken by an explosion of 'Up-up-up-keep her up!' 'Up Kerry!'; and the captain of the stroke oar – a stranger imported by ourselves, and possessed by ten devils each with a formidable second wind, would respond with a spurt in which he would, with short yelps of 'Double it–double it–double it' almost succeed in doubling it, and send the boat charging through the swell.

Three pound ten, my dear Jackson – six shillings a man – including interest on the price of the boat and wear and tear of ten oars, was what they demanded. They had thrown down their farming implements (they dont fish on Saturdays) to take to the sea for us at that figure.

I hardly feel real again yet.

Hindhead! Pooh! I repeat it in your teeth. POOH!!!

Celt and Saxon – you and me – I mean me and you – or is it you and I? Meredith and Anatole France! Is Box Hill a beehive cell 700 feet up? What does any Parisian know of Skellig Michael? Get out!

From a letter to Frederick Jackson

Chough

Robin Flower

1910

ROBIN FLOWER (1881–1946) was born in Leeds to parents who both had Irish ancestry. He was educated at Leeds Grammar School and later at Oxford. After joining the British Museum, he began to study Irish and completed the Museum's catalogue of Irish manuscripts. Flower came to Dublin in 1910 for a three-week study course. He travelled to the Blasket Islands for the first time and steeped himself in the local culture, earning the name Blaithín ('little flower') from the islanders. He is known for discovering and translating the works of Blasket writers Tomas O'Crohan and Maurice O'Sullivan.

Robin Flower

I set my face to the hill again, and now took my way against the slope, ascending slowly to the summit of the Island. There, almost on the highest ridge, where the land breaks abruptly towards the sea, an ancient people in days before any history had built their high place. Using the cliff-edge for the seaward front of their dún, they had drawn a semicircular trench to fence off their dwelling towards the land. And through a gap in the inner wall of this trench they had run a lesser ditch, dividing the inner space into two equal portions. The whole forms a cliff fort of the kind familiar along the range of the sea-wall of southern and western Ireland.

Let us leave it to the historians of the time before history to inquire who were the dark and strange people before the coming of the Celts who, vanishing, have left little more than these vast shells in which they lived to be their memorials. We cannot penetrate to the thoughts that thrilled them as they looked out over the cliff-wall across the shoreless sea towards the sunset. It may be that, when we stand in their place and, forgetting all the memories of our young civilizations, abandon ourselves to the unguided wantonness of

The Great Blasket Islands in the early part of the twentieth century, when they were still inhabited.

feeling, some shadow of the thoughts that moved them drifts across our minds, out of reach of our treacherous apprehension, and they live again for the moment in the latest of their successors. Standing there, as the sea-mists crept over the Island and shut out the visible world, I have at times lost consciousness of this present earth and felt the illusion of other presences in the wreathing swirls of clouds; my mind has filled with fragile thoughts insubstantial as the mist itself, and known the terror of that loneliness in which the greatest fear is that we are not all alone. But the frail mists fade rapidly into the sun, and the light of the living will frightens back into the depths of the mind those ghostly memories older than ourselves that live below the surface of our thoughts.

The dún has known other inhabitants than those its first builders. Roughly shaped stones hidden in the earth bear witness to later buildings, and these may well have been the homes of men of religion whose constructions still remain elsewhere on the Island and in the other islands of the group. There may be some truth, too, in the tradition of the islanders which claims so confidently that the Danes dwelt here. That the Northmen were on the Island we may be confident, and they can hardly have failed to make use of this strong place commanding both the landward and the seaward slopes. But history has nothing to tell us of that occupation, and no monuments remain to fill the gap of the written record. Below the fort the sharp wall of the cliff drops to a flat space, overgrown with heath, and fern, and sea-pink, and I know not what of the delicate and faint-hued island flowers. This space the islanders with a happy instinct call the garden of the dún. A path leading out of it to the left wanders down the cliff, and, if you have the head for heights, you may follow it and come at last to a hole under a flat ledge of rock called Sgairt Phiarais, Pierce's Cave, where, says the tradition, Pierce Ferriter, poet and warrior, hid from his enemies. Of Pierce's sojourn in the cave, and the poem he made there, we shall speak again.

Another path leads along the brink of the cliffs and climbs to the summit of An Cró, the highest point of the Island. Beneath to the sea are the 'bright stone dwellings' (*na clocháin gheala*) of that conversation on the hill. Loose stones lie about all over the ground, and it is plain that there must at one time have been a considerable settlement here. It may be that excavation would reveal the foundations of a church, but a cursory inspection does not yield any evidence of such a building to the inexperienced eye. Farther down towards the sea there is a little group of ruins the form of which is still discernible. These have been beehive huts of the customary Irish type. Of one there are still considerable remains, of a very interesting form. The building is half buried in the earth, and when you come to examine it you find that it was originally two-roomed, the rooms divided off from each other by an interior wall with a low doorway. Other remains in the neighbourhood are too fragmentary for description.

No record or tradition remains to tell what manner of men dwelt here when these buildings were new. But other such clocháns are to be found on Inis Tuaisceart and Iniscíleáin, and there can be little doubt that they had an ecclesiastical purpose. This is the country of St. Brendan. There across the water is the great mountain named after him, where the country people go on painful pilgrimage for the cure of all their ailments. And away beyond Sybil Head is the bay from which in their tradition he set out on his wild journey into the Atlantic, voyaging among marvellous islands, and coming at last to that icy peak where Judas Iscariot once in every year finds a day's solace from the pains of Hell.

From *The Western Island*

Stephen Gwynn

1912

STEPHEN LUCIUS GWYNN (1864–1950) was born in County Donegal. The grandson of William Smith O'Brien, he was educated at Dublin and Oxford. Elected nationalist Member of Parliament for Galway in 1906, he sat as a member of the Irish Parliamentary Party until 1919. An authority on eighteenth-century Ireland, Gwynn wrote biographies of Henry Grattan, Oliver Goldsmith and Jonathan Swift. During the First World War he served in France and received the Legion of Honour. He was also honoured by the Irish Academy of Letters shortly after his death.

A few miles down brings you into the valley of the Caragh river which flows out from Loughs Reagh and Cloon and after a course of some ten miles enters the long and deep Caragh Lake, whence another short run brings it to the sea. This is the valley which lies west of the Reeks, and, for my own part, I count this aspect of them finer that anything you will see at Killarney. There is a big, new hotel at the outfall of Caragh Lake on the railway, much frequented now: but all my time among these hills and waters has been given to a little oldfashioned anglers' inn, the Glencar hotel, on the reach of river between Bealalaw bridge and Lickeen rapids. Here you may fish for salmon at a nominal charge in one of the best waters in Ireland: on the evening when I got there this summer, they were jumping everywhere in the beautiful Long Range pool where the little Caragh joins the main stream; red, ugly fish, it must be owned, for this was in September and they had lain there since June without a fresh to move them – but still there were salmon and plenty of them. Or you can fish free of charge at Lough Acoose at the headwaters of Caraghbeg, in under the flank of Carrantuohil, with better prospect of a full basket than anywhere else known to me. The trout are not big anywhere in Kerry, but in Acoose they run to a good herring size, and the man who fished it the day when I was at Glencar got something over two dozen – a usual bag. My companion and I had gone farther afield, to the headwaters of Caragh itself, right up into the great ring of mountains through which the pass of Bealachbeama lets you out to the Kenmare side. Little need be said about our fishing, which was interrupted by the fact that our boat, leaking like a sieve, finally foundered while we were trying to get her ashore – a new boat too, wanting nothing but a couple of good coats of paint. Yet the chance which drove us off Cloon, while the boat was being got ashore and emptied, sent us up across a mile of bog to fish the upper lake from the shore; and what a lake! lying right in under the steep side of a mountain almost precipitous, where the eagles built till a year or two back, and for three parts of its circumference ringed about like the crater of a volcano.

It was a day of dry wind, northerly to north-easterly, and of hard lights: one lacked the magical enchantment of westerly air over the whole: yet for sheer grandeur I do not know that all my wanderings after fish in Ireland have ever taken me to so fine a scene.

That little hotel, primitive in its equipment but most friendly, has its attractions to offer all the year round, for the salmon fishing begins in earnest in February, and through the winter months there is rough shooting (grouse, cock, and snipe), to be had over the great expanses of heather and those broad belts of native wooding which grow about the river in its lower course. From the hotel down to the lake your path lies between this scrub of oak and holly and birch and a water, swift yet deep, where pool succeeds pool, each divided from the next only by strong rapids. You have no monopoly there: the river is fished from both banks and can be covered right across, though it needs a good man to do it; but it is practically a free fishing and the best free fishing river that I know in Ireland – absolutely an ideal spot for the holidaymaker who does not insist on being near the sea. You can walk from it all the finest mountains in Kerry since it lies in the very centre: and away west of you is Glenbeigh, another valley where decent quarters can be had amid landscape of the same type. Of the same type – but I cannot believe that anywhere in Kerry or out of it you will match the journey which convoyed me from Glencar to my next stage at the Caragh Lake hotel. It was inland scenery no doubt, but the breath and the feeling of the sea is over all this neck of sea-washed Iveragh, and that river valley seemed no more than an avenue through the hills leading to the gateway of ocean. We walked along the river bank, often shoulder high in fern, often stopping to pull the blackberry clusters, and we studied the pools set in, here among trees, there with open sward on both sides and moor stretching away behind. Below the rapids we took boat, and for a mile or more rowed through level bogland, with groups of Scotch fir, purple stemmed in the afternoon light, rising from the river bank. Between their trunks, or in the open gaps, we could see the peaked mass of Carrantuohil, rising in the south-east, the light on its high ridges, but the valleys and chasms on its sides deep in shadow. As we neared the lake the flat land broadened, and from across it came the aromatic, pungent smell of bog myrtle, distinct as the scent from a beanfield, but strong and tonic as brine. Then for an hour and half we paddled down the lake between mountain and mountain, winding round promontory after promontory into sight of reach after reach of the lake. Finally as we entered the wide northern stretch – for our course was due north – all the shore was seen divided into demesnes, big and little, each with its own wooding. The hotel lies farthest of all towards the river's outflow in the north-west, and whoever chose that site deserves credit, for across the wide shining water rise the whole ring of mountains – Carrantuohil away to the south-east, and all the other heights that close in the valley behind Cloon Lake and Bealachbeama spreading fanwise across the horizon as you look out from the pleasant terrace where palm and hydrangea grow. It is not so finished, not so exquisite, as Killarney; but I should rather choose it for a holiday. I sat on the terrace for an hour that Sunday and watched the sunlight fade off Carrantuohil: all was green and olive when we sat down, for it was a coldish evening and the air northerly; but cloud lay on the peaks, or rather caught the peaks intermittently as it drifted in wreaths across, so that at no time was the whole mountain visible. But gradually as the sun sank these wreaths became touched with a rosy glow, and below them what had been olive-green took on deep tints of coppery purple, rich and glowing, the purple gaining as the rose deepened on the cloud wreath; and higher and higher the shaft of light struck, reaching now only the very topmost pinnacles, till finally it faded out, and all lay before as in a sombre stillness waiting for the fall of night.

Nothing that I carry away from Killarney haunts me with the same fullness of beauty, but perhaps only because Killarney is no one's discovery; it has no secret lover. You might as well seek to praise Sarah Bernhardt's genius or Tennyson's charm of style. Yet I suppose each one will discern for himself some passing perfection, some special facet of that loveliness – as I indeed remember the wonderful, shadowed, lucid green of water reflecting darkly the bank of tall reeds which grow westward of the landing stage to which we rowed in after fishing: and remember, too, the singular sight of a man's naked body, as he stood poised before plunging in to bathe, some hundred yards from us; for the low sun caught his figure, outlined against the long line of dark foliage behind him, and made it at once the glowing centre of a beautiful landscape.

Salmon

From *Munster*

Harold Speakman

1924

AMERICAN HAROLD SPEAKMAN (1888–1928) served in the US Army in Italy during the First World War. He followed this with peacekeeping duties in Montenegro, described in his book *From a Soldier's Heart*. After the war he started to travel extensively and wrote several more travel books. In the summer of 1924 Speakman embarked on a walking tour through Ireland with a donkey and cart. Among the notable people he met on this trip were W.B. Yeats, Lady Gregory and Sean O'Casey. His journey was to take him to Kerry.

If you go to Killarney, wait I beg you, for a day of sunlight and cloud, and take the 'long trip' by coach and saddle horse and boat through the Lakes and the Gap of Dunloe. If the day is right, you will sample in a few hours much of the best of the varied scenery which the south of Ireland has to offer. The Killarney landscape may not be particularly august or splendid or imposing, but there is a deep tenderness about it and an indisputable charm.

You may see some pleasant, homely thing like a goat philosophically scratching his nose on the rope which holds him – which will make you forget that the town of Killarney isn't even within sight of the Lakes. And when you get to the top of the pass at Dunloe, there will surely be an old man to say, 'This is the next parish to Heaven, and as high as I'll ever get.' There will also be others who will want you to listen to an echo or buy a postcard or take a drink of milk-and-'mountain dew:'

If Anacreon – who
Was the grape's best poet,
Drank our mountain dew,
How his verse would show it!

And if you buy so much as twopence worth of their wares, you will receive the best of a very valuable blessing: 'Thank your Honor; a long life and good luck to you always.'

Or you may hear how 'the Colleen Bawn, a duck of a girl, was done to death by a little humpy man, she being thrown into the lake near a big stone which bears her name.'

And when you remonstrate and say that the Colleen Bawn was not drowned at Killarney at all, but far to the north in the River Shannon near Glin, the teller of the story may shake his head a little perplexedly and say, 'At least, I saw a play of it on the lake there, and it was grand altogether. There was a bit of a lad put on a handsome pale of hair, he being all dressed up like a girl. And in the middle of the play, the boat was near capsizing, and he fell overboard and almost drownded, and the manager was for hitting him over the head with an oar, he was that mad.'

Or it may be that in the evening you will take a small boat out to the lovely island of Innisfallen with its ancient ruin of the monastery where Brian Boru was educated so that later he might bring all the south of Ireland into one. There are strange, primitive faces carved over the doorways of the monastery, and arches so ancient that they have no keystones, and a holy water font, which, even in the driest of weather is not without water, and the tomb of an old abbot, hidden to all but the keenest observers, under the roots of an ancient yew.

Killarney! In spite of its commercialism, in spite of the fact that one is only a golden sponge to be squeezed as dry as possible and passed on, this traveler at least must remember it as a spot of innocent and strangely-compelling charm.

There is another traveler who should remember it too. Being feminine, she will perhaps recall it best by the fact that on the day she left Killarney, she was wearing a brand new leather collar, bearing upon each side two little, shiny, brass hearts.

We started off, not only with a new collar but with grease on our wheels. We started with an improved wooden 'straddle' for Herself's back. There was also grease on the groove of the straddle, grease on the sliding chains, and grease on my raincoat. If I had earlier found how much better an animal will do for a good night's housing, I had now learned, as with another awakening light, how much better that animal will travel if one makes it comfortable at the very beginning of a day's journey.

At a rise of the road, I turned for a final glimpse of the Killarney country. Crisp rolling clouds and a windswept sky. Below, the deep-ultramarine hills. A transfiguration of light, shining down upon a little Irish farm, with dark, feathery trees and a hilltop beyond . . .

There came to my mind a little Irish poem I had read, and I went on, neither whistling nor saying any word to Herself, because of the little house, and the poem, and the great yearning Irish sky.

Four ducks on a pond
A grass bank beyond
A blue sky of spring
White clouds on the wing:
What a little thing
To remember for years,
To remember with tears.

The Gap of Dunloe, a four mile-long defile between MacGillicuddy's Reeks and the Purple Mountain, has long been a popular excursion for visitors.

A man was coming up the hill with a powerful horse and a load of peat. When we met, he stopped and asked for the loan of a match.

'Will it light without the box? ' I asked as he took one (because his request for a match had brought down the rain, which is very delicately adjusted all about Killarney).

'It will!' he said vociferously. 'It will light in the middle of an English swamp – for it was made in Ireland.' And I went on chuckling, for after all, a match might easily light in the middle of an English swamp without lighting in that submerged Killarney weather.

To the left, veiled by gray and grayer and still grayer tones of mist, were the vast, uprolling sides of many pyramidal hills, each parallel to the others, hill beyond hill fading away into the distance, and above them a mighty cloud, sweeping like the wings of victory in a wide, majestic curve along their crests.

Then I came to a house where an old woman sat in the doorway smoking a pipe, and this was the first old woman I had seen smoking, so I stopped and passed the time of day with her saying, 'Good-day, mother; this is queer weather we're having.'

'It is. The spring has come back on us. And is it fishes you're selling?'

'No, I'm just on a holiday – '

'Glory be to God!'

' – from America, and – '

'Glory be! Wisha for *goodness* sake!'

'I thought I'd stop and bid you good-day because you are the first of the womenfolk I have seen smoking a *dhudeen*.'

She removed the pipe and gave a toothless, elliptical cackle. 'All the young girls do be smokin' now! Is it like that in America?'

'Like that, and worse. But how far up the road is Tralee?'

'And is it right out of America you come?'

'Yes, from New York City.'

'*My! You're plain for an American!*'

'Ah yes. We can't pick out our own faces, you know. This *is* the road to Tralee, isn't it?'

'It is indeed. Follow the straight road about six miles.'

I said good-by, and went back to the road . . . Did the old girl think we were all Adonises and Valentinos across the water? Just what did she mean, I wondered. 'My! You're plain for an American!' If she thought I was plain, I could show her a few others who . . .

Ah well . . . Only six miles more to Tralee . . .

From *Here's Ireland*

John J. Welsh

1928

JOHN J. WELSH took up walking as exercise at his doctor's suggestion. He started out doing a few miles a day, but soon developed the idea of taking a walking tour around Ireland, a country he had once visited briefly as part of a European trip. Welsh sailed from New York on the *Laconia* and disembarked at Cobh. With only a stick and haversack, he travelled around the coastal counties, including Kerry, before arriving back at Cobh.

In rain and with the Caseys' benedictions, I left at nine the next morning for Kenmare. Well on my road, I turned for a parting glance at unclouded Glengarriff and its environs. Down before me lay the placid bay of silver, dotted with emeralds and holding fast the rougher gem of a village at its shoulder. Only a British torpedo destroyer anchored on its bosom reminded me of man's distrust in man. All else was peace and quiet.

A landscape weird and wild, but alluring, caused to pass quickly the misting morning. Only falling waters, tinkling or murmuring, enlivened a stillness that was audible. In a glow of satisfaction I climbed gradually to the silent urge of the open road before me – to a diurnal symphony that reached my listening soul. I was away from the underworld of civilization, with its deceits, shams, inordinate appetites and lusts for money and power.

Though all about me had been remarkably bright, I was more pleased now that the rain suddenly ceased. Going into a tunnel, hewn through solid rock, my road stole up to Country Kerry and its quick-revealing charms. The hills of Killarney beckoned me to 'that Eden of the West.' I should be in Kenmare within the next three hours if – I was there much sooner!

I suddenly became enamored of a blushing rose, wasting her charms atop a stone fence. With no vandal thought, I had rather see her unsullied life go out slowly on my coat lapel. 'Man proposes' etc. My hob-nailed boots, somehow, did not fit rightly on a loose stone, which gave way. A twinge of pain came to my right ankle and black chagrin to my heart. Here was an end to my walking tour. The rose still blushed above me.

Dejected, I laced tighter my boot and tried to walk. Swelling ankle, throbbing against tightened boot, pained sharply. Having hobbled through another mile, I sat under a white thorn. Besides, it was hot again. Telling a passing young man of my plight and frustrated hope, I was solicitously advised by him.

'A bus, sure, will be along in ten minutes. You can get surgical attention in Kenmare – better ride to Killarney and you'll be certain. It could be worse. You'll be all right again.' His never-say-die spirit of hope that is Irish made me ashamed of my fears. I hailed and boarded the 'bus, stopping at Kenmare for dinner. Proceeding in the 'bus, I glimpsed the Gap of Dunloe, Upper Lake, Eagles Nest, greater Middle Lake, Colleen Bawn Rock and put up at the 'Arbutus Hotel' in Killarney – all done well within an hour after dinner.

The 'Arbutus Hotel' fortunately, had both hot and cold running water in the bedroom assigned me – a convenience one seldom knows in the hostelries of Ireland. The bowl-and-pitcher plan, as in most European countries, still prevails. For two hours I immersed my injured limb in warm water, which much reduced the swelling, temporarily wrapped it in adhesive tape and gauze and sought to buy an elastic support. The drugstore (medical-hall or chemist's, in Ireland) had no such thing. I saw that I should have to do my best without it till Tralee or Limerick City came my way. Besides, the ankle now seemed to be much better. With care in stepping out, perhaps I could make the grade. I was a happier *hombre*, greatly relieved in body and mind.

Poet-laureates and numerous other great writers have failed in every effort to have their readers imagine the full beauty of Killarney. Hence an overshadowed pen had better be still while the reader is saving for his contemplated visit to a spot where it is said 'angels fold their wings and rest.' Nor shall this poor narrative of a half-vagabonding foot-traveler savor of the promptings of a guidebook.

'Beauty is that which is pleasing to the senses or mind,' is the lexicographer's easy definition. Then, Killarney must be beautiful. So must be Glengarriff, the Vale of Avoca, Glendalough, the Glens of Antrim – even Connemara – even all Ireland. I was to see beauty – sublimity – in the vast, low-lying Bog of Allen.

Any natural scene, whatever its qualities, that raises the beholder's mind to reverent wonderment and the appreciation of Nature's God and his own impotence has the attributes of beauty. Any natural scene that interests, animates, exalts, is beautiful.

Natural scenes that inspire loftily – and most should inspire loftily – scarcely admit of comparison. Where is the recognized standard of merit to assist in one's just judgment? It is true that men, through the Greeks, the Romans and others, have an accepted standard of beauty in the human face and form, in architecture, etc. But where, I ask again, is the measure of Nature's scenic cast of feature or aspect?

So when a stately English lady in my hotel asked me whether Killarney is more beautiful than Glengarriff I could only reply that I had not the means by which to judge. Each spot was beautiful – just beautiful – to me.

My reader (who is saving) must not imagine there are only lakes at Killarney. Yet the lakes alone would compensate him for his coming here. It is the setting of these three glistening mirrors, rimmed in living green loveliness and in an outer frame of mountain grandeur with many contrasts and endless variety – under skies that are beautiful even in tears – that makes men wonder.

Isles, meeting-waters, rocks, cascades, old fanes, castles, gaps, black valleys, too, are Killarney's – touched or embraced by arbutus, holly, fern, ivy, moss and a world of green enchantment. The highest mountain in Ireland, Carrantuohill, is chief sentry here. And all this splendor is within the area of a few miles!

The neighborhood of Killarney abounds in warlike memories of such great chieftains as the McCarthys and the O'Donoghues. The ruins of Aghadoe, Innisfallen and Muckross silently bespeak its pristine ecclesiastical and intellectual greatness.

An enterprising guide will point out to you the authenticated little lake wherein St. Patrick drowned the last serpent of Ireland. There are many other interesting legends, notably that concerning 'Colleen Bawn'. Some are richly romantic and make one delighted with an ultra-imaginative people.

In the town I visited the Catholic cathedral, designed by Pugin. It is cruciform and built of limestone. With a massive, square tower and a fine spire, it stands as the brightest and most impressive of the buildings in Killarney. Then I was ready to quit this haunting spot of beauty.

From *Ireland Afoot*

H.V. Morton

1930

HENRY VOLLAM MORTON (1892–1979) began his journalistic career on the *Birmingham Gazette and Express* in his native city in 1910. From 1913 he worked for national newspapers in London, apart from military service in the First World War. Morton brought out five books about London between 1925 and 1927, and soon turned to full-time travel writing. He produced 35 books in all, several of them about Britain and Ireland, and became well known for his 'In Search of' series. Morton also travelled widely in the Middle East, Spain, Italy and South Africa, where he eventually settled.

If your bedroom is in the front of a house in Kerry you will be awakened while it is still dark by a queer, insistent pattering on the road outside. You look at your watch. It is 5 a.m. When you pull the blind aside you see herds of cattle going past in the moonlight. The drovers walk behind, bent over their sticks, and as they smoke their pipes they call now and then in early morning voices to the subdued dogs who skirmish on the fringes of the herd.

There is an interval, then along the empty roads walks a man driving a cow and her calf. He melts into the darkness. There comes a little cart drawn by a sleepy donkey. It contains a litter of pigs. There are more herds, then a donkey burdened like Atlas – just four thin, knock-kneed little legs beneath a great stack of hay. He patters off, to be followed by a donkey carrying brown squares of dry turf packed in two wicker baskets slung on either side of him.

You have seen enough to know that the whole countryside is awake for miles around. It is market day. (It is always market day somewhere in Ireland!) Women have been awake at 3 and 4 a.m. in hundreds of little white cabins far off in the hills, getting their husbands and sons off to market, preparing food while the men, outside in the dark, round up the cattle and pack the pigs in the donkey cart . . .

And all the time, as this strange procession of hill men and their beasts passes beneath your window, the moon sinks, growing paler every minute, the little chill winds that run before the sun bend the grass, and the air grows grey; and you feel that you have seen something from an Irish fairy-tale or something from the very beginning of history, something older than agriculture – the migration of herdsmen and their herds.

In the course of a day's motoring in Ireland you can see perhaps twenty market days, known, goodness knows why, as 'fairs.'

Some are in the abnormally wide streets of French-looking towns; others are in towns more physically attractive; others are held in mere villages; but the market day as we understand it in rural England does not exist, at least in the south of Ireland. Consider a market day in Wiltshire with the sheep pens overflowing and the fat cattle lowing in the market, while the farmers lean over the pens and make jokes and troop into the 'Nag's Head' to drink beer. Their daughters are buying silk stockings, their sons are buying a new wireless, their wives are packing brown paper parcels into a Ford motor-car. There is a robust family joviality about it.

In the little villages of Kerry market day means hundreds of tousled, mud splashed black cows standing with dazed expressions all over the main street, some on the pavement, some in the middle of the road. Now and then an indignant gombeen man comes out and smacks a cow out of his shop.

The market at Killarney, sketched by William Makepeace Thackeray nearly a century before H.V. Morton's visit.

Attached by bonds of self-interest to each cow is a man who adopts the same casual attitude. He is a tall, wild-looking fellow from the hills, leaning on a stick, his clothes are ragged, and his hat was once a bowlar. Sometimes the man leaves his cow and joins a group of men, but how he discovers his cow again in that queer mix-up of cows, all small and all black, is beyond my understanding.

The queer thing about these men – and this, I think, holds good throughout the country – is that if you picked the most bedraggled, the most villainous-looking, the wildest, the one who lost his razor in 1899, and the owner of a hat which is obviously the hero of a hundred tavern brawls, and spoke to him, you would find him worth talking to. This was the first lesson I learnt when I left Dublin. At first I talked down to moth-eaten characters beside the road as one would suit words to the understanding of an English yokel; but – they invariably replied like orators!

There is a fine touch of good breeding and an almost disconcerting air of culture about most of the tattered men who trudge the roads of Ireland.

To return to our market . . .

Donkeys chased by small boys, skip about among the melancholy cows. Many of these donkeys are too young to work which is the only brief happiness a donkey ever enjoys. At the side of the street are rows of small donkey carts, their bodies painted blue, their shafts bright saffron. Inside are slumbering pigs, maternal sows, and nurseries of pigeens.

The cow, the pig and the donkey are the props of the Irish countryside.

Such a market, spread haphazardly against the background of the white village street, a few tiny shops, and a public house, is an expression of country life at its barest. That man has walked fifteen hard miles from the peat bog with five shillings' worth of turf; another has tramped for many miles through the dawn with ten shillings' worth of hay.

These people scratch the barest living from a hard land, and their wealth is counted in pennies. Yet there is not one of them who would not rather drive his cow back again to the distant hills than accept less than he means to get for it. The Irish cannot compromise.

But they can argue! Watch a man who is anxious to buy a pig. He makes a careful survey of all the pigs on view, he prods them through the bars of the cart until they squeal and leap up; then, when his heart is settled on one surpassing pig, he approaches the owner and says:

'Good-morning. And it's fine weather we've been having, glory be to God.'

'It is.'

They talk about everything but pigs for twenty minutes. Meanwhile other candidates for the pig assemble furtively in the background. It is not etiquette for a buyer to break in on a conversation of this kind. Many a nose has been broken in Ireland because a man has not waited for another man to conclude his conversation with a pig-owner.

Eventually the would-be purchaser mentions airily, as if it had just come into his head, that a certain little pig in the cart is a good pig and might fatten well; and how much, he wonders, just as a matter of curiosity, might that little pig be worth?

He then decides to 'play tough.' That is to say, he lets it be known that he would buy the pig for five shillings less than the price named, and when the dealer has exhibited a polite indifference he moves off; and the next would-be buyer swoops down!

So the pig carts on market day are surrounded by a ring of men, all politely holding off until an argument has ended, all distrustful of each other, all anxious to buy the pig, all holding out, all 'playing tough.'

The pig is sold by a process of contraction and expansion in the generosity of buyer and seller. Frequently when they have reached the last argumentative fence a third party – the peacemaker – is called in to help them over. They pledge themselves to accept his decision. He hears the details of the transaction, splits the sixpence, and – the pig changes carts!

Most extraordinary in these markets is the absence of women. That is why they look such dull assemblies. Hundreds of men in black coats, hundreds of black cows. The women, of course, are miles away in the hills. They have no butter to sell, no eggs, no honey, no clotted cream, no cheese like the women of Somerset and Devon.

They wait at home on the bare hill-side for the man to come home with silver in his pocket. But sometimes he comes back with the sow or the pig, angry, independent, uncompromising.

I hope that sometimes he takes her back something from the village, but looking round the village shops I wonder what on earth he could take her! A pair of boots? A few yards of flannel? That is not the kind of present to take to a woman who waits for you in the hills all day! I think the only beautiful thing he could take to her from an Irish village shop is a little coloured picture of Our Lady.

From *In Search of Ireland*

The telegraph cable station at Waterville played an important role in transatlantic communications between 1884 and 1962. (Lawrence Collection R8295)

Signe Toksvig

1932

PLAYWRIGHT AND BIOGRAPHER Signe Toksvig (1891–1983) was born in Denmark and migrated to the United States with her family when she was fifteen. She won a scholarship to Cornell and graduated in 1916. While working at the *New Republic* she met Irish writer Francis Hackett. They married in 1918 and in 1927 moved to Ireland. When Toksvig's novel *Eve's Doctor* (1937) was banned by the Irish Censorship Board – suffering the same fate as Hackett's novel *The Green Lion* a year earlier – they left Ireland for Denmark. The outbreak of the Second World War kept them in the United States, and they finally settled in Denmark in 1952.

25 July. Lahinch to Kenmare via Limerick (shopped at Woolworth's), lunch on road, lost way near Abbeyfeale, it rained nearly all day, no room at Killarney, then a divinely thrilling mountain drive to Kenmare. Vegetation in riot, faery light, fantastic mountains, view of far gap, greeny golden light swooning on mountains, blue foreground, incredible. Every nook and inch a botanical garden, the ferns, heather, foxgloves, pines.

Upper Lake very lovely (!) 0 words. No words could justice it. But Killarney itself – *immonde*, full of priests.

26 July. Kenmare to Waterville, gave man a lift who said 'we're buggered up altogether' re the country's politics. So much beauty of colour and wild form along the coast that I give up. Waterville not so good. Fled from Butlers Arms. At Derrynane a very simple hotel and lunch – and there the most beautiful little sand bays and mountain views. We wanted to live there. Plants and trees luxuriant. Islets. Unspoiled, lost. Then from Kenmare to Glengariff, also an unparalleled drive, full of lone vast grandeur and eerie lights and corniche roads and a long tunnel. View of Glengariff from above. Rainy. But good intervals.

From *Signe Toksvig's Irish Diaries 1926–1937*

Virginia Woolf

1934

A LEADING LIGHT OF the Bloomsbury group, Virginia Stephens (1882–1941) was born in London. Her father, Leslie Stephens, was a distinguished critic and her mother, a nurse, worked among the needy. Virginia did not attend school, but was educated at home. With her husband Leonard Woolf, she founded the Hogarth Press, which published her first book, *Jacob's Room*, in 1922. Other novels followed, establishing her reputation as one of the major novelists of the twentieth century. In late April 1934 the Woolfs made a journey to the southwest of Ireland. Although at the time Virginia thought of finding a house here, she never visited Ireland again.

•

Tuesday 1 May Waterville [Butler Arms Hotel]. Too like its name; blowing the spray & the rain over a flat land, & a scattering of hideous 1850 watering place houses. Mist today, wind tonight; & L. opening the first Times to come our way, said George Duckworth is dead. So he is. And I feel the usual incongruous shades of feeling, one from this year, one from that – how great a part he used to play & now scarcely any. . . . Here I sit on my bed in the windy seaside hotel, & wait for dinner, with this usual sense of time shifting & life becoming unreal, so soon to vanish while the world will go on millions upon millions of years.

Wednesday 2 May Glenbeith [Glenbeigh Hotel]. On again, after an extremely interesting encounter at the windy hotel with Ireland – that is Mr & Mrs Rowlands; he is a giant, very shapely, small head, obliterated features; she small, abrupt, vivacious. They began directly, & so we talked, – they accepted us as their sort, & were gentry, Irish gentry, very much so, he with a house 500 years old, & no land left. 'But I love my King & Country. Whatever they ask me to do I'd do it' – this with great emotion. Oh yes, we believe in the British Empire; we hate the madman de Valéra.' There they live, 14 miles from Cork, hunting with an old retriever dog, & go to bazaars miles & miles away. . . . On to Tralee & saw the gipsies coming down the road & thought of G. being buried.

Thursday 3 May Adare [Dunraven Arms Hotel]. . . . To copy down conversation is not very interesting. People say the same thing over & over again. I wd like to describe the perfection of Irish conversation, which was Mrs FitzGerald's last night. She is exactly the great French lady – only living in a black jersey on an Irish bog. After dinner she came in, ostensibly to lend us a paper & offer advice, in fact to indulge her genius for talk. She talked till 11, & wd. willingly be talking now: about hotel keeping, about frigidaires, about her grandmother sitting on a chair in the kitchen & saying Thats done that wants another 2 minutes & so on, never stirring herself but somehow getting it done. We have the name of being good housekeepers. Then on about bogs, she has bought several fragments because now there may be money in it. However I can give no notion of the flowing, yet formed sentences, the richness & ease of the language; the lay out, dexterity & adroitness of the arrangement. There was the story of old Julia the cook, who had gone off home in a huff jealous of the young maids; had her daughter & the London husband on her, bought them gramophone records, & now wont own that she has wasted her savings. Mrs F. is one of those bluntnosed parted haired Irishwomen with luminous brown eyes & something sardonic and secretive in her expression. Talk is to her an intoxicant, but there is as Mr Rowlands said, something heartless about the I[rish]: quite cold indifferent sarcastic, for all their melody, their fluency, their adorable ease & forthcomingness. She was very much on the spot, accurate, managing, shrewd, hard headed, analytic. Why arent these people the greatest novelists in the world? – with this facility, this balance, this fundamental (now L. has joined in & is advising the 3 ladies. Are they American?)

Its very kind of you telling us: thank you very much. Now the wireless is brawling. Everything looks nice in fine weather. I think I'll go to bed. I want you to read this. One is the director of the others, severe, but apologetic, perhaps paid for.

But why isn't Mrs F. a great novelist? Certainly the salon survives at Glenbeith, the lust for talk, & finishing one's sentence – only with complete naturalness. For instance, explaining the bogs, 'saturated, now whats the opposite word?' Desiccated, L. suggested, & she adopted it with pleasure. She said one could never understand the Irish: one had to live as they did. They sit in their cottages talking about politics; they dont dance much; they have no amusements. They at once started to poach on her bog merely because she had bought it – otherwise it had been left alone for centuries. The bogs are full of trees, cant be self planted, so orderly, but now who has planted them? And they burn in a resinous way – go up – puf! – in a flash, like petrol. Suddenly she became severe & thought me a fool. 'What does this good lady mean?' Her grandmother was an innkeeper; she herself went away for 25 years; Oh, as my grandmother said, one becomes able to read peoples characters before they step over the door, & ones never wrong one way or the other. Her quickness was amazing. This morning the talk began & L. very slightly put out his hand. 'Oh I know that means you wanting to be off' – & so we parted from the last representative of the French salon of the 18th Century, this strange mixture of county lady, peasant, & landlady.

From *The Diary of Virginia Woolf*

Padraic Colum

1937

BORN IN LONGFORD, Padraic Colum (1881–1972) became one of the first Abbey Theatre playwrights with his plays *Broken Soil* and *The Land*. In 1914 he went to the United States, and in 1924 visited Hawaii to investigate Hawaiian folklore and to turn local legends into stories for children. Colum spent much of his life in the United States, lecturing and working for publishers. His best-known poems are 'The Old Woman of the Roads' and 'She Moved through the Fair.' He wrote many books on travel, criticism and biography. With his wife Mary he wrote *Our Friend James Joyce*. In the 1930s Colum visited Kerry and wrote this description of his travels.

From Mallow the roads run south and west into the Kingdom of Kerry. In the evenings one is always facing clumps of cattle coming home to the byres – Kerry cattle they are, remnants of the old Irish black cattle, small and used to sparse feeding. The hawthorn that lasts so long is gone, and, instead, we have the whiteness of the elder blossoms – hand-wide patches of blossom that have a penetrating smell. The elder bushes grow high along the roads. A girl, bare-footed and bare-legged, is climbing the road before us; she has the muscular legs of the mountain people. Here the girls and the women still cherish the shawl, wrapping it around them and putting it across their heads. And they have handsome fawny shawls with elaborate edges. Boots seem very heavy upon their feet. They walk barefooted two miles out of three, and put on their boots coming into the town, so that they will be respectable-looking at Mass.

This tract of Kerry reproduces the configuration of Ireland. Mountains surround it as they surround the central plain of the country. Within their boundary there is something of the Curragh of Kildare and something of the Bog of Allen; then there are green fields and shadowed meadows, and lakes and streams; there is the sea running its channels through a stretch of bog. The Kingdom of Kerry! Perhaps it has that title because it reproduces the features of the Kingdom of Ireland.

Always the people have before them the high mountains with their changing colours. These must influence their minds. And one notices in the Kerry people an intelligence more ready, an interest in learning more pronounced, a graciousness that is more than the graciousness of the people of other parts of Ireland. They have grave faults. They are mighty drinkers, and when drunk they can lapse into savagery. And they are noted for being untrustworthy witnesses in a court of law. They are a people adroit in parrying cross-examination. 'It might be,' 'It could be' is all that can be got out of a witness. The Kerry people regard the law as something to be evaded and circumvented; it will probably be a long time before they get away from this attitude.

The distrust of the law down here is probably related to a tradition of loyalty to their own customs and their own lords. In Kerry, be it noted, a few of the Gaelic families survived as landowners through the penal days – O'Connells, O'Donoghues and O'Mahonys – and kept their authority with the people. The chief of the O'Connells displayed a crooked knife as a sort of sceptre. 'A tenant would walk out and give up his holding at the bidding of the bearer of the crooked knife.' Even to this day around the mountains of Kerry there is a regard for the bearers of the old noble names. The shopkeepers in the small towns – even they – have a veneration for 'the old stock.' A man who drives his ass into the town will be received with respect by a shopkeeper who could give thousand-pound dowries to his daughters. The man will be one of the old families, an O'Sullivan or a MacGillicuddy, and in his cabin on the mountain he will have the bearing, the manners, and the *hauteur* of an aristocrat. The other evening I was on the road speaking with an old age pensioner who was leaving the town in an ass-cart. A young man came up to us. 'He is one of the oldest stock that comes this road,' he said to me impressively, speaking of the old man. 'Aye, indeed,' cried the pensioner, 'I am one of the old stock. I can trace my family back for three hundred years – aye, and beyond three hundred years. Seamus Ua Mongain – that's my name in Irish.' To go back to the people's attitude to the law. One evening I was standing in the street of a little town with a friend. A fight began in a corner, and my friend, who had a sprained ankle, suddenly made off. The people, instead of watching the fight, stampeded. No one wanted to be a witness to a possible action. 'Twould be unneighbourly to give evidence that would injure either party.

From *The Road round Ireland*

Robert Lloyd Praeger

1937

ROBERT LLOYD PRAEGER (1853–1953) joined the Belfast Field Naturalists' Society at the age of eleven and for the rest of his life remained keenly involved in botany. Educated in Belfast, he began his career there as a civil engineer. Praeger made many contributions to quaternary geology, and was a founder of the *Irish Naturalist*. A founder-member of the Geographical Society of Ireland, he also held positions in various other learned societies. He undertook many botanical surveys and wrote major scientific studies of Irish flora. In *The Way That I Went* he describes his wanderings around Ireland, with a particular eye on the natural surroundings.

There is another jewel in the Kerry crown, an animal unique, known only there, a resplendent creature called the Carrabuncle. It is true that it has never been seen by the cold critical eye of science, but Matthew Arnold reminds us through the mouth of Empedocles that 'much may still exist that is not yet believed.' The Carrabuncle is mentioned in Charles Smith's *Antient and Present State of the County of Kerry*, published in 1756, as having been seen in the Killarney Lakes – but he erroneously assumed that the name he heard belonged not to an animal but to the familiar precious stone. Henry Hart, when exploring the Kerry mountains in 1883, came on its track again, this time on Brandon. He learned that its home was in Lough Veagh (*Loch betha*, birch lake) where the people gather fresh-water mussels for the pearls which some of them contain. 'These come off an enormous animal called the Carrabuncle, which is often seen glittering like silver in the water at night. This animal has gold and jewels and precious stones hanging to it, and shells galore; the inside of the shells shines with gold.' Five years later, Nathaniel Colgan happened on Hart's informant, when climbing on Brandon, and obtained further particulars. The true home of the Carrabuncle, it appears, is Lough Geal (*Loch geal*, shining lake), not Lough Veagh. His informant had never seen it, but if you could only catch it you would get some things of great value that follow after it. The postman and the publican, interviewed by Colgan, confirmed the fact of the Carrabuncle's existence. But it is seen, it would appear, only once in seven years, and then it lights up the whole lake.

I have been five times at Lough Geal, but was unlucky as to date, for I saw nothing, and the lake was mostly inky black, with heavy clouds hanging on the dark cliffs which impend above it. But a very interesting side issue to the legend, as yet unexplained, pointed out by Colgan, arises from the reference by Alfred Russell Wallace in his *Travels on the Amazon and Rio Negro*, to the Carbunculo, a mythical animal of the Upper Amazon and Peru. Colgan was puzzled as to the connection (if any) between the Irish and the South American creature. The probable explanation of the presence of the name in these two widely separated areas lies in the fact that both regions were in intimate connection with Spain. A. Farrington tells me that till recently fishermen from the Peninsula brought to southern Ireland cargoes of salted cod obtained on the Newfoundland banks, which went in Cork by the name of *bockalow*, which is clearly the Spanish *bacallao* (Portuguese *bacalhao*), cod or ling – I well remember the horrible stuff we ate with unwelcome frequency in the Canary Islands under that name. It would seem that Carrabuncle corresponds similarly to the Spanish Carbunculo, meaning the precious stone we call carbuncle – though how the word came to be applied either in Ireland or on the Amazon to a water-monster is not clear.

The rare Killarney Fern, Trichomanes Speciosum

The floral beauty and interest of Kerry in the springtime I have endeavoured to describe in *The Botanist in Ireland*, and I can best pay tribute to it now by repeating what I wrote then: for the sake of non-botanical readers, I have substituted English plant-names for the Latin ones there used:

'To see the peculiar flora of Kerry in its most characteristic aspect the time to visit the area is not the usual holiday period of July and August, beloved of botanists, but the month of May and early June. Then the Large-flowered Butterwort, the glory of Kerry, is at its best, its great purple blossoms nodding in the wind over hundreds of square miles of bog and rocky mountain. "London Pride" and the Kidney-leaved Saxifrage are in full bloom too, decking the rocks, woods and glens with their slender red stems starred with white flowers. The Irish Spurge is at its loveliest stage, just attaining full growth, and forming luscious clusters of greenish gold along the streams and in all the rough pasture land. By the end of June it will be wholly green, with tubercled fruit and a straggling habit. The Royal Fern also is at its loveliest, golden brown, its strong shuttlecocks of fronds half expanded, with loose rags of brown fluff clinging to their straight smooth glaucous stems; it lines the streambanks and fences everywhere, and lights up the brown bogs. Alone among the rare species, the Arbutus is not at its best. Growth is only just beginning, the old leaves are yellowing and falling, and the half-grown fruit, so beautiful at a later stage, is still inconspicuous.

'Everywhere Gorse is blazing, with Broom following close behind. In the woods the delicate green of the young Birch contrasts with the old gold of the Oak and the grey-green of the Willows; the Holly, though full of flower, looking very dark in comparison. The shaggy young stems of the Male Fern add again a touch of golden brown, while half-expanded Lady Ferns and Bree's Fern are full green. The two species of Filmy Fern are still in excellent condition, *H. tunbridgense* separating itself at once from its ally by its bluish-green tint, and the broader rounded tip of its tiny fronds.

'In the lakes there is as yet little life. The Water Lobelia alone is sending flower-stems up towards the light. The Awl-wort, Shore-weed and Pipewort are still dormant, the curiously persistent old fruit-stems of the last lying criss-cross like straws on the fresh green mats of foliage.

'By the sea, the white sheets of Scurvy-grass have already passed away, but the rocks are bright with Sea-Pink and Sea-Campion, often in remarkable profusion, while the dunes are decorated with thousands of the yellow and blue flowers of the Sand-hill Pansy.'

To the botanist, Kerry will always stand associated with the name of Reginald William Scully (1858–1935), who gave us a book upon its plants which is the most complete account yet written of the botany of any Irish area. Scully was a doctor, but the presence of private means rendered unnecessary the adjunct of a practice, and while he remained a helpful member of his profession, he was able, under the incentive of A.G. More, to carry out during nearly thirty years a very complete botanical survey of this large and mountainous area, during which he added considerably to our knowledge of its vegetation. His *Flora of County Kerry*, published in 1916, forms a fitting memorial to an earnest and methodical worker, and a man whose old-world courtesy and scientific modesty lent to his companionship a special charm.

I am going to indulge in a grumble about Killarney – not about the lovely region of mountain and lake, but about the town which is its focus and gateway. It is all wrong; but indeed the wrongnesses are mostly its misfortune, not its fault. In the first place, it stands in the wrong place – on flat ground, with a lake two miles wide and five miles in length cutting you off from the paradise on its southern side – for to west, north, and east, the district around Killarney is quite dull. Nor does the town stand by the lake-shore but over a mile inland, with the high walls and dense trees of Kenmare demesne preventing for several miles even a glimpse of lake or mountain. The road which leads down to Lough Lene (*Loch Léin*) – the only one – offers to the visitor a mile and a half of flat straight dull thoroughfare, with flat fields on one side and a high wall on the other. It takes you to the cramped confines of the fine old ruin of Ross Castle, on the edge of the water; if you attempt to go to right or left – 'Sixpence, please!' The other roads leading from Killarney are dull too, especially the western one. The Kenmare road is somewhat better from the start, but you go four miles before the lovely wooded hills begin. Fortunately some of the hotels are well out on this side. The town itself is unattractive, devoid of the amenities which one associates with a great tourist centre as found in other countries: and while the principal streets are neat, the outskirts cannot claim exemption from a recent comment on the Irish provincial town: 'its most striking feature is its ruined buildings in various stages of decay. A decorative *motif* is supplied commonly by the display on suitable walls of rival political slogans.' It is just because I am an enthusiast as regards the beauty and interest of Ireland that I make these comments. Much-advertised Killarney, seen every year by thousands of visitors, should be in the forefront of effort to show a fair and smiling face to the strangers whom Ireland attracts to her shores from all parts of the world. As to those unfortunate topographical features which Killarney cannot help, they are by no means without compensations. If the beautiful wooded demesne were not reserved and 'Sixpence, please,' no doubt it would be bare agricultural land, with notices regarding trespass and barriers of barbed wire. And the four miles of road that intervene between the town and the Arbutus woods of the hills mitigate the enthusiasm of the crowds of invaders who otherwise might litter them with paper and cartons and broken glass, harry the wild flowers, and carve their names upon the trees.

Ross Castle was the seat of the McCarthys until 1652, when it surrendered to the English army.

So you will understand why, for my own part, I prefer to sojourn at quiet Kenmare, far from the madding crowd, and thence cross the mountain-ridge to the Upper Lake, entering the Killarney fairyland at its least frequented part. But if you stay at one of the excellent hotels well outside Killarney town, you will be in lovely scenery all the time, and the Kenmare road will lead you into the heart of the hills. If you are motoring, of course, you can afford to stop anywhere, for ten minutes will take you through the unexciting immediate environs of Killarney. And if you turn your back on the dull country north of the Lower Lake, what a lovely region lies before you! To the south the huge mass of Mangerton (*Mangartagh,* mountain of long grass?), with its enormous lake-filled cirque called the Devil's Punch-bowl. Close by, between Mangerton and Stoompa, is the Horse's Glen, long and deep, with three lakes between its rocky walls, and a grand cirque above the highest of them. It takes a big day's work to explore those two great coombs, and you must go on foot. A day for each of them will not be found excessive even by a vigorous climber. It is the remote tarn of the Devil's Punch-bowl that supplies Killarney with its excellent water – 'The grandest water in Ireland, sorr,' a local enthusiast told me; 'Just a drop of John Jameson in it and it will go down your throat like a torchlight procession, and warm the nails in your boots, begob!' To the south-west, beyond Torc Mountain (*Torc*, a boar) is the valley in which lies the Upper Lake. It has been excavated so deeply by ice in old days, that its floor is level for five miles into the mountains, so visitors to the Gap of Dunloe are rowed down the slow stream that occupies the valley-bottom, and on across the Lower Lake. This valley is for the botanist and zoologist the special attraction of Killarney – very sheltered, excessively humid, filled with luxuriant native woods of Oak, Arbutus, Birch, Holly and Mountain-Ash, under which the Saxifrages, Filmy Ferns and other interesting plants for which Killarney is famous run riot among a profusion of mosses and liverworts of extraordinary luxuriance and often of extreme rarity. And a feature that adds to the beauty and interest of these woods is this: they are not confined within bounds, like most that we know, but run up the hills to their natural limits, where exposure makes them halt; and we see the tree-edge fluctuating up and down along the mountain-sides between 600 and 800 feet according to the amount of shelter afforded by the conformation of the ground to the gales of winter. West of this unique valley rise the tall hills of the Purple Mountain group, with Tomies Mountain, densely wooded below, descending steeply into the waters of the Lower Lake; and beyond Purple Mountain, across the deep gash of the Gap of Dunloe, the Reeks tower up above everything else. It is a wonderful bit of country.

If you want to experience to the full the enchantment of Killarney get out on the lake on a calm evening (having contrived to leave your garrulous boatman behind), and watch the changing effects of light and shade on the towering hills and the water and the woods as sunset approaches. If you have been lucky, and have got a day of that indefinable astonishing Killarney atmosphere, you will admit that in your life you have never seen anything more lovely. But to be rowed about (fortunately motor boats are still almost unknown) one of a party of eight, with a running commentary such as 'Look now, there's the Elephant Island, right forninst ye. Do ye see his trunk, and his little eye. But he won't touch you, sorr. There was once a giant . . . ' – that keeps you firmly pinned down to earth, when you might be away in whatever sort of Elysium the enchantment makes for you.

From *The Way That I Went*

Sean O'Faolain

1939

JOHN WHELAN (1900–1991) was born in Cork and changed his name to its Irish equivalent after he became involved in the Irish Republican movement. He studied at University College Cork and at Harvard. After teaching in Boston and in England he returned to Ireland to pursue writing fulltime. As editor of *The Bell* he published the works of the best Irish writers of the time. His *Nest of Simple Folk*, published in 1933, established his reputation. O'Faolain's writings include ten volumes of short stories, novels, biographies on Constance Markievicz, Daniel O'Connell, Eamon De Valera, Hugh O'Neill, Cardinal Newman, an autobiography, and travel books.

Cahirciveen was shrouded in mist. The mountains behind it, up towards Caragh Lake, were a leaden wall of sky under the low clouds – unrecognizable as land. I do not think there is any town in Ireland so remote and yet so intact as Cahirciveen. Dingle, across the bay, runs it close. But Dingle is of a slightly different character; it is a fishing centre; it is more indigenous; it feels close to its hinterland out to the twelve Blaskets. Whereas Cahirciveen retains that definite alien quality in relation to its countryside which, at least to some degree, every town must in order to preserve its independence and its sense of superiority. After all, if a town loses all its snobbishness it becomes a village. Cahirciveen has no purpose but to be what the guide-books call 'an agricultural centre.' It is not residential, like Westport, and has no local Lord like the Earl of Sligo. It is not a holiday centre like Clifden. It is just a business town lobbed down on this toe of the wilderness and would never have been a town if the railway had not penetrated to it around 1870, and to Valencia beside it.

Really, Valencia made Cahirciveen, or rather, the Atlantic Cable Station thereon. The island was, as one might suspect, so-called by the Spanish. The Knight of Kerry owns it all except for a strip across the middle of it. Trinity College, Dublin impertinently owns that. I am not particularly interested in scientific matters but the image of that snaky line of cable being laid down, yard by yard across the bed of the rolling Atlantic, sometimes as much as two and a quarter miles down, is overpowering. Five efforts were made to lay it in the 'fifties and 'sixties, the cable snapping when only a few miles had been laid, or when three hundred miles had been laid, or losing insulation when a thousand miles had been laid, breaking when they tried to raise it, or reaching Newfoundland and falling silent mysteriously after a few months. The aristocracy which worked this machine from Valencia were always a strange little foreign colony – living an urban life of dances, bridge-parties, high teas, and so on, like a military settlement somewhere in India or Africa.

I had been cycling ever since Bantry, in grand weather as far as Darrynane. There the sun darkened and a threatening wind blew up from Ballinskelligs Bay. The rain fell in sheets of light mist as I entered Cahirciveen. I crossed the channel in a fog. The one half-hour during which the sun came out it shone purple on the wet slate quarries of Valencia – they used to polish billiard-table slabs out of these and export them – and I could see why the sea is said to surge, here, into waves more gigantic than any other part of Ireland. I stood on Fort Point and looked north-east across through a rainbow at Doulus Head, with its great unscaleable flat cliff-face rising out of the surge. The rollers came in like battalions of storm-troopers to crash on the shore of Beginish in wild spume. What it must be like in winter! I felt the colony needed its card-parties and its golf-links. Knightstown where I crossed back the half-mile to the mainland has a goodish hotel. There were some anglers. With a car on the mainland it would and does make an excellent summer resort for the discriminating few.

It showed no sign of letting up into a good day. I knew nobody in the town. So I gave up the road and took train for Killorglin. That long rail-journey up to Killorglin or down from Killorglin is one of those journeys one never forgets. The first time I did it, years ago, I was filled with excitement both by the thought that I was penetrating into one of Ireland's loneliest places, and by the sight of the wilderness itself. It was a dark day. The puffing train seemed in places to sway over the sea. The vast bay, shaking its white locks, was a threatening maw. The rough, boggy land to the left looked like the end of the world. I felt then, and I felt again to-day, that this is the proper side of the Magillicuddy Reeks from which to enjoy the magnificence of Kerry which is usually approached from Killarney. There are two good hotels near here at Caragh – the Glencar Hotel and the Caragh Lake Hotel. The first is a small, intimate, angler's inn. I stayed there and hated to leave it. The second is a big Railway Hotel. Here you are loftily perched above the great world of mountains, which, from Killarney, are seen merely in silhouette. The panorama is endless and it keeps changing endlessly under the roving light.

From *An Irish Journey*

The Franciscan Friary at Muckross, founded in 1448 by Donal MacCarthy Mór, was burned by Cromwellian forces in 1652.

Richard Hayward

1944

ULSTER-BORN RICHARD HAYWARD (1892–1964) wrote mainly travel books about Ireland. A specialist in Ulster dialect, he produced over one hundred records as a ballad singer, and wrote several plays. Hayward founded the Belfast Repertory Theatre and co-founded the Belfast Radio Players. He served as chairman of Irish PEN, president of the Belfast Naturalists' Field Club and president of the Ulster Folksong Society, and was also a committee member of many societies with interests in music, folklore, archaeology, geology and botany. His books include *In Praise of Ulster*, *Where the River Shannon Flows*, and *The Story of the Irish Harp*.

We awoke next morning to the great day of Puck, the first day of Puck Fair, the day of the Gathering, and even as we approached the main road along the hotel drive we could hear the rattle of carts going towards neighbouring Killorglin, (perchance Cill-Forglain – St. Forglan's Church) the patter of hoofs as the beasts were driven along to that great annual festival, and the cries and laughter of men, women and children as they exchanged sallies one with the other, or passed the time of day. It was all a grand excitement in this quiet country-side, and it must have been like this every year for countless centuries, for nothing seems to me more surely the survival of an ancient pagan feast than this age-old gathering under the patronage of a male goat, known in Kerry as a puck or pocán.

All young lovers fond of sporting, pay attention for a while,
Till I sing the Praise of Puck and cause you many a laugh and smile,
Where lads and lassies gaily in Killorglin may be seen
To view the Puck upon the stage, our hero dressed in green,

So here's to gallant Puck so gay,
Ah, he's the powerful fella,
No wind nor rain can wet his tail,
For it's waterproof an' yella.

It's on the square he puxes there in colours grand and gay,
There's not a fair in Ireland that can match his powerful sway;
You'll see gamblers in gyration, trick-o'-loop and other games,
Wheels-o'-fortune, ballad-singers, shootin' gall'ries for all aims.
Now all young men unmarried may next Shrovetide take a wife,

Puck Fair Killorglin at the turn of the twentieth century. During this ancient annual festival a goat is installed on top of a high platform. (Lawrence Collection R7939)

For by next Puck we'll have our land and Irish way of life,
No tyrant dare oppress us, our customs we'll hold still
With Puck above to bind us in one united will.

Apart from the accuracy of description in this racy old ballad, there is significant interest in the last verse, for there not only is the common custom of using Puck as an almanac – 'for by next Puck' – reflected, but in addition the atavistic character of the whole ceremonial is clearly indicated. Puck stands out as a pagan deity capable of bringing luck and success to marriage and of binding together in unity a gathering of people assembled to worship him, and although no one would be more surprised than this old ballad-singer, or these good farmers of Kerry, to know that they are taking part in what is virtually a pagan fertility festival, folk-memory, always astonishingly persistent, has been long enough in this case to preserve this antique celebration, undoubtedly associated with the goat-footed Pan, within the comparative safety of a ballad; and just as surely as a bee is preserved in amber, or a mammoth in a block of ice.

Puck Fair has always been held about the beginning of August, and August the First was the great central day of the month-long solar festival of Lugh, the Sun-god of the Tuatha De Danann, which was held at Tailtiu, the modern Teltown. So strong was the tradition in that place that hurling matches continued to be played there until recent times, and this ancient tradition has now been carried over into the present day Tailtean Games, a kind of Irish Olympics. Indeed the very month of August is known in Irish as Mí-na-lughna, and August celebration of this kind were common throughout the Celtic-speaking world, amongst other places at Lyons in Gaul, anciently known as Lugudunum, or the Fortress of Lugh. But Lugh was brought to Ireland by the Tuatha De Danann, and before the time of these invaders the Sean Tuatha, the older races of Ireland, had Sun and Corn and Fertility Gods of their own, chief amongst them being that Crom Cruaich to whom I have already referred earlier in this book. Crom was credited with having first brought wheat into Ireland, a common quality of a Corn God, and Lugh failed to displace him in the hearts and faith of the older races. It is true that Lugh, with his Sword of Light, became the resplendent Sun God of the Irish epic tales and romances and gave his name to the month of August, but Crom endured in the folk-tales and traditions of the common people. I have little doubt that Puck is the more modern equivalent of some other Corn or Fertility God who successfully resisted the intrusion of Lugh in this remote part of Ireland, surely the very place where the Sean Tuatha would have a good chance of survival, and his embodiment in the form of a male goat naturally associates him with the widespread cult of Pan, a God of agriculture, woodlands and the countryside, popular in the hearts of farming communities for countless centuries and under many names. This is my own personal feeling about Puck and I put it forward as nothing more than that. I do not even call it a theory. Many readers who have been to the fair will doubtless feel some of my ideas chiming with their own thoughts, but many more perhaps will find more satisfaction in the school of thought of which Dean Reidy is a worthy exponent, and see in Puck nothing more than 'the growth of a modern legend from the surmises of folklorists – a rural sarcasm at a wretched fair in a once-wretched town.' In the language of the fair ground itself: 'You pays your money and you takes your choice.'

The Puck fair is the last of the really ancient Irish fairs with a distinctive character, and its origin is so lost in the mists of antiquity, that one may immediately dismiss that rather silly story about the Cromwellian soldiery that was so obviously invented to explain its beginning. All we know historically is that James the First, in 1613, granted Jenkin Conway a patent 'to hold a faire in Killorgan on Lammas day and the day after,' a patent which was really a permission to continue a fair already held for centuries on those days; and that a subsequent patent granted in 1772 to his kinsman, Conway Blennerhassett, sought to abolish the Lammas Fair and to replace it with three fairs to be held in May, June and November. But in spite of prohibitions, proclamations and some small show of armed force, the people of Killorglin held their accustomed Puck Fair on August the twelfth and thirteenth, 1772, dates equal to August the first and second, old style, the calendar having been revised in 1752. Tradition dies hard in Ireland and very prudently Blennerhassett turned a blind eye on this forbidden fair and continued to hold the other three fairs with the greater success on that account.

Through the great kindness of Mr. O Shea, who owns the cinema in Killorglin, a spacious upper room, above his public house in the Square, was placed at my disposal, and it was there we went and unloaded the picnic lunch which Miss Bradshaw, in the best Huggard style, had prepared for us before we left the hotel. The situation brought back memories of a year ago, when I was in that selfsame room, with my moving cameras and equipment, waiting to photograph the Puck ritual for a film which has since been released. It all seemed much the same, the streets of the small town below jammed with people and beasts shoulder to shoulder, now a man jostling a cow to make his way into a pub, now a cow jostling a man to reach a bunch of grass growing from some old masonry; the tall wooden scaffold-like construction rising in front of my window, flagged and be-ribboned for the reception of His Majesty King Puck when the great moment arrived; the concourse of showmen and their stalls crowding the small square to bursting point; the movement of frightened herds with their loud cries and bellows; the streets and pavements in many places ankle-deep in cow dung; the rather savage feeling of sound and colour and raw humanity. It was all very primitive and lively and pagan-seeming and it was all intensely exiting. It was, in short, Puck Fair on the day of the Gathering. Tomorrow would be the Fair and the next day the Scattering, but one day at a time is good enough at this pressure.

The fairs and shows of Ireland have appealed to the poets of the country from remote times, and it is noticeable that when they are recorded in the epics and romances, the poetic phrase marches with more animation and with more life and blood in its step, than it does even when a great battle is being described and elaborated. And I could understand this circumstance as I walked about the sounding streets of this usually quiet little market place, for I had left my perch at the window for a space and was making my way down the long street to the foot of the town, where a stone bridge carries the highway over the wide-flowing Laune, the single outlet through which the Lakes of Killarney dispense with the surplus of their sweet waters. For wherever I went was colour and movement and animation, and no poet worth his salt could fail to be infected with the immense energy of it all. Horses and cattle, hounds and sporting dogs, pigs and sheep, little foals crying for their mothers, cocks crowing, dealers shouting and laughing and making wide gestures, sightseers getting in everybody's way, and the attendant train of show people with their flashy attire and alien-sounding language. And then over the bridge, along the road to right and left, were the caravans of the gypsies and the distinct and smaller portable habitations of the tinkers. A great riot of nomadic colour this, with swarms of children playing under the caravans, or about the openings of the lower tilts, and the buxom brightly-shawled women busy taking silver in exchange for news of dark-avised strangers whom they saw in the upturned palms of laughing country boys and girls.

On my way back I went into MacCrohan's store to look at the shattered fragment, standing behind the Provincial Bank, which is all that is left of the old Castle of Killorglin. This town was originally held by the Moriartys, but they were ousted by the McCarthys in the eleventh century, who in turn gave way before the Fitzgeralds. It was Maurice Fitzthomas Fitzgerald who built this castle in the thirteenth century and then handed it over with its manor to the Knights Templars. At the dissolution of that order the property reverted to the Fitzgeralds, but they lost it after the Desmond rebellion, and that Jenkin Conway already referred to, an English undertaker, received it as grantee and renamed it, and the town, Castle Conway. The Blennerhassetts came next, and in 1796 they sold out to Thomas Mullins of Burnham, the first Lord Ventry, from whom, in 1910, the place passed out of English control under the Irish Land Act. It seems hard to believe that this castle was occupied as late as 1830, for little more than a featureless gable remains. But Puck is as lively as ever and Castle Conway is Killorglin once again.

And now I went back to my room above the pub and we all gathered there to eat a late lunch and to await the procession which would herald the opening of the fair. Right under the window old Conn Riordan of Headfort, a man I have known for years, round many of the Irish fairs, as Conn the Laces, was playing a variety of three-card tricks, and Risteard Og begged to be allowed to go down to try his skill. I shouted down to Laces and evidently Risteard Og and he got on well together, for the young rascal soon came back with a beaming face and a pocket jingling with coppers.

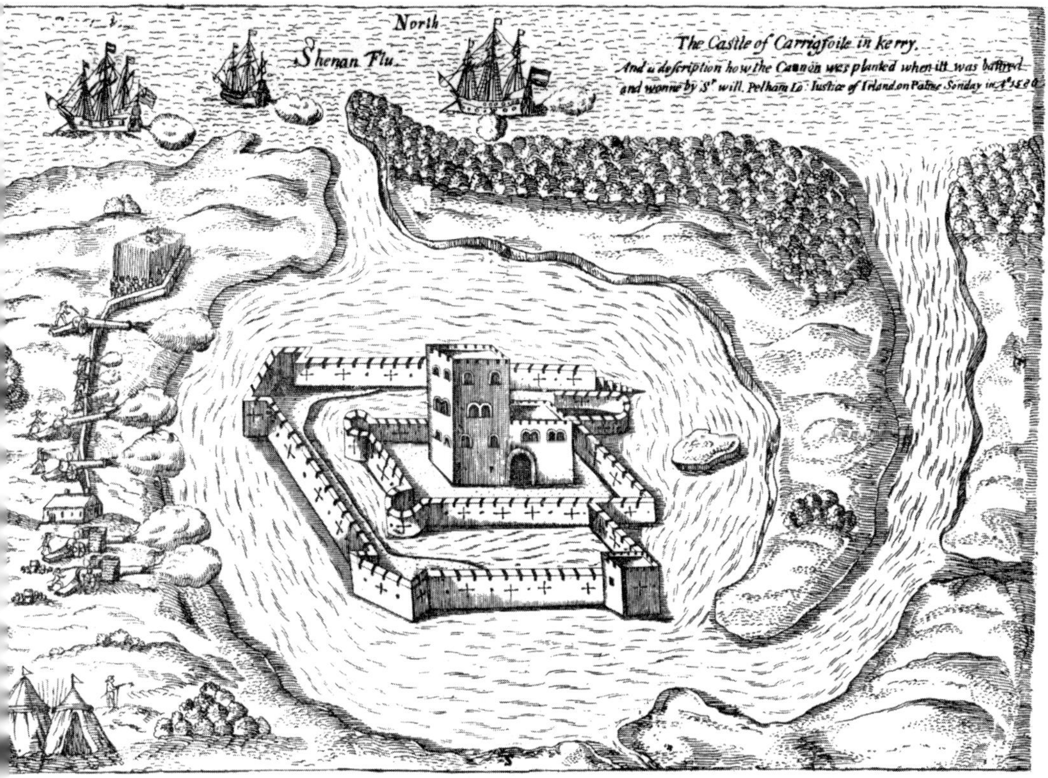

In 1580 Carrigafoyle castle was stormed from land and sea. The surviving Irish, Spanish and Italian defenders were all hanged.

And then the fun began. Conn the Laces broke into a wild, grinding growl – 'Ah-h-h-h here he comes, me bould Puck' – the music of fiddles and melodeons came from the far edge of the town – a sudden silence fell upon the crowd and one could actually feel that they were all listening to those distant strains – and then came something between a great corporate sigh and the sound the wind makes when it sweeps over the top of a fine crop of standing wheat – and with that babel broke loose. A line of six fiddlers, playing finely like one man and with a terrific sense of rhythm, started the Derry hornpipe, and a great fat fellow, 'with drink taken,' came from somewhere nearby and broke into the dance with much skill and spirit; but too much spirit of the one kind, for as the crowd widened out to make a circle round the musicians and the dancer, the poor fellow stumbled and fell flat on his back. He was a very big man, as I have said, but before the roar of laughter broke out to greet his discomfiture, he was on his feet again like a cat and into the dance for all he was worth. A great cheer broke out at this, for they are sporting people these Kerry farmers, and I must admit I added my own voice to theirs. Meanwhile old

Conn, sensing the competition, broke out into a great ballad, the tune of which, entirely unrelated to that of the dance or of the approaching band, quite evaded me:

Here's to Puck comin' down the hill
On a Sunday after Mass
Swearin' a mighty oath; me boys,
To scatter them all at Tobin's Cross:
Ah-h-h
Wasn't he the lovely one,
Wasn't he the lovely fella,
No wind nor rain will spoil his face
For his hair is long like a gauger's brace,
An' it's waterproof an' yella.

And then the other showmen started to bark, and the noise grew in volume so that it was difficult now to make sense of any part of it. One voice only came clearly through the din, the brazen voice of a great hand-bell, wielded by a roguish-looking red-faced man, atop of a box, with the clear lovely whistle of a blackbird on his lips and the merry eye of that sleek rascally songster. He seemed to be selling cough mixture and knives with glass-cutters set at one end of them. Not far away a rout of farmers crowded round a gypsy woman who was telling the fortune of a young girl, her upturned palm gleaming unnaturally white amongst the sea of sun-tanned

grimy necks and paws. Again the voice of the bell rang out – clangily – insistently – and that lovely blackbird trill floated high beside it, and on a soft breeze came again the sound of the band, nearer now and more coherently – 'twas 'The rose of Tralee' they were playing, but in march time and rather out of tune. And now a little donkey forced its way miraculously through the dense crowed, its crib of turf almost crying out that, fair or no fair, the ordinary business of life must go on.

A sudden blast of music came from my right and there I saw the head of the Royal procession, a little dark ass bearing a card between its long sensitive ears, with the question: 'Where is the Post Office?' scrawled across it; evidently a piece of local humour that was beyond me. Immediately behind this came a cart laden with vegetables and driven by a boy dressed as a chef, with a great notice above it proclaiming that this was 'His Majesty's Chef, ' and hard on the tail of this commissariat waggon marched the band, the musicians gaily clad in brightly-coloured paper costumes and hats, and now doing their worst with 'The Kerry Dance,' also in march time and a little more out of tune. And then came the royal coach, more brilliant than anything yet, crowded with bedizened courtiers and bearing in its midst His Majesty King Puck, a superb specimen of a dark-coated male goat with as fine a pair of horns as I have ever seen. Conn the Laces gave vent to a roar more prodigious than anything he had yet produced, and, whether by coincidence or design, the whole motley entourage came to a sudden stop, like a squad of soldiers obeying the brazen command of the traditional drill sergeant. The music stopped on the instant in the middle of a phrase and for a full ten seconds there was a dead silence that was unearthly in its abrupt contrast. Even the cattle were stilled and the raucous women at their stalls, and through the very air seemed to creep a deep sense of tradition, of the realization that now was the moment when the ritual of unnumbered centuries was to live again. It was ten seconds of extraordinary tension, and it was broken by the quavering note of a single distant violin, absurdly irrelevant and unspeakably fragile in the thin line of its stringy tone. And then one of the courtiers leapt from the Royal cart on to the base of the scaffold-like tower, and, as his Majesty was moved into position, the band resumed 'The Kerry Dance' and the multifarious noises broke out again. King Puck stood in a highly-decorated canopy crib, fitted with electric light for the nightly watches, and before this was hoisted to the lofty throne, another courtier came forward with a cardboard crown, the band changed over to 'The Rose of Tralee,' the crowd cheered mightily, and Puck was crowned for another year. Up and up went the crib, orange-coloured to match the topmost band of the four Irish flags that flew from the four corner-poles of the tower, and the cheering of the crowd and the playing of the band grew more and more frenzied with every foot of altitude gained. It was all too much for old Conn who threw his arms upwards with a grand dramatic sweep and roared out in his grinding growl of a voice: 'Ah-h-h-h, Puck me boy, if oo falls now oo'll never get up.' But Puck didn't fall, but stood there, aloof and unconcerned, high above the heads of his subjects, crowned king for three days and nights, and in his eyes and his whole bearing was that look of supreme contempt, coupled with a quizzical benevolence, which is rarely encountered save in the Royal tribe of Capra Hircus. A great movement and clamour spread about the crowded streets, the bell rang out again with the blackbird note beside it, the six fiddlers played 'The Harvest Home.' It was six twenty p.m. on the tenth day of August, in the year of Our Lord nineteen hundred and forty-four, or by our new dispensation, the First Day of Puck. The Fair had begun.

Back in the hotel that night all the dinner-table talk was of the fair, and a few of us made up a party to go into Killorglin some time after midnight. The scene then was almost incredible; crowds still thronged the streets; barmen lay sleeping over their counters, utterly worn out by the work of the day and relieved for a spell by some friend or relation; His Majesty stood erect on his high throne, now brilliantly illuminated: and the roundabouts and swings were thronged with merry-makers apparently endowed with boundless energy and an unquenchable lust for excitement and movement. It was close upon three o'clock in the morning when we left the town, and at that hour there seemed little diminution in the general fun and laughter: and one of our party, who returned to the fair after breakfast, told me that he saw many stout farmers lying asleep on the pavements, doubtless having dropped in their tracks in the midst of a high wassail which only sleep brought to an end.

From *In the Kingdom of Kerry*

J.P. Donleavy

c.1947

James Patrick Donleavy grew up in New York and served in the US Navy during the Second World War. In 1946 he came Dublin to study microbiology at Trinity College. He settled in the country and later became an Irish citizen. Donleavy achieved renown with his comic masterpiece *The Ginger Man* (1955) which was inspired by Gainor

Stephen Crist, mentioned in the following extract. Other novels include *A Singular Man*, *The Beastly Beatitudes of Balthazar B*, *The Onion Eaters*, *A Fairy Tale of New York*, *The Destinies of Darcy Dancer, Gentleman*, and *The Saddest Summer of Samuel S*. He has also written plays, short stories, sketches and non-fiction.

There were no documents and not much cash upon us on the impromptu toothbrush trip with Crist to the west. But it was my first extended stay in the Irish countryside. Kells Cove was no more than a house and cottage or two at the end of a path between boulder built walls and overlooking a tiny inlet on Dingle Bay. The nearest transport, a mile and a half away, was reached by a rutted dirt lane leading up to where the main road ran and at where a once daily train stopped in each direction at an isolated unmarked lonely spot at the foot of a dark rising mountain. On the main road there was a grocery tucked into the side of the hill, where Gainor Stephen Crist, Esq. already had opened an account for your best of bacon, eggs and tea to be supplied. And there was a pub. Two miles away across the fields as the crow flies and as Crist and I stumbled. Such forays necessitating a wet foot slog across treacherous bits of bog and upon an inebriated return it was a life risking venture. The nearest town was Cahirciveen another seven or so miles to the southwest along the coast. Crist, who was a ferocious walker, could transverse those miles in no time, twiddling his thumbs nervously in front of him as he did so. And waiting patiently as I would shout for him to let me catch up. But once he did stop dead in his tracks to call me up from behind and ask me to investigate something on the road ahead. It was a dead bird. Crist grew nervously white as the blood drained from his face. And I watched him detour down into a ditch, climb a wall and wade through nettles to circumvent this area of the road where the dead bird lay. I once asked him what would he do if a dead bird came to him in a box.

'Mike, I would kill the man who sent it.'

Cahirciveen itself on this sunshining day reminded me of a main street of Western cowboy territory. And as one entered it on foot, striding centre of the road, the curtains twitched at the windows. News of your arrival would have already reached the other end of the town. Where Crist was heading as he always did to a post office. If not to send something then to see if something desperately sought had arrived. Cahirciveen, although a spooky town, was one of Crist's most favourite places. Not least for its reputation of having more pubs per population than any other half square mile on earth. Except for the church and Garda Síochána, nearly every other building and shop, no matter what else it was for or sold, had a board supported between two barrels as a bar. Everywhere we entered the corks out of the Guinness bottles went pop. Thus producing an ambience

Killaghie church near the foot of Mangerton Mountain is reputed to be the smallest church in Ireland.

much to Crist's liking. We set off to walk the seven miles back and for some of it got a ride standing up in the rear of a lurching donkey cart which a young monosyllabic boy was driving. Who was suspicious and shy of his strange passengers. But as Irish custom would have it, you could not pass without offering a lift to another on the road. And back we came. Down the winding, twisting, stony lane. Through the trees the sound of a brook in this glen. Back to the bliss of this little house. From which you had only feet to take you somewhere. Only a candle to light your night. A bucket to hold your water from a stream. A turf fire to cook your meals. Nothing to get up for tomorrow. And no need to do anything today. Cloaked in this protection. With the West awake. Like strange, unseen lightning and unsounding thunder. Premonitions shimmering, tingling in the air. The haunting deathly strangeness. Of the hush out across Dingle Bay.

From *J.P. Donleavy's Ireland: In All Her Sins and in Some of Her Graces*

Olivia Manning

*c.*1950

OLIVIA MANNING (1908–1980), who had maternal roots in Ulster, came from a naval background in Portsmouth, Hampshire. Her first novel, *The Wind Changes*, was published in 1938. A year later she married R.G. Smith, a British Council lecturer, and went with him to Bucharest. Their sojourn in Romania and the Middle East during the Second World War provided rich material for her best-known works, which are known as the 'Balkan Trilogy' and the 'Levant Trilogy:' collectively they form a single narrative, *The Fortunes of War*. Besides other novels, Manning's writings include short stories, history, humour, and a travel book of her experiences in Ireland. She also contributed to many periodicals.

The next day I set out to cycle round the peninsula. Dingle is the most remote part of the ancient kingdom of Kerry and the most primitive area of Ireland. No 'bus goes out to Dunquin. Those who have neither car nor bicycle – and these would be the majority of the dwellers along the fifteen mile ride out to the westernmost point of the British isles – must get a lift on a cart or walk to Dingle to do their shopping.

As I cycled round the curve of the bay I thought of the poor sea monster that was stranded on the beach here at 'Dingle Ichough' on 3rd October, 1674. An old pamphlet tells us how it was found by one James Steward who ran to call the assistance of a couple who lived nearby. When they arrived the 'man and his wife were both almost astonisht at the sight of this strange Monster, and the Woman especially so far frighted that she would by no means permit her Husband should go near or meddle with it.' The cut shows the Monster upside down so it seems to have horns, but reverse the pictures and it is seen to be merely a giant squid. It was already at its last gasp. When the men put ropes round it, it did no more than catch feebly at their hands. They drew it above water-level, left it for the night and next morning found it dead. It was taken to Dublin and presented to 'several persons of Honour'; they, not receiving this strange gift until December, were glad to hand it over for public exhibition. The pamphlet tells us: 'We might now divert the Reader a little, and tell him that some Zealots hearing of a strange creature with several heads, ten horns and more than triple Crowns, took it for the Apocaliptical Beast, and fancied the Pope was landing in Person. . . . ,' but this pamphleteer, a man of sense, concluded that there was every reason to suppose 'the Ocean to be inhabited with as many several species of Creatures, as the

Earth; and that the vast wilderness of waters contains as many Monsters, and altogether as strange ones, as any in the Desarts of Afrique.'

The sun blinded me as I cycled along. It would be impossible to imagine a hotter day in these parts. All the distances were hazed with heat and there was no colour on anything. On the right the Dingle hills rose up towards Brandon, vague on this hot day; the road dusty, the sun pouring down from a sky pale and cloudless with heat. I passed gladly under the shade of the tree-grown prettiness of Milltown. Just outside the village there are two tall gallauns – one 5ft. high and the other nearly 8 ft. – that stand 5ft. apart as though they mark a grave. These are the Gates of Glory. No one knows how they came by their name, but not far away there is another gallaun known as the Milestone because it stands just a mile from Dingle. It is possible that some great prehistoric building here barred the road to the thickly inhabited headland beyond.

Next came the great curve of Ventry Bay where the sands lay firm as a silver collar and where was fought for a year and a day the great combat between Finn MacCool and Daire, King of the World.

From here a very long, hot, dusty road ran out towards Slea Head – somewhere along it I knew was the famous City of Fahan and the cliff-edge castle of Dunbeg, but I could see no sign of either of them. I came at last to a collection of cottages and small farms, and inquired the way. Dingle is one of the great Gaelic speaking areas of Ireland, but there is no village of Ireland now where an Englishman cannot get direction in his own language. It is said that when the civil servants and others started coming out to the west to learn Irish, the quick-witted Gaels picked up English in half the time their pupils took to learn Irish. I was soon crossing the rock-strewn field that led down to the great fort of Dunbeg. Dunbeg is much the same as the other prehistoric forts of Ireland with dry-stone walls, in places twenty-five feet thick. It stands very near the edge of the cliff that drops to the restless Atlantic. On the other side of the road, to be reached only by climbing up past a small farmhouse not marked in any way, is the site of the great prehistoric settlement of Fahan, called by the Dingle people 'The Town'. Here the hundreds of beehive-huts and walls are constructed of small, grey stones all sea-washed to a flat smoothness and cunningly placed to make the wall faces even and the huts slope neatly. The present day cottages of Coumenoole stand among the huts of a forgotten people, possibly ancestors of these peasants whose lives are almost as simple as theirs.

There are said to be nearly 500 of these 'clochans' scattered over the hillsides, but only the expert would wish to find all of them, for one is much like another, and the few huts reconstructed to show what they were like in use give the impression that life in a beehive hut must have been very limited.

As I came down from Fahan, the sky began clouding with a thunderous, headaching mist. When I turned on to the cliff road I had seen the grey outline of the north coast of the Ring of Kerry, but now the mist came down over it and I wondered if I would ever be permitted to see those fabulous hills. The water, a delicate blue-green, lay motionless as oil and I saw drift through it the fin of a basking shark. I asked a young woman with a child in her arms how far it might be to Dunquin. 'It might be six miles now,' she said, 'but it's a long time since I've been as far myself.'

I cycled on over the little ford at Glenfahan until the road cut into the cliffside round Slea Head. Somewhere along here the Great Blasket Island begins appearing with that slightly ominous, watchful look all large islands have when not far distant from the shore. The road turns under the enormous brow of Mount Eagle, and opposite are the Blaskets – the group of islands and rocks that is the most westerly land of our islands. The only inhabited island is the Great Blasket, 'the next parish to America,' that looks from here like a great snail's shell standing out of the sea.

An hour or so ago it seemed the most perfect day for the crossing to the island. Everything seemed in my favour. Not only was the weather mild, but this was a Sunday when the islanders were over to Mass and anyone of them would gladly row a visitor back in his curragh.

The Blasket community is hardworking but knows real freedom. There is no enclosed land on the island. When a new house is required, a man has only to choose his site and he and his friends build the house from rocks and driftwood, letting the problems of sanitation and water-supply solve themselves. He pays no rent, rates or taxes. The islanders tell you that the government favours them because they speak the best Irish in Ireland. They live by mackerel and lobster fishing and a little sheep-farming. The island owns communally three cows, and each cottager has his chickens and his potato and cabbage patches.

The people are friendly and warm-hearted, and have a great natural gaiety. Time was when the island was full of dancing, singing and story-telling – but now the young people are leaving. The world has changed and they no longer feel bound to accept the hard, primitive life and lonely winters of the Blaskets. Perhaps a fortune awaits them elsewhere – here they will always be poor. Ten years ago over a hundred people lived on the island, now there are only thirty-five; the school was closed in 1941; only one child remains.

Now as I looked at the swell growing on a purple-grey sea and saw the rain slide like a shadow to blot out the furthest rocks, I was afraid there'd be no crossing for me. Below Slea Head the sea churned against the wild, jagged rocks and the small incurving yellow strands. I cycled on quickly, not wanting to get drenched, and sped past Dunmore Head, the westernmost point of the Irish mainland and the burial place of the Prince of Ascule, son of the King of Spain, lost when his galleon, the Santa Maria de la Rosa, sank in Blasket Sound. A casket of gold was buried beside him and has not been disturbed to this day.

I did the downhill run into Dunquin in a matter of minutes over a boneshaking road that left me breathless.

Dunquin – Dun Caoin, the beautiful fort – the most westerly village in Ireland, is a collection of fishermen's cottages with a small, prosperous store kept by one of the famous characters of the west, Kruger Kavanagh. The rain had started to fall before I found his house: it was locked. All the houses were shut and locked and apparently deserted. While the rain teemed down I stood in a shed beside the house, feeling very depressed until, suddenly, the doors of the chapel burst open and the whole village, and most of the inhabitants of the Great Blasket as well, came out laughing and running in the rain. The islandmen bounded over to Kruger's shed and crowded into it until I could not look out. I managed to squeeze a way through and, seeing some people enter the house, I ran to it and was admitted with a welcome that could not have been warmer had I been the family's oldest friend. It was wonderful after the long ride, the rain, the sudden change from warmth to wind and cold, to come into the comfortable living-room with its range alight and all the unexpected appurtenances of a wireless set, photographs of Kruger's famous friends and copies of American periodicals – for Kruger is no ordinary countryman, if indeed any west of Ireland man is an ordinary countryman.

If you ask any man in the west if he's ever been away, he'll say no; after a while he'll probably admit that he did go to America once, but that was just across the water and not a journey in the nature of the word. Kruger had not only been to America but took there a personality that made history in New York.

I was pleased to see Denis O'Dea again. There was also a young man learning the Irish for the Civil Service. Kruger is a famous teacher of Irish and his home is a small college for students, civil servants, actors and others whose work requires good Irish. I was told that at night around the fire here there is more brilliant conversation, more wit, more delving into history and legend, and more original humour, than in any of Dublin's most brilliant centres. Listening to Kruger, I could well believe it, for he alone would keep a party going even if every one else in it was a mute. Soon he was telling me of the period in his history when he acted as

Gallarus Oratory on the Dingle Peninsula is a remarkably well-preserved early Christian monument.

publicity agent for a famous impresario. It is a well-known fact that the Irish run New York and Kruger with his quick tongue and wit, soon had his notices appearing in every paper 'for the sake of the old country and old times.' But that was only one of his many stories and told without Kruger's intonations they would lose their sparkle.

Kruger is not only a knowledgeable but a cultured man and his brother, the famous Sean a Chóta – 'Sean of the Kilts,' from the fact he wore the Irish Kilt – worked upon a massive Gaelic dictionary that was left incomplete at his early death.

While the rain poured down outside, Kruger made tea and talked, then his wife appeared, gentle and dignified, with the natural fine manners of the west. She looked after the company while Kruger went to serve the Blasket men who laid in their week's supplies after Mass on Sunday. Before he went, I asked did he think I could get across that day and he thought it unlikely.

'You'd get across maybe,' he said. 'But you might never get back. Many's the visitor has spent a month or more there waiting for the weather to change,' and he told me the story of the old Indian carpet seller who went to the Blaskets with his arms hung with rugs. While he was going round the cottages, the weather changed and he could not get back again. The islanders keep a guesthouse for stranded visitors and the Indian was put up there while the weeks passed and the winds blew a gale. The upshot was that he stayed on the Blaskets for six months and when he came off he spoke Irish as well as any of them. That's not the end of the story – for when he got back to Dublin he found a Gaelic conference in progress and decided to attend it. He went to the door but was refused admission – at which he swore so long and variously in Gaelic that he was invited in with all honours, for there was none of the delegates could speak the language as he did.

Later, when the rain had stopped, I walked with Denis to see the bathing place and the curraghs lying, black and sleek, upside down on the sand. The heavy sky drifted down at times and hid the islands, and at times they glowed copper brown in an oil-green gloom which heightened the electric colour of the bogland on the cliff top. When we returned, Kruger said they would drive me through Ballyferriter and over the mountains back to Dingle. I was delighted, not only to be saved the long bicycle ride back to Dingle, but to see the sights of the peninsula in such good company. As we drove, Kruger talked, not only about himself, but about this part of the wild Dingle peninsula with its rough, boggy ground, and the small scattered houses with the bare-footed children playing at the gates and the hens pecking the kitchen's earthen floor and the panniered donkey carrying in the turf. It was from cottages like this that somc of the most remarkable of Irishmen originated – from one came the present youngest Cardinal in the Church of Rome; from another a leading statesman, and from half-a-dozen different others, men who had risen to wealth and eminence in the States.

There are, someone once told me, twenty million Irishmen in the States, and most of them come from the Irish peasantry. When they left Ireland they met like a challenge the efficiency and energy of the new world, and soon equalled, and even surpassed, it, yet here life has remained unchanged for centuries.

This is the Ferriter country. We passed through Ballyferriter where the Inn is kept by Eileen Ferriter, a descendant of the great Pierce Ferriter, poet and leader of his people, a fragment of whose castle can still be seen near Sybil Head. In the distance, where the sea sweeps in to form Smerwick Harbour is the site of the ill-fated Fort-del-Oro.

The fluted line of cliffs from Sybil Point to Smerwick is one of the loveliest in all Ireland. The triple points known as the Three Sisters seem to fling back their heads from the sea like a team of horses. The walls of rock

Traditional modes of travel for visitors to the Gap of Dunloe in the mountains near Killarney were pony, trap or on foot.

that drop down to the sea are wild and broken, full of caves and great stacks rising like tusks from the waters. Those who have sailed round this shore say that it is a journey of wonder and fear, the cliffs overwhelming in their magnificence, would offer no harbourage in a storm, and storms are so sudden and frequent here that a yachtsman setting out, takes his life in his hands.

Beyond Ballyferriter we turned off into the hills to find the Oratory of Gallerus. We got out of the car and Kruger led us up a lane that was really a small stream-bed down which the stream, swollen by rain, gushed furiously over the pebbles. We waded through it, using whatever we could find for stepping-stones until we came on the Oratory standing in a field, as neat and flawless as though it had been built yesterday. It was a small building – 22 by 18 1/2ft. – untouched by time, the dry stones perfectly shaped and fitted together to form a building rather like an upturned boat. The effect is of perfect workmanship and artistry that fills one with satisfaction. The inside, which is as finished as the outside, is lit by a semi-circular window. These drystones have been put together with such skill that the Oratory has stood in its grassy field for thirteen hundred years, and there is no reason why it should not stand as long again.

The village of Kilmalkedar near the Oratory is full of the monuments of history and pre-history for which the peninsula is famous.

From the Oratory the road crosses a bleak mountainside, one of the few really deserted areas of the peninsula. Kruger entertained us so we scarcely noticed our surroundings. I asked him about the basking shark I had seen. Was it, I wondered, the same sort as that in the dramatic scene in 'Man of Aran.' Kruger laughed, for the old sharks, he said, were harmless creatures and no one hunted them at all these days. As for the 'Man of Aran' shark, far from being the dangerous monster it was claimed to be, it was only a stuffed skin – no genuine shark being obliging enough to put in an appearance while the film company was on the island.

The weather, having done for my trip to the Blaskets, was brilliant again next day when two visitors from Cork, Michael and Una Gill, took me over the Connor Pass to the fishing lakes of Ballysitteragh. When we reached the pass where I had stood on my first afternoon, the scene looked very different in this early light. The shoulder of hillside which rose like a cliff from the right of the road was slate black in shadow while the valley below lay tender as gauze. We drove down the steep hill and came out into the sunlight of the bogland plain. Michael Gill stopped at the Guards Station at Cloghane to inquire from whom he should get permission to fish the loughs. A large, friendly Guard, lounging at the gate, assured him:

It's all right, I'm sure. There's no need to trouble at all. No one will be saying a word to you. . . . '

The Guards have none of the ponderous self-importance of English police. They wear their authority lightly. The long occupation of Ireland and long revolt, has given a peculiar virtue to police and priests, both of whom come from the people and have their sympathies with the people rather than with the powers that be.

Climbing over rocks and heath, jumping boggy patches, escaping brambles, we got up to the plateau where the lough lay shallow and smooth with cattle standing motionless in the water and the great points of Brandon and its neighbours looming so close, their dangers glossed by the bright light, it seemed a short and easy walk would take us to the top.

On our return we passed near the scene of the Bloody Banquet of Castlegregory. The village, that lies some eight or nine miles along the flat, sandy coast from Cloghane, is named after Gregory Hoare, who built a castle there in the sixteenth century. Old Gregory was at enmity with his neighbour, William Moore, and would not let his son, Black Hugh, marry Moore's daughter, Ellen, with whom the boy was in love. During a fit of rage, Gregory became paralysed and lost his reason, and Black Hugh at once took the opportunity to marry Ellen. When the wedding party, with the bride's father at its head, reached the Hoare castle, Gregory came tottering out and refused the guests admission. Moore, incensed, pushed aside the old man who there and then fell dead upon his own threshold. Silenced and shocked, the revellers dispersed, and the wise women of the village foretold that the marriage would end in tragedy. All went well, however, for a few years until the arrival of Grey in the district to clear up the Fort-del-Oro affair. Ellen was strongly partisan, but Black Hugh prudently decided to support, in appearance anyway, the stronger force. When a company under Colonel Zouche, that included Spenser and Sir Walter Raleigh, arrived to spend the night at Castlegregory, Hugh ordered a feast and, fearing she would speak her mind, locked his wife in her room. Ellen's absence was noticed, and when the wine had gone round several times, his guests began to laugh at Hugh and make jokes about jealous husbands who kept their pretty wives from meeting English officers. Black Hugh, whose temper resembled his father's, had to control himself, but when a servant came to tell him that someone had got into the wine cellar and turned on the taps of the casks, he leapt to his feet and rushed downstairs to find Ellen calmly flooding the floor with wine.

'Do you think you can keep me a prisoner in my room,' she said, 'while you feast with the enemies of our country? I'd rather pour your wine on the good Irish earth than give it to these English swine'. Hugh, beside himself with rage, drew his knife and stabbed her to death. He was arrested by his guest, Colonel Zouche, and next morning, as he was taken from his castle for trial before the Lord Deputy, fell dead upon the very spot where his father had fallen on the ill-omened wedding-day.

From *The Dreaming Shore*

Frank O'Connor

1950

FRANK O'CONNOR was the pseudonym of Cork-born Michael O'Donovan (1903–1966). He first worked as a railway clerk and librarian and was imprisoned for his activities with the Republicans during the Civil War. O'Connor served as a director of the Abbey Theatre and as visiting professor at several universities in the United States. He first achieved success with short stories published in *The New Yorker*. In addition to several short story collections, O'Connor wrote *Guests of the Nation*, *Crab Apple Jelly* and *The Big Fellow*, a biography of Michael Collins. In the late 1940s he travelled throughout the west and southwest of Ireland and wrote *Munster, Leinster & Connaught* about his journey.

Kerry is remarkable for its scenery – when you see it, which, owing to the appalling weather the county enjoys, is very rarely. It is a continuation of the mountain and lake country on the West Cork border, and it can be ravishing, particularly at evening, when the golden light brings up the deep blues and browns of mountain, sea and lake. If it would only stay dry for a few days on end it would be the finest country in the world.

There is not much to see except the scenery; the towns, with the exception of Tralee, are terrible. Outside Tralee there is the old ruined diocesan centre of Ardfert, with the remains of a rather fine Early English cathedral and abbey and bits and scraps of excellent Romanesque. The builders of the cathedral made an attempt to take in the decorated front of the Old Romanesque cathedral, but the shooting was bad, and they only scored a near miss, which makes the front look very odd indeed. Near the shore of Dingle Bay in one of the wildest spots in Ireland, Kilmalchedar, is the ruin of another beautiful little Romanesque chapel, on the site of a very early anchoritic monastery.

The capital is Killarney, which the Romantic movement turned into a sort of tourist resort. In itself it is a depressing hole, too wealthy for its lack of taste, and infested by hotel-keepers, touts, jarveys and boatmen, all with a glib flow of patter which also probably goes back to the Romantic movement. But on the lakes or on the hills above them you are in the world of Scott and Vigny. The most striking spot is the little twelfth-century church of Aghadoe, which has a doorway whose design you can trace through the little church of Clonkeen outside Limerick to the Church on Holy Island in Lough Derg. It commands a tremendous view of lakes and mountain.

From *Leinster, Munster and Connaught*

The Black Valley, also known as Cummeenduff, lies in the mountains to the southwest of Killarney.

Honor Tracy

*c.*1950

THE NOVELIST AND TRAVEL WRITER Honor Tracy (1913–1989) was born at Bury St. Edmunds, Suffolk and educated in London. Before she became a full-time writer she worked first in publishing, then as a foreign reader for a film company. During the Second World War she specialised in Japan at the Ministry of Information. Tracy was a journalist in Dublin from 1946 to 1950, and then a foreign correspondent for British newspapers. Her first book, *Kakemo: A Sketch Book of Post-War Japan*, appeared in 1950. Among her other works are *Silk Hat and No Breakfast, The Ballad of Winter in Castille*, and *Castle Reef.*

The journey to the Blasket Islands was not a very long one in space. Every clear day I saw them from the garden of the house, over the blue waters of the bay, lying out in the Atlantic at the western tip of the Dingle peninsula, dark shadows on the sea. And then all at once they would be invisible, curtained off by the mist. A motor launch would have reached them in half an hour: they were barely twenty miles away as the crow flies. But there was no motor launch and the flight of Irish crows is of academic interest only and without relation to human affairs. There was nothing for it but to rise rather earlier in the morning than I care about and to take, as a beginning, the little green train to Tralee. To cover those thirty-nine miles the little train, pausing thoughtfully at each tiny station, took two hours and twenty minutes; and there was something fine in the leisure of its pace, in its refusal to be hurried, to take itself or its passengers seriously.

At Tralee a wait of three hours for the Dingle bus offered fresh opportunities for meditation; and at Dingle it was disclosed that there was no bus at all to Dunquin, thirteen and a half miles away and the nearest point on the mainland to the Blaskets. There was a bus to Ventry, about half the way along, but it went only twice a week. The local taxis were busy with a wedding or a funeral – in the excitement of it all I have forgotten which. But in Ireland people take an interest in their fellow beings, and never more so than when these are in some kind of difficulty. Their aim then is not only to soothe but to encourage. Urging me not to give way to a facile despair, they led me to the Ventry-Dunquin road and explained that if I would only start walking along it, a turf lorry, a private car or a pony trap was sure to come by – and that before I was fairly out of sight – and take me wherever it was that I wanted to go.

How that Irish kindness, that friendly concern, does warm the heart and ease the mind! How rare, how precious, it is in the world of today! The glow of it was not extinguished – not really – when five hours later I limped into Dunquin with the skin off my heels and a vague sense of having absent-mindedly filled my suitcase with lead. In all that time I had not seen a solitary vehicle, and hardly more than a dozen men working in the fields or on the bog. A young man let me rest my bag on his donkey's back for the time that our ways ran together and entertained me with stories of how the 'flu had carried off all the old-age pensioners the winter before: to the satisfaction, he assumed, of the government fellas in Dublin. And once I went into a little pub by the wayside and asked for a glass of rum to revive my spirits. The old lady behind the bar was incredulous.

'Rum! You never said rum!'

'I did.'

''Tis terrible strong!'

'I hope so.'

'Did you ever take it before?'

'I did.'

Richard and William Morrison designed the neo-gothic castle at Ballyheigue for the Crosbie family in the early years of the nineteenth century.

The old lady looked me up and down and called to someone sweeping the yard outside, 'Mary! Come in, will you? She wants rum.'

Mary came in and said, 'And isn't she right? Isn't rum a very fine drink?'

Warmed by this tolerance, I explained my difficulties and she cried, 'Now isn't that the divil? You missed a ride with the schoolmaster by inches. You'll never walk it, mind.'

And many times in the long hot afternoon I thought I agreed with her. But trudging along on that apparently endless road I saw things which, inside a car, I should certainly have missed. At the end, the very end, it ran up a mountain and down again; and pausing on the saddle with the busy little mountain breeze cooling my ears, I looked back the way I had come, and there were the many rounded peaks of the Kerry Hills swimming in the blue haze of evening, wave upon wave of them, more beautiful than they had ever seemed before, remote and mysterious as the mountains of the moon; and I looked forward down the last lap to the cottages of Dunquin, with the Great Blasket Island lying three miles out like a fat, tawny seal in the fading sunlight, and beyond it, An Tearaght, shaped like a bell, rising from the water with the subtly enchanted air that hangs about the rocks of Leonardo da Vinci.

A whole day had passed in covering the eighty miles round the shores of the bay, and the slow painful method of it was perhaps a better one than shooting across the water in a boat. The world I was entering was separated from the one left behind by more than a twelve-hour journey. Gradually the little cottages dotted about on the hillsides had grown fewer, looked poorer; the faces of the people became harder, more finely modelled; the flowers, the blarney were forgotten, speech became direct and candid. It was an austere, a bitter world in which everything spoke of poverty. Even the animals looked weary of the struggle to get a living as they hobbled painfully along the roads, a front leg shackled to a back to prevent them from straying, and pulled hungrily at the meagre blades of wayside grass.

It was a dying world, too, inhabited by old people living on memories or young ones longing to be away. They could hardly wait, those young people, to exchange their simple, wholesome, laborious lives in that lovely corner of earth for the high wages and debased pleasures, the bustle and confusion, of an English or American town. To be sure, I was to meet that evening in Dunquin three bright young things who appeared to be thoroughly enjoying themselves: but they were not natives. One was a student from Dublin University; one was a vivacious young actress from the Abbey Theatre; and the third . . . dear me, the third! He came from the cottage where I was going to stay and greeted me, a young man in corduroy trousers and gaily checked shirt, with bristly blond hair and calm expressionless features. Surely I had seen that face, not once but many times, before? And yet I hardly expected to find it here. Gaelic streamed from the lips, uttered with the unmistakable intonations of the New World. Its owner had come from California, six thousand miles away, to learn the Irish language in one of the few recesses where it is still spoken every day. There was no particular reason for it, for he was not of Irish descent, and he could hardly be hoping to further a business career in the States: his was the pure, disinterested passion of a real scholar. But I had to tell him I knew not a single word of it and, losing all interest in me, he retired at once, nor was the conversation resumed at any moment of my stay.

The undergraduate and the actress were learning Irish, too. He could not take his degree without it; it was as important to her career, and indeed rather more so than a talent for acting. There was something about the lively, business-like intrusion of people like these into a melancholy, shadowy, decaying outpost that was very comic; and something that was faintly macabre. Every year all through the summer they come and go, poking busily about in the relics of a dying culture. Reverently they copy into their notebooks the evening gossip of old fishermen, with awe they hang upon the prattle of tiny tots: and at the end of it all the little gold ring goes up on their lapels, they are Irish speakers now and voilà! they have one more qualification to become an egg-tester or a pathologist, an inspector of taxes or a politician, at the earliest opportunity . . . .

There was a cloudless sky next morning and the sea was a brilliant cornflower blue. I perched on a rock and waited for the island postman's canoe to put out to sea, coming to fetch the letters and ferry me back with him. But he never came that day, nor the next, nor the one after that. In fact, he telephoned to the mainland to say he should not come at all until the wind had dropped. It began to look as if I must pass my summer lying on the rocks and peering out to sea, shrivelling in the sun like a stranded fish. It did not seem possible that the weather could ever be finer or the sea calmer. At last I was driven to make an arrangement with a local man, which I had hoped to avoid, for if there is one thing the simple Kerryman likes better than a little easy money, it is to make a fool of a stranger. He was a fine, upstanding young fellow with honest blue eyes that looked straight into mine, and the sum that he named was a small fortune. He pointed out that it was little enough and that only the summer before an American gentleman had cheerfully paid twice that amount. Saying that I would think it over, I retired to consult a woman of the islands now living on the shore and to whom I had been introduced by one of the clergy: two good reasons for expecting a valid opinion.

'God forgive him!' she cried, clapping a hand over her mouth and at once added the eternal Irish formula, 'I haven't said anything, now, mind you.'

So I told the young man I should wait for the ferryman after all; but after a protracted negotiation, oriental in its ruse, its use of the go-between and its careful preservation of face on both sides, a bargain was struck with neither party feeling too badly.

The prudence of the island postman became a little easier to understand when I saw the craft in which we were to make the voyage. She was long and narrow, made of nothing but tarred canvas stretched over a delicate wooden frame, and she danced about on the waves as light as a feather, or wriggled uneasily if anyone made a move. We shot out over the clear green water, past the black jagged rocks with white surf foaming angrily at their base, and made for the open sea. The two boatmen laughed and sang and made jokes with each other as their oars flew through the air as if, after all, to leave their little farms or potato patches, their digging or turf-cutting for a few hours was not quite the grave matter, the harm to their interests, they had thought it might be when we discussed the fee:

and in less than an hour they passed shrewdly between the two guardian rocks and pulled in to the runway.

It was not the right day to visit the island: you could not get a true picture of its life on a day like that. The people seemed to be the favoured inhabitants of a paradise. Sunlight twinkled on the water like a million gold coins set spinning; the little fields were bright with flowers; the air was full of the singing of larks and the lazy tumbling of the waves. The sea and the sky ran into each other in a blue that was deep and intense and yet radiant; the sand on the beach was dazzling white; and the whole scene, the islands and the rocks and the gently rounded hills far away over Dunquin had the gay, summery shimmer of Mediterranean lands. But no keen Latin minds were at work here to make the most of natural advantages. No luxury hotels or villas fronted the strand, no large ladies in striking beach clothes toyed with Cinzano beneath gaily striped umbrellas or gambolled with shrieks of merriment at the water's edge. Nothing was to be heard but the cry of birds and the sound of the sea, and nothing human seen but a few bent figures toiling on the land.

I went up the steep winding track into the village. The cottages were built on the side of the hill and with every turn of the track you found yourself looking down on the roofs of those you had just passed. Many of them were in ruins, now, tumble-down crofts of coarse gray stone shouldering each other, miniatures of the ruins lying about all over Ireland. The little house where Tomás O'Crohan wrote his famous book, *The Islandman*, has been stripped of its roof and lies crumbling away in the weather; that of Peggy Sayers, another island author, is standing yet, but Peg herself was on the mainland where, blind and crippled, she kept her bed. The school, where fifty children once learned their lessons, is closed except on Sundays when the old people, who can no longer make the crossing to Mass in Dunquin, go there to say prayers. There was only one child on the island now; they pointed him out to me as something of a curiosity, a bright-faced little man sitting in a canoe on dry land and pretending to row. And the storytellers and the singers and all who made the renown of the island have long since disappeared.

I climbed still higher, up to one end of the village where lived an old lady to whom I was bringing a letter. She was only just out of bed and still combing her few white hairs, for these people are not early risers unless there are cows to be milked, and she had had to sell her cow the Christmas before. She spoke very few words of English but succeeded in making me understand that I was to come again in an hour's time when she would have cleaned the house and made the tea. And off I went, wandering about and talking to all in sight, and came back to find the kitchen as neat

Although many visitors assumed Valentia Island was named for the Spanish city, it derives from Beal Inse, the Irish name for the channel that separates it from the mainland.

as a new pin, with a kettle singing on the hook over the turf fire and a place laid at table with an egg-cup and spoon, and my heart sank, for Ireland is greatly addicted to eggs and this one would make my third that morning. The kitchen was in harmony with the austere spirit of the island, being for all its cleanliness equally devoid of comfort and ornament; the floor was of stone and the chairs of wood, and the white walls were bare except for a holy picture or two, a certificate of the family's devotion to the Sacred Heart and a photograph of the late Dr. Robin Flower, the Irish scholar. It is touching to see how the islanders treasure the memory of that English friend of theirs. They speak as if it were only yesterday that he last came to see them, and ask at once if you are going to see the place where he is buried. In fact he was never buried at all, his ashes having been scattered from one of the island heights as he willed them to be; but in the eyes of the people the ceremony must have had something a little pagan about it, and they perhaps use the circumlocution out of affection for him and their good manners.

The kettle boiled at last, but my prayers succeeded and the hens refused to lay. The old lady was ashamed of them, but there was no help for it, and when I had finished my second breakfast she walked up with me to the top of the hill and we saw, glowing in the sun, the other islands, empty and lifeless as this one was soon to be. And we came down again, and she showed me her little estate, and the sheds with fishing tackle and tools and freshly cut wands of pussy willow that her sons made into lobster pots, when they came back from their day on the bog, cutting turf. Then we had to say good-bye, good will being no substitute for language, and real communication between us being impossible.

On my way down to the tiny harbour a fine young man with dark curls and a broad white grin called out to me; and I confessed, yet again, that I had no Irish, and he replied at once that I was very much better without it. And he went on talking in the beautiful lively English of native speakers, saying how much he wanted to go away, and what a wonderful place London must be, and lamenting that there were no girls on the island. 'No girls at all, think of it,' he said, gravely; and I did think of it, and of him, too, of his charm wasted among the seagulls there and of the brilliant position in a Dublin government office which, with his mastery of the Gaelic, he might have been filling.

The boatmen rowed away over the sparkling sea. I had paid my visit to the Great Blasket Island, the first and perhaps the last. It may be that when I come this way again I shall hear that all the islanders have found the homes they are looking for, and have been absorbed in the life of the mainland. And mingled with the relief of greater comfort and greater security, there will be a melancholy, a sense of having fallen from high destinies: for the islanders share in the human passion for being a little special, a little different from the man next door, and the kindly disparagement in their voices as they speak of the mainland folk is delightful to hear.

I had not been with them when the weather was wild and the wind screaming round their lonely cabins; or when some one fell ill, or a woman began labour, and the doctor could not cross to them; or when the body of one of them was recovered from the sea. Unless one had, one could form no idea of what it is like to be a Blasket Islander. But I carried away a memory of friendly, courageous people, civilized with none of the aids of civilization, yet primitive enough to have kept the sense of wonder, of awe and reverent delight in the natural world alive in their hearts: accepting the end of their way of life with philosophy: indulgently amused at being the object of interest to so fortunate a being as an outsider.

From *Mind You, I've Said Nothing*

Oriana Atkinson

1955

ORIANA ATKINSON (1894–1989) was raised in New York and started publishing poetry at a young age. A contributor to many periodicals, her employment also included social service and personnel work, and a stint in a munitions factory. Her best-selling book *Over at Uncle Joe's* was an account of ten months' residence in Soviet Russia with her foreign correspondent husband at the end of the Second World War. Another best seller was *Manhattan and Me*. Among six other works are a novel, *Big Eyes*, and a historical romance, *Twin Cousins*, with Catskill settings.

From the crucifix you begin to drop downhill to Killarney. The landscape gentles and a blush of faint green begins to color the fields and rocks. Through Healy's Pass there is nothing but grinning, dead-bone rock. But now kind earth slowly takes over. The way is steep and the curves are numerous and a little harrowing, but the relief of vegetation and open sky is so keen that danger is easily forgotten. Slowly, slowly now the rolling hills open into little valleys. Then, if your driver is Irish, like our driver, Sean O'Brien, he will draw up dramatically and say impressively: 'There it is. There's Killarney.'

A string of small dun lakes lying in the folds of a string of colorless hills. After Healy's Pass – poor little Killarney!

Sean O'Brien, reading from his omnipresent guidebook, said, 'Killarney means "The Church of the Sloe."'

'Slow?' I said. 'Church of the *Slow*?' I looked so bewildered that Sean and Miss Witlov laughed.

'"*Sloe*" is a wild plum,' Miss Witlov told me mildly. 'So "Killarney" must mean "Church of the Wild Plum."'

It's a pretty enough name, I suppose, but it seems to me that they might have chosen something more impressive for a place that has become world-famous. It's lovely in Irish – 'Killarney' couldn't be lovelier. But 'Church of the Wild Plum' doesn't seem at all adequate to me.

There on the outskirts of the town of Killarney we had paused at a place called 'Ladies' View' and we could see at once why it was called that. Probably, after Healy's Pass, this was the first place where a really timid lady might look over the panorama with pleasure. And now from Ladies' View we looked across to the Macgillicuddy Reeks. Macgillicuddy's Reeks surprised us a lot.

When we were planning our trip to Ireland, Miss Witlov and I had studied the map of Ireland and had rolled the sonorous Irish names deliciously on our tongues. We had wondered then about the Macgillicuddy Reeks. I thought they were reefs of rock, shoals along a dangerous shore. But they are mountains and now they were all around us. Sean said that one of those mountains was the highest in Ireland – Carrantouhill.

We discussed the reason for this mountain range's having been called 'the Reeks.' We thought perhaps 'reek' meant smoke or mist, because Edinburgh in Scotland is called 'Auld Reeky,' and Edinburgh is a smoky city. These were smoky, misty mountains, half hidden by blowing, smoky mists. (Later I indignantly rejected the explanation of an unsympathetic American with whom I was trying to discuss the meaning of 'reeks.' 'It's my opinion,' he said, 'that Old Man Macgillicuddy was such an unpleasant character that they could only do his reputation justice by naming mountains after him. "Macgillicuddy reeks to heaven – Macgillicuddy reeks high as those mountains!" That's what the Irish meant. It's perfectly simple.')

The plain truth of the matter turns out to be that a reek is a round-topped mountain. Who Macgillicuddy was I never did find out.

Near the Ladies' View there was the usual ruined castle. At one time I would have thought that any castle would pique my interest and attention, but such is human nature that I had already become somewhat callous to these ancient buildings. In Ireland they're all over the place. They dominate and sadden many an Irish town. Yet the people who live in their very shadows seem to know little or nothing about the ruins. 'That's more of Cromwell's work,' you will be told, as though the dust and disaster of his passing was still in the air. I was sorry that I had not paid more attention when my hard-working history teachers tried to pound the story of Cromwell into my head. I resolved to find all about Cromwell as soon as I could. A man whose bloody thumb print is plain all over any country is worth investigating. I began to sympathize more fully with our own Southerners who are still bitter about Sherman's terrible march from Atlanta to the sea and all the other times of the torch and the terror in the War Between the States. In our South, the surrender to overwhelming odds happened in 1865; and although the memory of this sad time is still bitter in many hearts, the country itself has long ago wiped away most of the scars and ravages left by that war. After all, as Americans count time, 1865 is very long ago. In Ireland the work of Cromwell's men stands plain to see in every field and town the country through: 1641 is today in Ireland.

Before the road near Ladies' View was another reminder of times gone. This was a small stone cross, one of the hundreds standing pathetic and solitary by mountain paths and valley streams. 'Wherever you see one of the crosses,' Sean told us, 'that's to mark the place where some rebel died fighting for Irish freedom.' I don't know why one lonely little rebel cross should be so much more impressive that a whole cemetery full of crosses. Yet somehow the sight of one simple stone tears the heart and reminds the visitor that here, at this very place, freedom gave a throb just before one heart ceased to beat in her defence.

After you get settled in your hotel and make a few excursions around the neighborhood, you may perhaps feel more enthusiastic about it and sympathize with Michael Balfe, the Irish composer and poet who wrote these lines in its praise:

By Killarney's lakes and fells,
Emerald isles and winding bays,
Mountain paths and woodland dells,
Mem'ry ever fondly strays,
Bounteous Nature loves all lands,
Beauty wanders everywhere,
Footprints leaves on many strands,
But her home is surely there.
Angels fold their wings and rest
In that Eden of the west:
Beauty's home, Killarney,
Ever fair Killarney!

Killarney's loveliness cannot be denied; its sweet vistas, opening mistily against cloud-filled skies, remain in the memory forever after. Yet you, like me, may feel that there are other places in Ireland equal to, if not surpassing that world-famous Killarney. The beauty of Glengarriff tears the heart; Limerick has a charm all its own; Tipperary is worthy of the homesick song written in its honor. But it's hard to break the news to an Irishman. It assaults an old myth and spoils an ancient dream. When an Irishman sighs 'Ireland' most of the time he means 'Killarney.'

The town itself is frankly a tourist town. It draws its life from catering to tourists from other parts of Ireland, and from what the Irish call 'cross-channel' visitors, not liking to pronounce the word 'English,' no doubt. Lately more and more Americans are discovering Killarney, stirring up mixed emotions in their Irish hosts.

The Irish are eager to have more visitors from the 'dollar areas' – Canada and the United States. Killarney is polished up and smartened and the 'Welcome' is plain on the mat. But the over-all air of this holiday place is not one of raucous, unbuttoned enjoyment. It is, as everywhere else in Ireland, gentle and restrained. The Irish have strict ideas about propriety in public places and they never forget them. Their velvet voices

The ruins of the old mansion at Carhan near Caherciveen where Daniel O'Connell, the Liberator, was born in 1775.

are never raised and prim decorum is always observed. The heavy hands of church, teacher and parent guide Irish behavior. Nobody shouts at you to 'hurry-hurry-hurry to fill your face' with hot dogs or hamburgers or hot buttered corn. There is one so-called Coca-Cola booth, but Americans can hardly recognize the national tipple. Concy Island, Broadway, Atlantic City, Hollywood, the sly, sleazy honk-tonkity of New Orleans just could not happen in Killarney. Killarney is well behaved, calm and refined. Americans may be surprised by all this, but they admire it and find it a nice change from American playplaces.

From *The South and the West of It*

Kate O'Brien

1958

KATE O'BRIEN (1897–1974) was born in Limerick and educated locally and at University College Dublin. She first worked as a journalist and translator. Her first work was a play, *Distinguished Villa*, which ran for three months in London in 1926. Her novel *Without My Cloak* won the Hawthornden Prize in 1931, establishing her reputation as a new voice in Irish literature. Deeply interested in Spanish literature, O'Brien travelled frequently in Spain and wrote several books with Spanish settings. Her best-known works are *The Land of Spices*, *Mary Lavelle* and *That Lady*.

Yet such as it is in its haphazardry – do I leave it and stroll home from Cork to the Shannon shore without as much as a step aside into Kerry? I shall have to. I funk Kerry. It is, I suppose, the most renowned for beauty of all the thirty-two counties of Ireland. Antrim may be a runner-up; and Sligo most certainly should be – for Sligo is magnificently strange and lovely. But I have known it, this now renowned Yeats country, very briefly so far, and only with my hurrying eyes. I do not know Sligo to stay about in, to walk and talk in, to delay and consider; and as for Donegal, its great northern neighbour, I have only once just barely got my toes over the border – so of neither of these proven Paradises of the eclectic can I venture even inwardly to form an impression.

With Kerry I am not in so poor a case. The Kingdom being part of Munster and bordering Limerick I have found myself astray amid its splendours now and then: I have stayed in Parknasilla and in Glenbeigh: I know Caragh Lake and Castleisland and the Dingle Peninsula and The Ring. I can identify Brandon's gloomy head: I have seen charming Waterville and Daniel O'Connell's sad Derrynane, and I know the road into beautiful West Cork. But so far I do not know Kerry with anything like love. The loss is mine. But no one can love *all* the manifestations of beauty.

Many years ago, when I fell in love with Spain someone more travelled than I said to me: 'It is improbable now that you will ever really love Italy.' It was to be long before I put this surmise to a test – but I thought it a poor one; for how, on the evidence, could one *not* love Italy?

I found that one need not – while being enchanted, overwhelmed, delighted, amused and sometimes exalted and exultant.

Kate O'Brien

For contrary Spain had conditioned me deeply; irrationally but in bare truth she held my heart, against all the boundless and riotously civilised splendours of her sister that she so coldly contradicts. It seems true that because of Spain I have not fallen in love with Italy.

And because of Clare and Connemara I have not given any of my heart to Kerry. But Kerry, like Italy, has the heart of the whole world – so one absentee from her felicities will not be missed. It is a proud region, prouder that its voluptuous aspect may suggest – and it has cause for pride: for its part, always forthright, often tragic, in Irish history; for its leading place in literature and language, its Courts of Poetry, its great Pierce Ferriter and Egan O'Rahilly and Owen Roe O'Sullivan, its conservation of the people's lore and stories and of the living Gaelic speech – all of this with Kerry's twentieth-century intelligence and liveliness give it place and distinction among the counties. And when all this is said and more besides, it owns, it *still* owns Killarney. For which the whole world owes it something. But then the whole world comes, from time to time, to pay that something. And I understand that Kerry is not shy in collecting beauty's fees.

I remember Muckross, near Killarney. The abbey, a neglected Franciscan ruin beside the Torc Lake, commands a graveyard of the O'Sullivans; and I by chance attended a funeral there of one of the name, many years ago. The child we had to bury was, if I remember, no more that fifteen years old or so. She was one of many sisters and brothers, all young: her mother was a very beautiful dark woman of Limerick, her father a fair man, of Killarney. It was late autumn, cold: last, flaming leaves hung from desolated trees, white mist circled beyond the ruined monastery over the lake; the crooked tombstones were all but hidden in rich, decaying grasses, weeds. The whole of Kerry had crowded through the rain, high and low, to honour the awful sadness. Priests went about their business in white surplices and the grave received the slim coffin.

I shall always remember the frieze that mourning family made against the cloister wall – all in black, and the black and the gold heads of the sisters, the mother, black-mantillaed and bent; the straight young boys bareheaded, very still. They seemed for one moment of farewell to the little sister as if eternal, as if standing there to represent all human loss, all patience, all unanswered question. And the rain streamed down on their mourning elegance, their brief, immortal grace.

Not long afterwards, in the Old Vic Theatre in London, watching Orphelia's funeral in Tyrone Guthrie's production of *Hamlet* in modern dress – when Hamlet was played by an unknown young actor called Alec Guinness and the Queen by our Irish actress, Veronica Turleigh – as the rain dripped down over the tombs on the stage and off great black umbrellas held above the heads of the ladies of the court by footmen, and when Gertrude, beautiful, slender, all in black, bent over the grave – 'I had thought to deck thy bridal bed . . . sweets to the sweet . . . ' and the flowers fell from her hands – I remembered Muckross Abbey and another funeral, Shakespeareanly presented, in real rain and real grief.

From *My Ireland*

Brendan Behan

1962

BRENDAN BEHAN (1923–1964) was born in Dublin to a family steeped in the nationalist movement. He joined the Fianna at the age of ten, and the Irish Republican Army at fifteen. In 1939 he was arrested in Liverpool for carrying explosives and served three years in Borstal, which provided the inspiration for his *Borstal Boy*. Deported in 1941, he was sentenced in Ireland to fourteen years for shooting a policeman with intent to kill. This experience gave him material for his play *The Quare Fellow*. Released on an amnesty, Behan worked as a house painter while writing articles. In 1958 a London production of his play established his reputation, which was confirmed by his second play, *The Hostage*.

I worked in this area once – in Caherdaniel – on the pious task of trying to restore Daniel O'Connell's old home. He's by way of being a saint now in Ireland, but that didn't make the shop-keepers put their hands in their pockets, between their visits to Lough Derg and Croagh Patrick, to help on the work, and the old house is still there falling into rack and ruin, if I may coin a phrase.

Near by, at one part of a very lonely road overlooking the bay, there was a shooting – about twenty years ago – and the police came down in droves but couldn't find out anything about it. So one policeman dressed as a tinker, and he went to an old lady living beside the house in which the shooting took place. The shot must have nearly deafened her.

'Would you give me some hot water,' he said, 'for to make a cup of tea, if you please?' Which she did and they carried on a conversation in Irish. During the talking, he said to her: 'I'm a tinker,' which aroused her suspicions immediately for tinkers, as a rule, don't speak Irish – but as she hadn't very much English he had to speak Irish to her. He talked about the weather, the crops and one thing and another and 'Tell us,' he said, 'wasn't that a terrible thing that happened up in the house yonder when the man was shot?'

Brendan Behan

'Oh,' says she, 'I never heard anything of that,' though, as I say, the shot must have deafened her barring her being deaf already which she didn't seem to be. So he asked her a lot of questions and to each one of them she answered she didn't know, she didn't know.

'Tell me, ma'am,' says he, 'do you know anything?' And he pointed out over the Atlantic Ocean to the Blasket Islands lying out in the bay and he said, 'Tell me, ma'am,' he says, 'do you know the names of those three islands out there?'

'I couldn't tell you, sir,' she said, 'They weren't there when I'd gone to bed last night.'

The same Blasket Islands form the last points of Europe before America. Up to 1946 or so there were still families living on the biggest island – not getting much of a living, as far as we call it living, but contented enough with the little they could get from the few sheep they could keep. Three books – good ones – came out of this small community of a few hundred people. One of them entitled simply *Peig* was by one of the oldest of the islanders, Peig Sayers. She was married to a man of English descent – how people with names like Sayers and Perkins and Piggott got to these outlandish places I don't know, except that the English must be as good at travelling to strange places as the Irish. Peig, in fact, wrote two books, but perhaps the two books from the Blaskets best known are: *The Islandman* and *Twenty Years A-Growing*. The first is by Tomás Ó Criomhthain and was translated into English by Robin Flower, a Keeper in the British Museum, who himself wrote two of the best books ever written about Ireland: *The Irish Tradition* and *The Western Island*. The other was written by Maurice O'Sullivan, a policeman (if I have to say a good word for him myself) which also appeared in Penguins, some years ago. All three are dead now, the Lord have mercy on them, because as Ó Criomhthain said, we shall not look upon their like again. Nobody lives on the islands now; they have all been moved to the mainland with the help of Government grants and the like, but nobody can say if they're any way happier or not.

Years ago, when the last inhabitants of the Blaskets were moved to the mainland, I was lying on what passed for a bed in Mountjoy Jail in Dublin doing fourteen years. I thought of the wonderful kind people they were and the free and independent, if frugal, lives they and their ancestors had on those islands, their eras of quiet happiness there on the uttermost fringe of Europe, and I wrote, in Irish, a poem lamenting the death of the islands. In translation, it goes roughly like this:

The great sea under the sun will lie like a mirror,
Not a boat sailing, not a living sign from a sinner,
The golden eagle aloft in the distance the last
Vestige of life by the ruined abandoned Blaskets.

The sun will be gone, the shadow of night spreading
As the moon, rising, through a cloud coldly stretches
Its ghostly fingers over the silent earth
Where, wracked, the shells of the houses stand deserted.

– Silent save for the birds all homeward flying
Glad to be back, their heads on their breasts lying,
And the wind soughing, softly a half-door swinging
By cold wet hearths, their fires forever extinguished.

The Dingle Peninsula is still one of the places where Irish is spoken as the everyday language of the people and even then, it's only on the far tip of the Peninsula. You get the older people, though, still coming in to Dingle who have nothing but Irish and, of course, some of the pub-keepers there make it their business to know what they are being asked for. Kerry Irish is a bit different from what they speak in the West Galway or Donegal areas – though not any more different than the German they speak in Prussia is different from what they speak in Bavaria; and God knows what Zomerzet man would understand a word out of a Yorkshire man's mouth, lavin' aside, your honour, the varieties of English spoken in Scotland or Wales, which as the world and his mother knows, are outlandish enough for anyone's lifetime.

One of the simplest examples I can give of the difference between the dialects is, indeed, the name of the language itself. Anglicised, the name of the Irish language is Gaelic; but it is only in Donegal that you will find the pronunciation remotely approaching that Anglicised version. . . .

The Dingle Peninsula is one of the most beautiful parts of Ireland – long silver strands deserted even in high summer, and I hope it remains that way, though the tourist people seemed determined to turn the place into a kind of English south coast. Ballyferriter, the last village before America, is a place I know well with its four good pubs resting snugly under the shadow of Mount Brandon or, if I may say so with proprietary pride, Brendan's Mountain – named from St. Brendan the mariner who is said to have discovered America about five or six hundred years before Columbus. A very decent and civil people, the Ballyferriter people – I remember one year being in a pub there late at night, during the time when the old licensing laws obtained. The pubs were supposed to shut at half past ten but, if you had travelled more than three miles – to have your pint among that kind congenial company – you were entitled to have the benefit of the *bona fide* provisions of the law up to midnight. None of us there that night lived further than a mile away, I need hardly say. At about eleven o'clock, the barman asked us if we'd mind moving outside and up the mountain a bit, as the police had sent word that they intended to carry out a raid at about a quarter past eleven. The barman, having replenished our glasses, led us out the back door and told us to go on up about a couple of hundred yards, and not to make too much noise while we were out there, as it would only upset the police if they had to take any action against either proprietor or patrons. It was a lovely starlit night and warm, too: and one of my most cherished recollections is of sitting out there on the side of Mount Brandon, looking at the mountain opposite called the Three Sisters framed against the clear moonlit sky and the quiet shimmering Atlantic, a pint of the creamiest Guinness in my hand as I conversed in quiet Irish with a couple of local farmers. After about three-quarters of an hour, the police having finished their business, the barman came out and beckoned us back and, with the relaxation of the nervous strain we had undergone, what could we do but sing until two o'clock or so – the memorable haunting Irish songs of the area, to which I was coaxed into adding a number of my own native songs from Russell Street, Dublin.

Further west than Ballyferriter is Dunquin, famous for the guesthouse of the legendary 'Kruger' Kavanagh, the friend of many Hollywood film-stars, various American gangsters, boxers, politicians and similar sporting personalities. The late Monsignor 'Paddy' Browne, President of University College, Galway, until his death a couple of years ago, used to stay all summer in a bungalow near by, which now, I think, is owned by his niece, Máire MacEntee, daughter of Ireland's Deputy Prime Minister and now married to Conor Cruise O'Brien. 'Paddy' Browne was a mathematician but he also was a fine Irish-speaker and scholar, and translated many classical Greek plays into Irish as well as Dante's *Divine Comedy*.

From *Brendan Behan's Island*

Robert Mitchum

1969

ACTOR ROBERT MITCHUM (1917–1997) is best remembered for his tough guy roles, especially in westerns and war films. Born in Connecticut, he was riding box cars at the age of twelve, and at fourteen he was sentenced to a Georgia chain gang. He started out as an extra, then graduated to B-Westerns in the early 1940s. Best known for such films as *The Story of G.I. Joe*, *Out of the Past*, *The Night of the Hunter*, and *Cape Fear*, Mitchum came to the Dingle Peninsula in 1969 to play the role of the schoolteacher in David Lean's film *Ryan's Daughter*.

By the time I got there, all of the accommodations were pretty much taken up. I don't know where David was living. Bobby and Sarah had a place. Johnny and Mary Mills had a pleasant little cottage. So, they gave me a hotel. It had nine rooms numbered one to ten – I never could figure that out. Upstairs, at one end of the hall, the sign said 'Bath' and 'T-I-L-E-T' – at the other. It was $450 a month. Furnished it with a bunch of directors chairs. All the stand-ins would stay there. Visitors would stay there. In Ireland it doesn't get dark in the summertime until 10.00 p.m. By the time crew would come back, when I wasn't working, I'd be cooking. There was no place to eat around there. I had a dozen people for dinner every night.

From *Mitchum: In His Own Words*

Rebecca West

1971

BORN IN LONDON to a family that originated in North Kerry, Cicely Fairfield (1892–1983) took the pen name Rebecca West, from a character she once played in an Ibsen play. West soon gave up the stage to become a militant feminist journalist. She dared attack the established thinkers of the day, including H.G. Wells with whom she later had a son. On the eve of the Second World War, West travelled to the Balkans and wrote *Black Lamb and Grey Falcon* about her time there. After the war she covered the Nuremberg trials and wrote *The Meaning of Treason*. In 1971 she travelled to Kerry to visit the houses where her ancestors had lived, and wrote her impressions in a letter to her brother and sister-in-law.

Life has been stirring – I went at the beginning of September to Ireland with Lettie to visit the tombs and homes of our ancestors, which was really a beautiful trip, and the more pleasant because the distances are so short – you can't motor more than 100 in a day, you run out of space, not as anywhere else of time. The country was lovely. Cork and Kerry (where my father's people lived) have fuchsia hedges and vast patches of wild montbretia and datura, and the Dingle Peninsula (which was the seaside place where my father always went as a little boy) is like a blanched, bone-coloured Greece. The lovely little 18th-century house where my father was born, has been completely gutted by a prosperous dentist who has been able to express his aesthetic self; but the very nice house where the last Denny to live in Kerry lived (as parish priest where there were in fact no Protestants) has been bought by a Washington lawyer who has retired there, and it reveals itself as a most beautiful small house. Ballyseedy House (where my cousins lived and from which my grand-father and grand-mother were married) is a lonely hotel but a most amusing house – it is a beige Regency house, and beside it apparently a Tudor palace two storeys high. The Blennerhassetts built the house in 1832, the Palace was then solely ruins about 4 ft high. They built up to two storeys high and put turrets on – as a screen for the stables. The funny thing about Ireland is that there are lots of houses – large and small – which have been allowed just to fall down through sheer neglect. There are agricultural cottages quite near my grandfather's shooting-lodge, but when my grandfather moved out, nobody went to live there and the roof just fell in, and it is a ruin (a lovely little house, doll-sized). It really is a strange feeling – it's as if one was on a Western frontier in U.S.A. and the extending forces had not gone on to California and the Pacific but had retired. There was some hope for us, I thought, in

Rebecca West

the way that the Fairfields and the Dennys and the Rowans and the rest of our family did do useful things in this wild place – they had built harbours and canals and roads. But it was hateful now – only sometimes something dangerous showed – I got out of the car when we were in a lovely little village called Sneem, and there were boys in the road scuffling and playing with pistols. A woman grinned at me and said happily, 'The lads are playing they're in Belfast.'

From a letter to Edmund and Vita Fairfield

Philip Ward

1972

PHILIP WARD WAS born in Harrow and studied at London, Perugia, Coimbra and in Lebanon. Ward began his career in librarianship, working in London, Libya, Egypt and Indonesia, before becoming an editor, translator and publisher. A prolific writer, Ward has travelled widely and is the author of numerous travel guides. Among his writings are poetry, plays and short stories. Non-fiction subjects are diverse, such as library science, cataloguing, literary appreciation, bookbinders and a dictionary of common fallacies. He has also contributed to several books. Some of his works appear under the pseudonym Darby Greenfield.

If I were to suggest, to top Baron Munchausen's *Narrative of his marvellous travels,* that Rudolf Erich Raspe (who wrote it) was employed in Muckross copper mines and died here of scarlet fever, I suppose you wouldn't believe me, unless you checked the entry for his burial in the local parish register. Well, the date to check is 19 November 1794, where the great story-teller, liar and embezzler is described as a 'miner.' There's glory for you.

Now if you were to emerge from Killarney's railway station between Park Road and Countess Road, you'd pass the Hill of the Martyrs. That's where they hanged Piers Ferriter. Did you ever tell how it was? Well now, Piers Ferriter was a passionately pro-Irish landlord of Anglo-Norman descent, as you'd guess by the name, and did a few great deeds, like the taking of Tralee in 1641, but at the end he died by treachery. He was the last Kerry captain to submit to Cromwell, and in history Cromwell broke his promise of safe-conduct and hanged him in 1653. The fiction is better.

Hunted by everyone, he gave everyone the slip until one fine day they cornered him and brought him for execution to Killarney. A priest gave him a fragment of the consecrated wafer, and told him to keep it under his tongue, for until he spat it out or swallowed it down he could not die. Three times they strung Piers Ferriter up and three times the rope broke. In the old days such a miracle meant certain salvation for the noose's victim, but as he swaggered off a free man he suddenly stopped with a shout of defiance. 'I'll never live to be called the leavings of a rope' and as he spat out the holy wafer he offered his neck to the noose again, for the last time.

Off the road from Killarney to Killorglin I bore right and uphill to Aghadoe, where a 13th-century round castle stands in the middle of a moated square. Northeast of the castle is the 12th-century church in the grounds of S. Finian's monastery established five hundred years earlier. Two grave-slabs portray the Crucifixion and the Descent from the Cross, and you can see an Ogham stone in the chancel. The church is interesting for the clumsily-reconstructed west doorway, but the round tower is no more than a stump. The view from here is remarkable, Killarney town hidden behind trees low on the left, Lough Leane embracing Ross, Inishfallen and Rabbit Islands, and the highest hill in the distance to the right Carrantuohill (3400 feet) in the range called the MacGillicuddy's Reeks. That's where we're making for now.

Beaufort Bridge, roughly halfway to Killorglin, has a sign-post to the Gap of Dunloe. A car can go as far as 'Kate Kearney's Cottage' but then, unless you walk, you'll take a slow jaunting-car (there are always a dozen available) or ride a horse to the Gap. According to Killarney tourism authorities, there is a fixed rate of £1 per person return for a seat in a car or on a horse, and cars are legally entitled to take this route, though woe betide the independent spirit who tries to dispute either matter with the jarveys. Specify that you want to go to the Upper Lake in the jaunting-car, otherwise you are likely to turn back without an explanation after three miles. The Gap reminded me inevitably of the *Siq* through which riders to Petra pass on their way to 'the rose-red city half as old as time' but if Petra is well-nigh waterless, Dunloe sees three lakes rising, one after the other: Black Lake, Cushwally and Auger, under the looming cliff of the Purple Mountain. The boat trip from the Upper Lake to Lough Leane is one of the pleasantest ways of spending a summer afternoon imaginable, but there are some rapids to negotiate before the meeting of the waters of Muckross Lake and Lough Leane.

North Kerry starts at Tarbert, with its hourly car-ferry from Killimer in Clare. Out of Tarbert you can head for the coastal resort of Ballybunion, where the bank clerks pretend they're drunk and the parish priests pretend they're sober, or the market town of Listowel, the literary capital of Kerry that has given Ireland George Fitzmaurice, Maurice Walsh,

The ruin of a 16th-century castle, once a Fitzmaurice stronghold, overlooks the popular bathing strands at Ballybunion.

Seamus Wilmot, Joe O Connor, Bryan Macmahon, Tim Danaher and above all John B. Keane.

I made straight for the pub run by John B. Keane, the best Irish playwright since Brendan Behan. In his ironic *Self-Portrait*, he tells how he was christened John, and later added the B. for Brendan, saint of travellers. Once, when he was attending a posh premiere of one of his plays in Dublin, he came more and more restive as the Dublin actors failed to bring alive the nuances of his West Kerry characters, and when he heard a genteel city voice say 'heaps of turf,' he was heard to call out from the row in some anguish, 'hapes, man, *hapes* o'bluddy turf' and predictably brought the house down.

On another occasion he was invited to see a company giving his first play, *Sive*, in English in Galway while his *Big Maggie* was on in Irish at the Taibhdhearc in the same city. He went to *Sive*, but to his astonishment the producer had cut a whole scene with tinkers, a scene which adds greatly to the impact of the play. He was muttering about this in stage whispers for some time until a line which went something like 'I hear voices,' upon which John B. roared out, 'You . . . well *do* hear voices. Where the . . . hell are my . . . tinkers?' upon which the performance collapsed in disarray, the audience yelling their approval of the author's intervention.

From *Come with Me to Ireland*

Peter Somerville-Large

1980

PETER SOMERVILLE-LARGE was born in Dublin, to a West Cork family. Educated at Trinity College Dublin, he spent the next decade abroad, working at such jobs as gold miner and wharfee. He has written extensively about Ireland in such books as *The Coast of West Cork*, *From Bantry Bay to Leitrim*, and *The Irish Country House*. He has also written books about his journeys to distant places: *To the Navel of the World* relates his travels in Tibet and Nepal, and *Tribes and Tribulations* his journey in Yemen. When Somerville-Large was in his teens, his father bought an island off the Kerry coast and he spent many summers there.

On another overcast winter day I arrived in Killarney by the Dublin train. I had come down just before St. Brighid's Day, the first day of spring, to witness old traditions that survive in Kerry.

A shrine on the platform proclaimed 'God wishes to establish in the world devotion to the Immaculate Heart (Our Lady of Fatima)' above the official notice 'All change here for Tralee and Castlemaine.' In the Gents, each cubicle was topped by rows of ferocious spikes like spears to keep out invaders. I went over to the comfortable and decorous Great Southern Hotel and sat on a sofa in the pillared lobby to drink coffee. I recognized the hall porter whom I had known years ago. His uniform flashed with silver and gold under the chandeliers. Among the green velvet sofas we remembered mutual dead acquaintances.

'Oh, he's long gone . . . '

'The children didn't come to much . . . a couple took to the drink . . .'

'God rest . . . '

'Drink took him . . .'

'Ah well, he was a nice man.' There was no gloom in the sweet melodious Kerry voice.

The scent of chips wafted down the street where outside the cinema a queue formed in the rain to see a film called *The Black Bitch*. There was evidence that St Brighid's Day offered opportunities for commerce. In souvenir shops St Brighid's crosses were attached to cards full of explanation. 'St Brighid's feast is at Candlemas when the days are so much longer that a candle can be dispensed with . . . The days are then a cockstrike longer, the footsteps of a cock on a gentle evening when his crop is full . . . ' What did it mean? Could a tourist – if any existed in February – make sense of it? Outside the chip shop a group of small itinerant children dressed in gaudy clothes stood in the rain. A boy in a blue dressing gown, his face blackened, wearing the suggestion of a mask, huddled beside two girls in bright pink dresses and crumpled leather boots. Across their noses was pinned yellow gauze.

'Something for the Biddys,' they whined.

'Those kids hunt in packs,' the shopkeeper selling crosses complained. 'They take advantage of the saint. The Council should do something . . . it's bad for business and gives a bad impression to visitors.' Besides him a notice for the Biddy Ball offered Bar Facilities and a prize for the Biddy of the Eighties.

The bus took me to Loo Bridge where brown hills were scattered with grey rocks and spotted yellow gorse and amber water roared and frothed under the bridge. There were a few farmhouses, some old tobacco signs and herds of wet cattle belonging to hill farms hidden in sticks of winter fuchsia. Dominating the place were two rounded hills, the Paps, Da Chich Anann, the breasts of Anu or Danu, Celtic goddess of plenty, responsible for the fertility of Munster. Her sister deity, Brighid, was Celtic patroness of poetry and learning. Brighid's Christian namesake took on ancient mythology and ritual. Her feast day, the 1st of February, coincides with Imbolg, the pagan festival of spring. She was born at sunrise, neither within nor without a house, was fed with the milk of a magical white cow with red ears, and used to hang her wet cloak on the rays of the sun.

Under the breasts of the goddess of plenty Mrs. Lynch was supervising the celebration of the first day of spring. She was dressed in a belted mackintosh and a black hat and scarf and her face was painted. The pagan schoolhouse was packed with Biddys. Everyone was dancing to music provided by an accordion, a mouth organ and a tin whistle. There were a good many children with masked faces, boys and girls dressed in pinafores and scarves. A man from Radio Telefis Eireann making recordings was also dressed up, in an old coat with a silk scarf draped across his face. He held the microphone to a girl who sang in Irish in praise of Brighid. Next a boy in a skirt sang like a linnet, Brighid's own bird, a song about Irish resistance to English perfidy. Then there was more dancing, arms pressed to sides, thump of feet before the fire.

Outside a full moon rose over the Paps. 'It's a good Brighid's evening. That will mean a good harvest.' The people love St Brighid round here, added Mrs. Lynch, who had been to hiring fairs as a girl and could remember the time when crooked rush crosses were made to protect man and beast and not to be sold to tourists. Born in the sixth century Brighid united the pagan and Christian worlds. The little cowherd ousted her pagan namesake, the stern patroness of divination, prophecy, healing and the smith's craft.

All the Biddys were outside now. A boy dressed as a girl carried a collecting tin and the brideóg, a large pink doll wrapped in an orange shawl wearing a mitre decorated with St Brighid's cross. They were getting into cars to follow the saint's wanderings around the countryside. The first farmhouse they came to was empty, but at the second they were welcomed in. The woman of the house watched the group dance while the RTE man made his recording before they were given tea, bread, butter and cake and coins were thrust into the tin. Then on to the next farmhouse and more dancing, more waves of music from the musicians, more tea. The dancers romped on the concrete floor; a dog barked, hens cackled in their runs and St Brighid's night passed away into another year.

From *The Grand Irish Tour*

Edna O'Brien

1986

EDNA O'BRIEN grew up at Tuamgraney, County Clare, and wrote from an early age. She studied at the Pharmaceutical College of Ireland in Dublin, and practised pharmacy for a short time before devoting herself to writing. She quickly established her literary reputation with the publication in 1960 of her first novel, *The Country Girls*, soon followed by the novels *The Lonely Girl*, *Girls in Their Married Bliss*, and *August Is a Wicked Month*. O'Brien has since published many more novels, as well as writings that include short stories, poetry and plays.

Heavy snow had begun to fall. The slated roofs looked like houses from somewhere else. The Brandon Mountain with its cope of snow had all the majesty of the Himalayas. I was setting out for a jaunt in a pony and trap with my inebriate friend of the night before. He had promised to give me the low-down.

True to his trade, he had words of praise for all nationalities, then said that I seemed very educated and that I must be a schoolteacher. He decided to call me Edwina because he once knew an Edwina with a face like mine.

'Tallywack and tandem,' he shouted as he took hold of the reins, and warned me to sit well back in the seat for balance. The little cob, excited at the novelty of a journey in stark winter, set out at a dizzy canter.

'A brave gay morning it is, Edwina,' he said.

'A fierce cold morning,' I thought, wondering how long we would stay out and lamenting the fact that I did not see adversity as a source of inspiration.

'Jesus, we'll make a day of it like the gintry,' he says, as he swerved into a side-road, sensible from the point of view of avoiding traffic but perilous for the little cob who was without shoes. Hedges bulged and sagged under the weight of snow and the tiny fields were like virginal cubes without even a bird's faint track. The silence was so immense that one felt it would be possible to alert a friend across the sea in America.

'Make a wish now, girl, 'cos we're crossing a sthrame.' Then he expressed his own wish, which was to win the sweep, but countered it with the fact that health was everything, that health was a gift from God.

'You're handy with the pencil,' he said, as I wrote down some sage utterances, such as 'A friend is worth a thousand enemies.' He seemed disappointed because I was not a Yank, as he had a pile of cousins in America and more in 'Toranto' and born gentlemen they were and when they came in the summer they drove around with him and stayed out till all hours. For no reason he then launched into song, having a hoarse and tuneless voice.

'Very nice,' I said, to be civil.

'Christ, 'tisn't a song at all, only an auld 'rincain.' He knew singers though, real tallywack ballad singers, 'Christ can they drink, they get sober on whiskey, they're so used to it and 'tis a bad drink, whiskey is, unless you have a cold, and sure this time of year you couldn't go long without it, 'tis like hay to a horse, and yes the country had picked up a pile, and there was good dole and sure the money crowd come in the summer, mad about Ireland because 'tis frightful old, 'tisn't in book or paper how old it is, but that there is nowhere on God's earth to beat it.' Other homilies followed, such as that the Irish are easily led but can't be driven, and that the wind does be fresh in the mornings.

We passed two people, Germans who were out for a constitutional and whom he hailed with lavish and loving expostulations. Soon after, a bungalow with 'Chien Féroce' on the gate, a fact corroborated by the bounding arrival of four snarling and primeval dogs, who avalanched upon us with a venom that sent the poor cob teetering to her knees. We had to get out of the trap, to contend with the cob's excitability, our own nerves and the beasts who seemed not to have been privileged to sniff human flesh ever in their lives before. What with that, the freezing cold and the harum-scarum state of the road, it was timely, nay essential to repair to a hostelry. Before we did so, my companion pointed across to the estuary where the boats had come to take the famine emigrants to America and, momentarily moved by this memory, he said there was a castle not far away, Rahinnane, built by local labour, and that the strength of the mortar was due to the fact that it was mixed in with the blood of the people. Then he made me run a few yards to look at a windmill that was being restored by a group of students and would be a real eye-catcher for tourists because they would be milling flour there next year and the whole world wanted to get back to nature.

Our arrival in the hostelry was somewhat precipitate since they were not ready for early-morning callers even though it was near noon. A pub is one thing at night and another thing altogether in the raw unaerosoled morning. The pyramids of glasses along the counter, a consignment of ashes in the grate and, on the hearth, chairs and stools turned over and the daughter of the house, aged six or seven, playing unmolested on the Moon Patrol video game. The billiard table looked a picture of abandonment and the whole place needed an influx of merry customers. A young boy was engaged in the task of tidying up, but had a desultory approach, his interest being consumed by a video of rock musicians on a television screen which was positioned so high up that it hurt the neck to keep looking at it. The video he had made himself, a *compote* from various programmes, and made more with an eye for frenzy than any notion of continuity. Never mind, my friend of the high-roads was blissfully happy, being now the proud recipient of a pint and a hot toddy, with another on the way and the reins under the leg of the table, and every so often an unholy yell delivered to let the cob know that he hadn't forgotten her and that he was still 'master.'

'You didn't show the white feather,' he kept saying to me, praising my fortitude at coming out at all, my apparent absence of hysteria when the dogs descended on us and my appreciation of the beautiful and ancient countryside. In my heart I was aching to go home, until it suddenly occurred to me that this was home, this country of hills and promontories, this country of stone walls, old oratories, new grottoes, seedy hostelries, lonely schoolhouses, laser discos, automatic milking parlours, tufted islands and people ravenous for company. A shaft of sadness went through me, both at my inability to change things and my refusal to accept them as they are.

'You didn't show the white feather, Edwina,' he kept saying and, now fortified by hot toddies and careless of protocol, he was back to the transports of the previous night, thou'll wife in jail, grabbing one's arse on the mountain and all the heady Dan McGrew bravado.

It would need more than a fleet of mobile libraries to change Ireland. It would need a hundred Sigmund Freuds to unravel the Gordian knots of guilt and anger and darkness and tortuous sex.

From *Vanishing Ireland*

Niall Williams & Christine Breen

1990

DUBLINER NIALL WILLIAMS met his wife, artist Christine Breen, who grew up in New York, when they were both students at University College Dublin. In 1985 they gave up careers in New York for a rural life at Kilmihil in County Clare, where they settled at Christine's great-grandfather's old cottage. The couple have jointly written four books about their County Clare experiences: *O Come Ye Back to Ireland*, *When Summer's in the Meadow*, *The Pipes Are Calling* and *The Luck of the Irish*. Williams is the author of the novels *Four Letters of Love* and *As It Is in Heaven*, and two plays, *A Little Like Paradise* and *The Way You Look Tonight.*

Back in Kenmare we walked with Deirdre around the pretty triangle of streets that make up one of our favorite Irish towns. Kenmare nestles in the crook between the outstretched arms of two magnificent mountainous peninsulas. It's a haven between the mountains, and its shops and restaurants are lively, bright, and decorative. Quinn's on the corner is a maze of woolen sweaters. The Purple Heather serves good food and is all bare stonework. Besides this, in the Park Hotel, the town boasts one of the finest hotels and restaurants in the country.

In early evening, Deirdre safely asleep at Mrs. Dignam's with a baby-sitter listening for her, Chris and I slipped from the house for a second drive into memory. Once, ten years ago, on the mildest Valentine's Day anyone could remember, we two had taken a train from Dublin together and come courting into Kerry. Our stay was two days in a marvelous old house by the water. No one else was there, and with every place closed in February, the naturally secluded feeling of the house was doubled. We were our own Diarmuid and Grainne, reading poetry and escaping west into the green rush of early Irish springtime. We walked miles by hedgerows and ditches. We talked morning, noon, and night along country roads where daffodils were already rising, took knowing nods and salutes from passing farmers, and waved and saluted back in the growing knowledge that yes, truly, we would be married. Here, in a place not half an hour from Cuil Aodha, where I had stood, as a boy, gazing at the countryside, full of questions, had come one of the answers. Kenmare: courtship, love.

Under the glow of a midsummer sky, we drove west from Kenmare on the Sneem road to see if we could find that house by the water again. Chris and I remembered Marino House as a fine two-storey building with a great sitting room and a roaring fire where we could sit and talk and take evening mugs of cocoa from a kind woman whose spirit had seemed fairy-godmother-like to both of us. As we drove out of town the whole feeling of the road along the peninsula came flashing back to us, its green richness, the sense of water, and the fragments of view through the trees of mountains and hills across the Kenmare River. We drove slowly, inching into our shared dream, and I felt the landscape conspire with our mood. This was a place of entrancement even if it had not already held a place in our hearts. The red and purple saucers and spires of wild fuchsia sprawled in high hedges. Teori De I had heard them called in Irish, the tears of God. By summer's end all roadsides would be edged red with their flowers, struck down by the rain. But for now they bloomed in a magical evening light as fine as any we had seen in Ireland. Under tree-shadows and by leaf-light, smelling the sea and the tangled woodbine, we at last found the long road into Marino House. It was almost a mile in from the main road, a narrow one-car track to the water's edge. We turned a bend and drove slowly up to the front of the house. And there it was, almost everything – the steps to the arched stone porch of the main door, the clinging ivy, the window, within which was 'our' sitting room. The low sounds of water still lapped all around. The only thing that was different was the little cluster of foreign cars in the carpark. I pulled up at the side of the house and we sat there, unable to decide whether to go in or not. We sat outside and looked; then we drove away. That night in Mrs. Dignam's, with a light in the sky that seemed undying, I wrote: 'First day of our jaunt, two drives to two places of memory, Cuil Aodha and Kenmare, Innocence and Love.'

From *The Pipes Are Calling*

Sources

Giraldus Cambrensis Giraldus Cambrensis, *Topographia Hiberniae*, quoted in Edwin, third Earl of Dunraven, *Notes on Irish Architecture*, George Bell, London 1874, vol. 1, p. 36.
Thomas Stafford Thomas Stafford, *Pacata Hibernia, or a History of the Wars in Ireland*, ed. Standish O'Grady, Downey & Co., London 1896, vol. 1, pp. 144–146. (First published 1633.)
Dionisio Massari Mgr. Massari, 'My Irish Campaign,' *Catholic Bulletin* vol. 7, 1917, pp. 159, 217–219.
William Petty Marquis of Lansdowne, ed., *The Petty-Southwell Correspondence* 1676–1687, Constable & Co., London 1928, p. 153.
Samuel Molyneux TCD MS 885 fol. 20–30, as quoted in K. Theodore Hoppen, 'Samuel Molyneux's Tour of Kerry, 1709,' *Journal of the Kerry Archaeological and Historical Society*, no. 3, 1970, pp. 71–74. Reproduced by permission of The Board of Trinity College Dublin and the Kerry Archaeological and Historical Society.
Charles Smith Charles Smith, *The Antient and Present State of the County of Kerry*, Dublin 1756, pp. 172–177.
Richard Pococke Richard Pococke, *Richard Pococke's Irish Tours*, ed. John McVeagh, Irish Academic Press, Dublin 1995, pp. 166–168. Reprinted by courtesy of John McVeagh and Frank Cass Publishers.
Richard Twiss Richard Twiss, *A Tour in Ireland in* 1775, London 1776, pp. 115–119.
Arthur Young Arthur Young, *Arthur Young's Tour in Ireland*, ed. Arthur Wollaston Hutton, George Bell, London 1892, vol. 1, pp. 348–352.
Daniel Beaufort TCD MS 4030 pp. 8–11, as quoted in Gerard J. Lyne, 'Rev. Daniel A. Beaufort's Tour of Kerry, 1788,' *Journal of the Kerry Archaeological and Historical Society*, no. 18, 1985, pp. 190–192. Reproduced by permission of The Board of Trinity College Dublin and the Kerry Archaeological and Historical Society.
Jacques Louis de Bougrenet De Lactocnaye, *A Frenchman's Walk through Ireland* 1796–7, trans. John Stevenson, McCaw, Stevenson & Orr, Belfast 1917, pp. 100–113.
George Holmes G. Holmes, *Sketches of Some of the Southern Counties of Ireland*, Longman, London 1801, pp. 115–124.
Isaac Weld Isaac Weld, *Illustrations of the Scenery of Killarney and the Surrounding Country*, Longman, London 1812, pp. 193–197.
John Carr John Carr, *The Stranger in Ireland, or a Tour in the Southern and Western Parts of That Country in* 1805, London 1806, pp. 355–363.
Edward Dubois Edward Dubois, *My Pocket Book; or Hints for 'A Ryghte merrie and Conceitede' Tour*, Vernor, Hood & Sharpe, London 1808, pp. 129–137.
James Bell James Bell, 'Sketches of the Life and Experience of James Bell,' p. 63, BV Bell, James, New-York Historical Society. Quoted courtesy of The New-York Historical Society.
Lewis Dillwyn From TCD MS 967, as transcribed by Gerard J. Lyne in 'Lewis Dillwyn's Visit to Kerry, 1809,' *Journal of the Kerry Archaeological and Historical Society*, no. 15/16, 1982/3, pp. 87–89. Reproduced by permission of The Board of Trinity College Dublin and the Kerry Archaeological and Historical Society.
Thomas Moore Thomas Moore, *The Journal of Thomas Moore* 1818–1841, ed. Peter Quennell, B.T. Batsford Ltd., London 1964, pp. 85–86.
Alexander Nimmo From *Minutes of evidence taken from select committee appointed to inquire into the disturbances in Ireland.*
Walter Scott Walter Scott, *The Letters of Sir Walter Scott* 1825–1826, ed. H.J.C. Grierson, Constable & Co., London 1935, pp. 199–200.
John Lockhart D.J. O'Donoghue, *Sir Walter Scott's Tour in Ireland in* 1825, Gowans & Gray, Glasgow 1905, pp. 76–78.

Hermann von Pückler-Muskau A German Prince, *Tour in England, Ireland and France in the Years* 1826, 1827, 1828 *&* 1829, trans. Sarah Austin, Massie Publishing Co., Zurich 1940, pp. 300–304. (First printed 1833.)

William Wordsworth From letter to the Wordsworth family, 17th September 1829, quoted in *The Letters of William and Dorothy Wordsworth*, ed. E. de Selincourt, vol. 5 *The Later Years Part 2:* 1829–1834, rev., arr. & ed. Alan G. Hill, Oxford University Press 1979, pp. 135–136.

Jonathan Binns Jonathan Binns, *The Miseries and Beauties of Ireland*, Longman, London 1837, pp. 111–115.

Georgina Chatterton Lady Chatterton, *Rambles in the South of Ireland during the Year* 1838, Sanders & Otley, London 1839, vol. 1, pp. 214–224.

Michael Condon From Michael Condon's diaries quoted in Bernard J. Canning 'Michael Condon's Visit to Derrynane, 1839,' *Journal of the Kerry Archaeological and Historical Society*, no. 17, 1984, pp. 95–98. Reproduced by courtesy of the Kerry Archaeological and Historical Society.

William M. Thackeray William Makepeace Thackeray, *The Irish Sketch Book of* 1842 in *The Works of William Makepeace Thackeray*, vol. vii, Elder & Co., London 1877, pp. 362–366.

Johann Georg Kohl J. G. Kohl, *Ireland, Scotland and England*, Chapman & Hall, London 1844, pp. 67–71.

Asenath Nicholson Asenath Nicholson, *The Bible in Ireland*, Hodder & Stoughton, London 1926, pp. 213–222. (First published as *Ireland's Welcome to the Stranger*, 1847.)

William Bennett William Bennett, *Narrative of a recent journey of six weeks in Ireland in connection with the subject of supplying small seed to some of the remoter districts*, Charles Gilpin, London 1847, pp. 127–131.

Thomas Carlyle Thomas Carlyle, *Reminiscences of My Irish Journey in* 1849, Samson Low, London 1882, pp. 129–143.

Thomas B. Macaulay George Otto Trevelyan, *The Life and Letters of Lord Macaulay*, Longmans, Green & Co., London 1876, p. 531.

John Windele Royal Irish Academy MS 12.C.11, pp. 627, 635 and 637, as quoted by Peter Harbison in 'John Windele's Visit to Skellig Michael in 1851,' *Journal of the Kerry Archaeological and Historical Society*, no. 9, 1976, pp. 127–129. Reproduced by courtesy of the Royal Irish Academy and the Kerry Archaeological and Historical Society.

Harriet Martineau Harriet Martineau, *Letters from Ireland: Reprinted from the Daily News*, J. Chapman, London 1852, pp. 189–193.

Isabella Beeton From Isabella Beeton's diary quoted in Nancy Spain, *Mrs Beeton and Her Husband*, Collins, London 1948, pp.149, 154–156.

Daniel Gooch *Diaries of Sir Daniel Gooch Baronet*, Kegan Paul, London 1892, pp. 90–92.

William W Barry An Englishman (William Whittaker Barry), *A Walking Tour round Ireland in* 1865, Richard Bentley, London 1867, pp.217–220.

Bernard H. Becker Bernard H. Becker, *Disturbed Ireland*, Macmillan & Co, London 1881, pp. 282–284, 288–293.

E de Mandat-Grancey Baron E. de Mandat-Grancey, *Paddy at Home*, trans. Alice Pullein Morton, Chapman & Hall, London 1889, pp. 156–159.

Marie-Anne de Bovet Marie-Anne de Bovet, *Three Months Tour in Ireland*, trans. Mrs. Arthur Walter, Chapman & Hall, London 1891, pp. 162–166.

Bertha Beatty Bertha Beatty, *Kerry Memories*, The Channing Press, Dawlish 1939, pp. 35–38.

John Millington Synge John M. Synge, *In Wicklow and West Kerry*, Maunsel, Dublin & London 1912, pp. 67–82.

Michael M. Shoemaker Michael Myers Shoemaker, *Wanderings in Ireland*, G.P. Putnam's Sons, New York & London 1908, pp.163–165, 167–169.

George Bernard Shaw Bernard Shaw, *Collected Letters* 1898–1910 ed. Dan H. Laurence, Max Reinhardt, London 1985, vol. 2, pp. 941–943. Reprinted by courtesy of The Society of Authors on behalf of the Bernard Shaw Estate.

Robin Flower Robin Flower, *The Western Island*, Clarendon Press, Oxford 1944, pp. 31–33. Copyright © Oxford University Press. Reprinted by permission of Oxford University Press.

Stephen Gwynn Stephen Gwynn, *Munster*, Blackie & Son Ltd., London 1912, pp. 44–49.

Harold Speakman Harold Speakman, *Here's Ireland*, Robert M. McBride, New York 1925, pp. 70–75.

John J. Welsh John J. Welsh, *Ireland Afoot*, Gorham Press, Boston 1931, pp. 51–54.

H.V. Morton H.V. Morton, *In Search of Ireland*, Methuen & Co. Ltd., London 1930, pp. 122–125. Copyright © Marion Wasdell and Brian de Villiers. Reprinted by permission of Methuen Publishing Ltd. on behalf of Marion Wasdell and Brian de Villiers.

Signe Toksvig Signe Toksvig, *Signe Toksvig's Irish Diaries* 1926–1937, ed. Lis Pihl, The Lilliput Press Ltd., Dublin 1994, p. 201. Reprinted by courtesy of The Lilliput Press.

Virginia Woolf *The Diary of Virginia Woolf*, ed. Anne Olivier Bell with Andrew McNeillie, Hogarth Press, London 1985, vol. 4, pp. 211–214. Reprinted by permission of The Random House Group Ltd.

Padraic Colum Padraic Colum, *The Road round Ireland*, Macmillan, New York 1937, pp. 473–476.

Robert Lloyd Praeger Robert Lloyd Praeger, *The Way That I Went: An Irishman in Ireland*, Allen Figgis Ltd., Dublin 1969, pp. 364–370. (First published by Hodges, Figgis, Dublin 1937.) Copyright © The House of Figgis Ltd. Reprinted by permission of The House of Figgis Ltd.

Sean O'Faolain Sean O'Faolain, *An Irish Journey*, Longmans, Green & Co., London 1940, pp.124–126. Copyright © Sean O'Faolain 1940. Reproduced by permission of the Estate of Sean O'Faolain c/o Rogers, Coleridge & White Ltd., 20 Powis Mews, London W11 1JN.

Richard Hayward Richard Hayward, *In the Kingdom of Kerry*, Dundalgan Press, Dundalk 1946, pp. 228–236.

J.P. Donleavy J.P. Donleavy, *J.P. Donleavy's Ireland: In All Her Sins and in Some of Her Graces*, Michael Joseph/Rainbird, London 1986, pp.129–131. Reprinted by permission of J.P. Donleavy.

Olivia Manning Olivia Manning, *The Dreaming Shore*, Evans Bros., London 1950, pp. 63–71.

Frank O'Connor Frank O'Connor, *Leinster, Munster and Connaught*, Robert Hale Ltd., London 1950, pp. 196–197. © The Estate of Frank O'Connor. Reprinted by permission of PFD on behalf of The Estate of Frank O'Connor.

Honor Tracy Honor Tracy, *Mind You, I've Said Nothing*, Methuen & Co. Ltd., London 1955, pp. 147–156.

Oriana Atkinson Oriana Atkinson, *The South and the West of It*, Random House, New York 1955, pp. 31–35. Reprinted by permission of Russell & Volkening as agents for the author. Copyright © 1955 by Oriana Atkinson, renewed 1983.

Kate O'Brien Kate O'Brien, *My Ireland*, B.T. Batsford Ltd., 1958, pp. 178–180. Reprinted by permission of Chrysalis Books.

Brendan Behan Brendan Behan, *Brendan Behan's Island*, Hutchinson 1962, pp. 67–68, 70–71, 74. Reprinted by permission of The Random House Group Ltd.

Robert Mitchum Robert Mitchum, *Mitchum: In His Own Words* © 2000 by Gerald Roberts, p. 148. Excerpt used by courtesy of Proscenium Publishers Inc., New York.

Rebecca West Reproduced from a letter from Rebecca West of 29 September 1971 (Copyright © Rebecca West 1971) by permission of PFD on behalf of the Estate of Dame Rebecca West.

Philip Ward Philip Ward, *Come with Me to Ireland*, The Oleander Press, Stoughton, Wis. 1972, pp. 197–199. Reprinted by courtesy of Philip Ward.

Edna O'Brien Edna O'Brien, *Vanishing Ireland*, Jonathan Cape, London 1986, pp. 20–21. Reprinted by courtesy of Edna O'Brien.

Peter Somerville-Large Peter Somerville-Large, *The Grand Irish Tour*, Hamish Hamilton, London 1982, pp. 10–12. Reprinted by courtesy of Peter Somerville-Large.

Niall Williams & Christine Breen Niall Williams & Christine Breen, *The Pipes Are Calling*, Soho Press, New York 1990, pp. 141–143. Reprinted by courtesy of Niall Williams & Christine Breen.

Picture Credits

By courtesy of the National Library of Ireland, the following Lawrence Collection photographs: p. 13 R10 460 Dingle, Main Street; p. 109 R10 577 Valentia, Clock tower and Harbour; p. 114 R8226 Listowel, Fair Day; p. 128 R4275 Ballybunion, Lartigue Railway; p. 132 R4582 Port Magee, fish curing; p. 158 R8295 Waterville, Head Office Cable Station; p. 173 R7939 Killorglin, Puck Fair.

By courtesy of the National Portrait Gallery, London: p. 9 Sir William Petty by Isaac Fuller; p. 27 Daniel Augustus Beaufort by Unknown artist; p. 45 Sir John Carr by William Brockedon; p. 62 John Gibson Lockhart by Daniel Maclise; p. 110 Isabella Mary Beeton by Maul & Co; p. 112 Sir Daniel Gooch, 1st Bt by Sir Francis Grant; p. 205 Kate O'Brien by Mary O'Neill.

By courtesy of the Royal Irish Academy: p. 105 John Windele's Skellig Michael sketches, from RIA MS 12.C. p. 653.

By courtesy of the Irish Historical Picture Co.: p. 142 On the Blasket Islands.

Pictures on the pages listed are from the following books:

p. 15, p. 84 John Barrow, *Tour around Ireland* 1836;
p. 37, p. 122, p. 193, p. 199 Marie-Anne de Bovet, *Three Months Tour in Ireland* 1891;
p. 74, p. 93, p. 101 Georgiana Chatterton, *Rambles in the South of Ireland* 1839;
p. 204 A Cosmopolite, *The Sportsman in Ireland* (illus. by P. Chenevix Trench) 1897;
p. 56, p. 60, p. 215 J. Stirling Coyne and N.P. Willis, *The Scenery and Antiquities of Ireland* (illus. by W.H. Bartlett) 1842;
p. 46, p. 51 Edward Dubois, *My Pocket Book* 1808;
p. 22, p. 53, p. 59, p. 115, p. 164, p. 182 Mr. & Mrs. S.C. Hall, *Ireland: Its Scenery, Character, etc.* 1841;
p. viii, p. ix An Oxonian (Samuel Hole), *A Little Tour in Ireland* (illus. by John Leech) 1859, p. 28, p. 118, p.149, p. 157, p. 178;
p. 20, p. 41, p. 71, p: 87, p. 131, p. 139, p. 171, p. 187, p. 189 Richard Lovett, *Irish Pictures* 1888;
p. 195 J.P. Neale, *Views of the Seats of Noblemen* 1818;
p. 117 Robert O'Callaghan Newenham, *Picturesque Views of the Antiquities of Ireland* 1830;
p 1, p. 17, p. 71, p. 88 Charles Smith, *The Antient and Present State of the County of Kerry* 1756;
p. 4, p. 7, p. 177 Thomas Stafford, *Pacata Hibernia* 1633;
p. 43, p. 78, p. 155 W.M. Thackeray, *The Irish Sketch Book* 1842;
p. x, p. 19, p. 26, p. 33, p. 137, p. 167 Isaac Weld, *Illustrations of the Scenery of Killarney* 1812.

Acknowledgments

We gratefully acknowledge the kind co-operation of copyright owners, and invite contact from one not found through enquiries. We also thank the following institutions and people who have been helpful in the compilation of this book.

New York Public Library, The New-York Historical Society, Trinity College Dublin, National Library of Ireland; Gráinne MacLochlainn, National Photographic Archive; Mary Kelleher, Royal Dublin Society; Siobhán O'Rafferty, Royal Irish Academy; Theresa Whitington, Catholic Central Library; Michael Costelo, Kerry County Library; Tim Cadogan, Cork County Library; Kieran Burke, Cork Central Library; staff of Boole Library, University of Cork; Society of Friends Library, London; Hester Swift, Law Society Library, London; Guy Holborn, Lincoln's Inn Library, London; Michael Marshman, Trowbridge Public Library; Susan Wilson, Lancaster Public Library; Val Craggs, Sunderland Public Library.

Beara Action Group, Isabel Bennet, Josette Cadoret, Joseph Coencas, Anissa Fox, David Durell, Peter Harbison, Patrick Kelly, Jennifer Lewis, Gerard J. Lyne, John McVeagh, Jean Paul Michaud, Paddy O'Conor, Ted O'Sullivan, Simon Prichard, Lisa Reswick, Barbara Simon and Kerry Stevens.

Index

Bold indicates illustrations

Abbey Island 18
Abbeyfeale 50, 75, 158
Achill 108
Aghadoe **53**, 153, 192, 214
Antrim 205
Ardfert 11, 35, **37**, 38, 192
Ardtully 6, 8
Auger Lake 214

Balfe, Michael 203
Ballinskelligs 104, 139
Ballinskelligs Bay 117, 170
Ballybunion ix, 124–126, 214
Ballycarbery 119
Ballycarnahan Castle 18
Ballydonegan Bay 18
Ballyferriter 129, 133, 188, 210
Ballyheigue 10, 11, 38, 73, **195**
Ballyristan 73
Ballyseedy 212
Ballysitteragh 190
Bananeer Castle 16
Banna 11
Bantry 99
Bantry Bay ix, 55, 112
Bealachbeama 144, 146
Bealalaw Bridge 144
Beaufort Bridge 214
Beginish 170
Behan, Brendan ix, 207, **208**
Berehaven 18, 111
Bianconi, Charles ix
Black Lake 214
Black Valley **193**
Blackwater River 16, **19**, 38
Blasket Islands 141, 143, 185, 187, 188, 193, 208, 209. See also Great Blasket Island
Blennerhassetts 175, 176, 212
Blennerville 53
Bolus Head 104
Boru, Brian 148
Brandon 163, 164, 184, 191, 205, 210, 218
Brandon Bay 10, 11
Bray Head 117
Broadford 12
Brown, Samuel ix
Browne, Paddy 210

Caherciveen 75, 76, 77, 107, 109, 116, 117, 169, 170, 181
Caherdaniel ix, 207
Cahir 75
Cambrensis, Giraldus vii, 1
Caragh Lake 144–146, 169, 170, 205
Carew, George vii, 2, 3, 5
Carhan **204**
Carrantuohill 43, 44, 67, 68, 130, 144, 145, 146, 153, 202, 214
Carrigafoyle Castle **177**
Castlegregory 191
Castleisland 45, 46, 50, 53, 205
Castlelough 99, 102
Castlelough Bay 111
Castlemaine **4**, 13, 14, 15
Cloghane 190, 191
Coleman's Castle 111
Coleman's Eye 40, 41
Colgan, Nathaniel 164
Colleen Bawn 147, 153
Colum, Padraic 161
Connor Pass 190
Coulagh Bay 18
Coumeenoule 184
Cow Rock 112
Crist, Gainor 181
Croker, Thomas Crofton viii
Cromwell, Oliver 203, 213
Cushwally Lake 21

Derrycunihy Cascade **56**
Derrynane ix, 18, 75, 76, 77, 91, 92, **93**, 117, 118, 159, 170, 205
Devil's Punch Bowl 34, 167, 168
Dingle vii, 5, **13**, 14, 15, 34, 70, 126–129, 134, 169, 184, 188, 194, 205, 209
Dingle Bay 116, 181, 182, 192
Dingle Peninsula 183, 188, 209, 211, 212
Dinis Island 26, 27, **137**
Donegal 205
Dublin 184
Dunbeg 184
Dunkerron 16
Dunloe, Gap of viii, 42, 99, 100, 110, 138, 147, **149**, 152, 168, **189**, 214
Dunmore Head 131, 186, 183
Dunquin 133, 134, 183, 185, 186, 194, 195, 198, 210
Dursey Island 18

Eagle Rock 39
Eagle's Nest 24, **26**, 27, 31, 110, 152

Edgeworth, Maria ix, 63, 103
Edward VII ix
Emmet, Robert 118

Fahan 184, 185
Feale River 113
Ferriter, Pierce 143, 188, 206, 212, 213
Ferriter's Castle 129
Fitzgerald 3, 15, 107, 176
Fitzgerald, Ida 160, 161
Fitzmaurice 2, 3
Flesk River 56, 111
Flower, Robin viii, **141**, 199, 208
Fort del Oro 188, 191

Gallarus Oratory 88, **187**, 189–190
Galway 107
Garfinny Bridge 73, 75
Gill, Michael & Una 190
Glena Mountain 24, 28, 39, 69
Glenbeigh 145, 159, 160, 205
Glencar 145
Glenfahan 185
Glengarriff 67, 95, 151, 153, 159, 203
Glin 147
Great Blasket Island 131–135, 141, **142**, 143, 185, 186, 195, 198–200

Hart, Henry 163
Healy Pass 201
Herbert, Mr. 24, 26, 49, 96
Hoare, Gregory 191
Hoare, Hugh 191
Hog Island 18, 20
Horse's Glen 167

Inch 14
Innisfallen 29, 31, 58, **60**, 62, 65, 69, **90**, 111, 136, 148, 153, 214
Inny Bridge 71
Iveragh 117

Kavanagh, Kruger 186, 187,188, 189, 190, 210
Keane, John B. 215, 216
Kells Cove 181
Kenmare ix, 9, 23, 55, 67, 95, 96, 97, 120, 152, 158, 159, 167, 221, 222
Kenmare, Lord vii, 29, 31, 49, 57, 58
Kenmare Bay/River 5, 22, 24, 34, 116
Kerry, Knight of 11, 15, 104, 107, 116, 169
Kerry Head 10, 38
Kilcatherine 96
Kilcrohan 16, 18
Killagh 15
Killagie 182
Killarney viii, ix, 24, 34, 47, 48, 57, 60, 62, 64, 67, 68, 78, 95, 97, 98, 110, 111, 115, 116, 122, 135, 137, 146, 147, 148, 152, 153, **155**, 159, 166, 167, 192, 201, 203, 204, 213, 216
Killarney, Lakes of 22, 24, 26, 27, 31, 34, 39–42, 58, 62, 64, 65, 68, 69, 101, 102, 103, 111, 134, 135, 136, 147, 159, 163, 167, 168, 176, 214
Killorglin 75, 170, 172, **173–180**
Killoyra 94
Kilmakilloge 96,
Kilmalkedar 190, 192
Kinard 71, 72, 73
Knightstown 117, 170

Ladies' View 201, 202
Lamb Head 119
Lansdowne, Marquis of 96, 120
Laune River 76
Lawlor, Shea 99
Lawlor, Shine 98, 99, 100
Limerick 8, 34, 35, 50, 203, 205
Listowel ix, 86, 89, 113, **114**, 124, 214
Listowel Castle 2, 3, 61, 86
Little Skellig 19, 139
Lixnaw 11, 12, 58
Lixnaw, Lord of 2, 3, 58
Loo Bridge 217
Loop Head 124, 130
Lough Acoose 144
Lough Cloon 144, 146
Lough Geal 164
Lough Reagh 144
Lough Veagh 163
Ludlow, Edmund vii, 39, 69

MacCarthys 167, 176
McFineen 8
MacGillicuddy, Miss 78, 82
MacGillicuddy's Reeks 40, 43, 57, 97, 100, 114, 168, 170, 201, 202, 214
Macroom 8
Magheries 11
Mahony, Michael 104
Mallow 161
Mangerton 22, 24, 25, 34, 97, 102, 167
Massari, Dionisio vii, 5
Mathew, Theobald 80, 86
Milltown 184
Minard Castle 14
Moore, Eileen 191
Moore, Thomas viii, **57**
Moriartys 176
Mouse Island 65
Muckross 23, 24, 30, 31, 34, 49, 102, 123, 153, 213

Muckross Abbey 25, 30, **33**, 62, 97, 102, **115**, **171**, 206, 207
Muskerry, Lord 39, 69

Newcastle 75
Nicholson, Asenath ix, 89
Nimmo, Alexander ix, 59
O'Connell, Daniel ix, 76, 77, 91, 92, 102, 107, 117, 118, 204, 207
O'Criomhthiann, Tomás 198, 208
O'Dea, Denis 186
O'Donoghue 28, 30, 39, 62, 65, 66, 162
Old Weir Bridge 40, **41**
O'Sullivan, Maurice 208
O'Sullivan, Murthy 106
O'Sullivan's Cascade 31, 58
O'Sullivans 206

Paps, the 217
Parknasilla 138, 205
Peel, Robert 112
Percy, Richard
Port Magee **132**
Priest's Leap 54
Pückler-Muskau, Hermann von ix, 63
Puffin Island 2
Pugin, Augustus 153
Purple Mountain 168, 214

Rabbit Island 214
Raleigh, Walter 191
Raspe, Rudolf Erich 213
Ratoo 11
Rinuccini, Cardinal vii, 5, 6, 8, 9
Ronayne's Island 41, 58
Ross Castle vii, **22**, 27, 28, 39, 42, 43, 48, 64, 69, 111, **167**
Ross Island 30, 39, 58, 69, 111, 214
Roughty River ix

St. Brendan 143, 210, 215
St. Brighid 217, 218
St. Crohan's Cave 16, 17, 18
Sayers, Peig 198, 208
Scarriff Island 104, 117
Scott, Walter ix, 60, **61**, 62, 103
Scully, R.W. 165, 166
Shannon River 10, 11, 38, 89, 147
Shaw, George Bernard ix, 138
Skellig Islands 23, 104, 112, 130
Skellig Michael 1, **20**, 22, 91, 104, **105**, 106 107, 138, **139**, 140
Slea Head 186
Sligo 205
Smerwick Harbour 14, 130, 188
Smith, Charles vii, viii, 12, 69, 163
Sneem 16, 21
Spillane, Mr. 110, 116
Stafford, Thomas vii, 2
Stag Island 29
Staigue Fort 16, **117**, 118
Stoompa 167
Sybil Head 130, 143, 188
Synge, J.M. viii, 126, **127**

Tarbert 83, 214
Tearaght 133, 195
Templenoe 16
Three Sisters 130, 188, 210
Tipperary 203
Tisdall, Rev. 54
Tomies Mountain 24, 69, 168
Torc Mountain 168
Torc Waterfall **87**
Trahan, Gerald 48
Tralee **17**, 34, 61, 63, 86, 114, 115, 192, 194
Trench, Mr. 120, 121
Tuosist 96, 97
Turk Mountain 24, 26, 39
Twiss, Richard viii, 21

Valentia Island ix, 89, 90, 93, 106–**109**, 111, 116, 169, 170, **199**
Ventry 14, 184, 194
Victoria, Queen ix

Waterville 117, 159, 205
Weld, Isaac 19, 33, 42
West, Rebecca ix, 211, **212**
West Cove 119
Wilmot, Charles 2, 3, 5
Wordsworth, William ix, **67**

Zouche, Colonel 191